TRAVELS WITH FRANK LLOYD WRIGHT

GWYN LLOYD JONES

TRAVELS WITH FRANK LLOYD WRIGHT

LUND HUMPHRIES

First published in 2017 by Lund Humphries
Office 3, 261A City Road
London
EC1V 1JX
UK

www.lundhumphries.com

ISBN 978-1-84822-226-7

A Cataloguing-in-Publication record for this book is available from the British Library.

Designed by Crow Books
Printed in Slovenia

Acknowledgements: Professor Murray Fraser, University of Westminster, LKE Ozolins Studentship, RIBA, Giles Worsley Travel Fellowship, Studio Egret West, the Frank Lloyd Wright Foundation, Cary James, Val Rose and the team at Lund Humphries, all the home owners, guides and friends who assisted me along the journey.

Dedicated to Amanda, Joshua and Olivia.

CONTENTS

Introduction

ROUTE FINDER

Frank Lloyd Wright was born in Richland Centre, Wisconsin, just two years after the end of the American Civil War in the age of the horse and cart; he died nine decades later in the age of commercial jet travel. Wright therefore not only experienced the rapid compression of space and time that such revolutions in methods of travel offered, but was also a participant in this globalising movement. The act of journeying has, of course, for centuries been an inherent method for inspiring architectural thought, and in his later writings even Wright acknowledged the role of travel in conceptualising 'organic' architecture. In his book, *A Testament* (1957), he reflected: 'I have learned about architecture by root, by world-wide travel and by incessant experiment and experience in the study of nature.'[1] However, Wright adopted a rather detached and impersonal view of travel as an experience, and preferred the study of abstracted 'nature' when reflecting on his trips.

The Italian architect, Carlo Scarpa, claimed that 'Architects are full of journeys,'[2] likewise, Zaha Hadid reflected on her 2009 commission in Rome, 'There can be no progress without an element of uncertainty and without a sensation of embarking on a journey into the unknown.'[3] These quotes eloquently describe the element of excitement, trepidation and mystery that any new trip can generate, even in these days of mass tourism. Travel and cross-cultural dialogues are an important part of architectural 'progress' and have been throughout history. This book takes us on a journey with Frank Lloyd Wright to six very different countries outside America and will not only reflect upon how Wright's own personal encounters with new cultures moved him, but also, by my re-enacting them, show how he in turn disturbed these indigenous settings. The purpose of the journey was to take Wright beyond his American masterpieces, and open up a dialogue with 'organic' architecture and the wider world. I wanted Wright to be my companion as I travelled the world reflecting on 'organic' architecture as a globalising force. Following a broadly chronological sequence, the book is anchored around Wright's trips abroad at critical junctures in his career. Thus, we first follow Wright's visits to Japan and Germany and demonstrate how they informed and framed his early 'Prairie Style.' Next, we investigate Wright's visits to Russia and Britain as part of his efforts to promote his global 'Usonian' manifesto, based on what had already become a highly dispersed society in the USA. The final sections of the book pursue Wright to Italy and the Middle East in the locus of Kuwait as part of his 'Legacy' period.

Ever since I started studying architecture, I have found Frank Lloyd Wright to be a fascinating character. Like most, my architectural school did not include Wright in their curriculum; this may have been because he was always the outsider, too idiosyncratic to be taught seriously. His rebellious streak, his refusal to follow the prevalent architectural cultural trends, and even his reluctance to explain 'organic' architecture properly, appealed to me – I liked to identify with his non-conformity. His early architecture combined a dynamic form with an intimacy of scale and warmth of material that responded to a natural setting and was, I found, at once progressive and unpretentious. I had first written about Frank Lloyd Wright for my architectural dissertation, in which I undertook a road trip across America that followed Wright's annual journey from Taliesin North to Taliesin West and I reflected on 12 different states of America and Wright's architecture across the continent.[4] He was likewise my companion on this most recent odyssey, and it was a natural way to follow on from our earlier road trip, but this time I was to consider Wright outside America and how his 'organic' architecture might embrace many different cultural settings. With sponsorship from the Royal Institute of British Architects (RIBA), my travels for this book took five years to complete, beginning with a visit to Japan in 2005, exactly 100 years on from Wright's first journey overseas.[5] I attempted to follow Wright's routes as closely as I could; Wright's journeys and consequently my trips were short and focused, although to reach Japan and Europe Wright had to endure long sea voyages, while I made full use of international flights. On other occasions, however, I did take the time to make a three-day train journey to Russia and a 12-day road trip to Italy.

Within the book, the concept of globalisation is used as an armature to evaluate Frank Lloyd Wright's architecture within different national and regional contexts; it allowed me to make new connections across different cultural fields and to disturb the traditional means of discussing architectural history, making it more fluid and informed. In addition, it shows how Wright's 'organic' architecture was developed from a number of mediated global encounters, for example, the Prairie Homes were in fact derived from traditional Japanese architecture, the 'English Free Style' and the American 'Shingle Style.' Globalisation is particularly relevant an idea because it unsettles the traditional notion that culture is related to a fixed location.[6] Furthermore, it offers a contemporary method of evaluating Wright's 'organic' architecture from a multi-perspective view. In doing so, it makes new links that provide a more nuanced understanding of Wright's architecture. As well as acknowledging Wright's global fame, the book includes local tales of resistance. While returning to the sites previously visited by Wright, I met and talked with people who are living and coping with his organic architecture. In doing so, Frank Lloyd Wright's architecture is revealed and challenged, and new perspectives are uncovered.

A BRIEF HISTORY OF FRANK LLOYD WRIGHT

Franklin Lincoln Wright, as he was christened, was born to a Welsh mother and an American father of English descent in 1867, and he was named after the victorious Civil War president. Wright's father was an itinerant preacher and solicitor, and the family moved several times along the eastern seaboard of America to pursue new opportunities to preach or to practice law. His parents then separated and Wright and his mother went to join some of their family, of Welsh stock, in rural Wisconsin. During his teenage years he changed his middle name to that of his mother's family, to become Frank Lloyd Wright, showing an early capacity for self-reinvention.

Wright's first architectural position in Chicago was with Joseph L. Silsbee in 1887, an architect who practised in the American 'Shingle Style' of the period, and who had worked for the Lloyd Jones family in Spring Green, Wisconsin. Silsbee was also an avid collector of Japanese artefacts and was familiar with the Boston 'Orientalist' set and it may well have been him who exposed Wright to the fashionable Japanese arts of the period (Wright himself later became a dealer in Japanese art). Wright was always highly ambitious, and so in 1888 he began working for the progressive and innovative practice of Adler & Sullivan. There he immediately struck up a close rapport with Louis Sullivan, who is said to have been equally smitten by the youthful Wright.

Wright married Catherine Tobin in 1889 and built a new home in the affluent Oak Park suburb of Chicago with money he borrowed from Sullivan. To support his growing family in Oak Park, Wright began to moonlight on private jobs. When Sullivan found this out, they quarrelled, and – depending on rival accounts – Wright was either fired or else left in anger. In 1893, Wright set up his own practice and subsequently decided to add on a studio to his house in Oak Park. In doing so, he experimented both with the internal spatial order of his home and with the external manifestations of a freer layout. Indeed all of his early domestic work shows a desire to 'deconstruct the box,' as he termed it, in search for more fluid forms of spatial continuity. There were, of course, many other cultural ideas involved in his early architectural development, and there were numerous instances when Wright turned to Japan for architectural ideas.[7] The Ho-o-den house by Masamichi Kuru exhibited in the famous Chicago World's Fair of 1893 came to influence Wright's ideas about internal spatial continuity and lightweight frame construction.[8] Essentially, the Ho-o-den house showed Wright the potential of breaking down the 'load-bearing box' of Western architecture into something far more expressive – the Prairie House.[9]

Perhaps not surprisingly, Wright's first venture outside America was to travel to Japan with some former clients, the Willitses, in 1905; it has also been suggested that the trip was intended to save his floundering marriage to Catherine. A century later, in 2005, I retraced Wright's initial visit to Japan by following a very similar itinerary to the one that Wright recorded in a remarkable set of photographs. Wright returned several times again to Japan, including trips between 1913 and 1923 when he was designing and building the Imperial Hotel in Tokyo, a building primarily conceived for

Street view, Ward Willits House, Highland Park, Illinois (1902) by Frank Lloyd Wright

foreign visitors, but also to promote Japanese interests beyond. In addition, Wright undertook a number of residential commissions in Japan and he also continued to trade – as he had done by then for many years – in Japanese *ukiyo-e* woodblock prints. His built projects in Japan therefore provide a unique insight into an early global encounter in which Wright, who was so clearly inspired by Japanese art and architecture, got an opportunity to build his own interpretation of that culture. And yet, Wright never properly understood Japanese space or architecture, and his objectification of space was an example of 'cross-cultural confusion.'[10] However, it is these confrontations that can lead to a new direction in architectural and cultural 'progress.' I made one significant detour from his 1905 tourist route, to visit the Yamamura Villa in nearby Kobe that was designed by Frank Lloyd Wright (1918) – a site of a cultural translation where Wright's Western-style villa encloses a sequence of Japanese-inspired interior spaces.

By the time that Frank Lloyd Wright designed the seminal Robie House in south Chicago (1908–10), he seemed to have sensed already that he was coming to the end of his 'Prairie Style' era. He even appears psychologically to have been seeking out a new form of challenge. In 1909, Wright dramatically left his wife and six children – along with his friends and unfinished projects – and travelled to Europe with the wife of a former client, (Martha) Mamah Cheney. They went to Germany, where he published two-volume Wasmuth Folios; comprised of lithographs and photographs, they were effectively a summary of his 'Prairie Style' career. The Folios were in truth a vanity-publishing venture that was aimed largely at the American market, and their reception in Europe was, at most, incidental. I extended Wright's journey of 1909–10 to include visits to the old Imperial capitals of Paris, Amsterdam, Berlin and Vienna, so as to situate Wright's ideas and work as part of the early ferment of architectural modernism, prior to the First World War. Despite having produced a series of designs and ideas that were clearly more progressive than those of his European colleagues at this time, Wright seemed unable to disseminate his thoughts beyond the Wasmuth Folios – there were, for instance, no lecture tours, journal articles, architectural gatherings or public exhibitions linked to this trip. Wright's influence on European modernism is still very much questioned today, but he clearly played a role in setting the scene for the new architecture. But what was his role? His work was openly embraced in Holland both by the rationalist De Stijl School and the far more expressionist Amsterdam School. Yet Wright operated on the margins of European modernity on either side of the First World War, and was viewed as an outside contributor. Ironically, this was a distanced role that Wright later even came to embrace as his destiny, in turn causing him to become one of the most trenchant critics of what became known as 'International Style' modernism.

In 1911 Wright returned to America along with Mamah Cheney to a life of notoriety and frequent press intrusion – provoking him to build the personal sanctuary of Taliesin out in rural Wisconsin. Wright turned to his Welsh ancestry to name his new home, and to re-invent himself again, claiming that 'Taliesin was the name of a Welsh poet, a druid-bard who sang to Wales the glories of fine art.'[11] Shunned by the public because of his affair, his practice in Chicago declined notably. But soon his life was disturbed by greater tragedy. A deliberate fire at Taliesin in 1914 and the massacre of seven people, including Mamah Cheney and her children, by a deranged servant, destroyed the dream of rural contentment. Needing to move on once more, Wright began another relationship with Miriam Noel, whom he eventually married in 1923. He had also begun to work on many residential commissions across America, such as the 'Textile Block' houses in California, during the 1920s. When his marriage failed only a year later, there was bitter wrangling over the divorce settlement, amidst accusations of desertion and cruelty. Then, in 1925, Wright met Olgivanna Hinzenberg, a Montenegrin divorcee and mystic. They soon moved in together to the recently repaired Taliesin in Wisconsin. It can be argued that each of Wright's romantic relationships fulfilled different needs: Catherine gave the young Wright civility and a solid family; Mamah Cheney remained his true love, tragically lost; Miriam gave him emotional and financial support at a vital moment; and, finally, Olgivanna provided a deeper spiritual dimension that appealed to, and fuelled, his ego.[12]

Meanwhile, in his professional career, foreign publications from Holland and Germany started to reframe his architecture. The lavish 1925 publication by the Dutch expressionist journal, *Wendigen*, acted as a critical reappraisal of his work for those in Europe. Now a number of leading European modernist architects went to pay homage to Wright at Taliesin, and he loved the adulation. This led Wright to engage in alternative design approaches during the 1930s. He began lecturing regularly around 1930 and he published the first version of his own life story, simply called *An Autobiography*, in 1932. However, it was the launch of the Taliesin Fellowship in that same year that finally eased Wright's financial problems – as his young tutees had to pay handsomely to study with the 'master' at Taliesin, providing him with a new impetus and source of income. Wright duly proceeded to reinvent himself yet again as the grand architect of the new American car-based suburban landscape, and in this way his 'Usonian' period emerged. Wright's Broadacre City concept was clearly inspired by Roosevelt's 'New Deal,' plus it responded to other alternative ideas about reforming American society in the wake of the 1929 Wall Street Crash. Following the shock of the subsequent Great Depression, Wright developed and promoted his decentralised urban plan – Broadacre City – that he planned to extend over the whole American continent. Broadacre City was based on the equitable distribution of utilities and land throughout America, and would allow all its citizens to have one acre of land as a birth right. This remaking of the American landscape he called 'Usonia' and it was supported by the freedom offered by the car. Broadacre City came to serve as the collectivised expression of Wright's global ambition for 'organic' architecture – i.e. it was his idealised vision of community, democracy, society, and architecture all rolled up into one.

Yet Wright still remained outside the architectural and political mainstream, and from that stance he was not afraid to criticise the American

Perspective views, Herbert Jacobs House, Madison, Wisconsin (1936) by Frank Lloyd Wright

government and its institutions during the Great Depression. This brought Wright a degree of admiration from the Soviet Union and in 1937 he was invited to attend the First Soviet Congress of Architects in Moscow. Ever looking for a chance for self-promotion, he took Broadacre City – his answer to dispersed agrarian society – over to Russia as a globalising force. Wright, like many disaffected intellectuals in the West in the late 1930s, viewed the Soviet Union as a means of establishing a better society; in Wright's case, it was his own democratic 'organic' ideal that he believed transcended both capitalism and communism. Curiously the Russian architectural avant-garde had also by then embraced a dis-urbanist alternative to centralised cities, meaning that two conflicting ideologies identified similar plans for the new society. By the time of Wright's visit in 1937, Stalin had begun persecuting intellectuals, especially those in the avant-garde, in his infamous purges. I arrived in Moscow 70 years later in the search for any traces of Wright's 'organic' architecture. I also extended my trip to include Magnitogorsk in the Russian Urals, a steel-producing city that was planned in the 1930s by the dis-urbanists, so that I could compare it with Wright's Broadacre vision. Magnitogorsk reflected the changing, and often muddled, political machinations during the Soviet period, with Russian centralised bureaucracy struggling to impose its will on an emerging city, meaning that its realisation was very different from its conception.

Wright's notable architectural successes in the 1930s with Fallingwater (Pennsylvania; 1934–7), Johnson Wax Administration Building (Wisconsin; 1936–9) and his new second home, Taliesin West (Arizona; 1938) in the desert, confirmed him as a leading architectural practitioner. He was invited to edit a full edition of the *Architectural Forum* in January 1938, which further consolidated his global reputation. Later that year, Wright was asked to occupy the Sir George Watson Chair on behalf of Sulgrave Manor, an Anglo-American institution seeking to bind the US to Britain. As part of this honour, Wright was required to give a number of public lectures in London, he duly presented four unrehearsed and provocative talks at the RIBA in 1939. In Britain, I visited the utopian community of Ashbee's Guild of Handiwork in Chipping Campden, the postwar Welfare State creation of Brynmawr Rubber Factory in Wales, and the new town of Milton Keynes. In addition, I visited homes that had been inspired by Wright to understand how his architecture had been adapted to Britain.

Wright's later career proved to be relatively prosperous, with the Guggenheim Museum in New York (1943–59) acting as the spatial and professional crescendo. However, the value of what I term his final 'Legacy' period remains contested. At the end of his career, Wright's celebrity found itself called upon for a variety of architectural projects, with perhaps the single most intriguing example being the Wright retrospective entitled *Sixty Years of Living Architecture* which was held in Florence, Italy, in 1951, and then went on to tour worldwide. The exhibition was conceived by the US government as a subliminal piece of Cold War cultural propaganda, with Wright's ongoing creative virility being portrayed as a bulwark against the collectivist values being proposed by Italian communists. From Florence, Wright was also taken to see the Venice School of Architecture – then under the joint stewardship of its head, Giuseppe Samona, the design professor, Carlo Scarpa, and the architectural historian, Bruno Zevi. Wright's 'organic' architecture was strongly supported by these eminent Italian figures. Hence in Venice he was lionised as a true star and received a number of awards. I recreated a Grand Tour to Italy with Wright, visiting Venice, Florence and Rome. There were many traces of Wright's work in these cities and beyond, where architects had followed Zevi's call to establish an alternative 'organic' tradition in Italy.

Interior courtyard view, 'How to live in the Southwest', David Wright House, Phoenix, Arizona (1950) by Frank Lloyd Wright

In one of his final commissions Wright was invited to Iraq in 1957 to design a new opera house for Baghdad. This scheme also carried elements of political intrigue, plus many regional tensions, since the ruling Hashemite monarchy was seeking to forge links with America to bolster their vulnerable position against emergent Arab nationalism. As a young boy in Wisconsin, Wright had read the fantastical *Arabian Nights* tales and now he was being given the opportunity to prove that he really could be Aladdin, just as he had imagined during his childhood. His opera house design was duly expanded into the Greater Baghdad Plan and Cultural Centre, a full-scale 'Arabic' fantasy, but also prophetic of our current search for cultural identity. I visited Kuwait, Dubai and Abu Dhabi along the Persian Gulf to analyse Wright's architectural fantasies within the Middle East, especially in the way they seem to seek to project a new modern identity. The recently completed Burj Khalifa in Dubai tries to echo Wright's Mile High Tower (1957), and indeed possesses a similar triangulated plan and dramatic stepped profile. While there, I also visited an exhibition at the Emirates Hotel in Abu Dhabi on the Saadiyat Island Cultural Quarter development, this being a scheme that replicates Wright's proposal for the Baghdad Cultural Centre.

'ORGANIC' ARCHITECTURE – FROM LOCAL TO GLOBAL

Wright's 'organic' architecture beyond America negotiates a paradox. It was purportedly founded on close personal responses to different sites which the architect knew well, yet it became a brand of generic architecture that appeared to travel seamlessly across the globe, with little real understanding of the cultures being affected. Another problem with 'organic' architecture is that Wright never fully explained what 'organic' architecture was; it seemed at once to be both obvious and elusive, and not many commentators have sat down and tried to deconstruct the concept in all its multi-faceted glory. Wright himself did not initially use the term 'organic' architecture at the start of his career. Indeed, one of the first instances was to conclude his 'Prairie Style' manifesto essay, 'In the Cause of Architecture' (1908), with a tantalising phrase about his future aspirations, 'As for the future – the work shall grow more truly simple; more expressive with fewer lines, fewer forms; more articulate with less labour; more plastic, more fluent, although more coherent; more organic.'[13]

For Wright, 'organic' architecture was developed from an understanding of nature both in its 'external' and 'internal' manifestations. 'External' nature was expressed in four interrelated components: the response to the nature of the site; taking one's inspiration from natural forms; displaying natural materials honestly; and being responsive to local climate.[14] Thus, in its essence, 'organic' was seen as being derived from the site and its environment, which would be as we would expect. Furthermore, Wright had contemplated the abstract 'internal' character of nature in his essay on the 'Japanese Print' (1912), in which he saw inherent abstract geometries as self-defining and self-propagating features.[15] Wright also believed there existed an internal pre-disposed logic that allowed nature to grow into new forms in balance with external natural forces. Wright, thus, in effect rephrased Louis Sullivan's famous declaration, 'form follows function,' so that it became the holistic concept of 'form and function as one.'[16] This combination of 'external' and 'internal' nature seems to be a wonderful means for deriving an architecture that was critically situated, environmentally responsive and which possessed an integral harmony. It is a philosophy that certainly seems to articulate most people's idea of 'organic' architecture. Yet, for Wright, it was not a static concept, and over his career 'organic' architecture developed into a 'cumulative' approach that became universal as time passed.[17]

I believe that underlying Wright's concept of the 'organic' architecture was an early and long-lasting engagement with globalisation. Early in his career, Frank Lloyd Wright manipulated the concept of globalisation, as he synthesised traditional Japanese architecture, the 'English Free Style' and the American 'Shingle Style', to invent the Prairie House. He extracted architectural and cultural ideas from England, Japan and America within the cultural void of the American Midwest and gave them a new 'Prairie' suburban identity. It seems that Wright had realised that globalisation offered not only opportunities to travel, but also to extract, sample and combine other cultural ideas. I believe that the 19th-century expositions – whereby different nations produced a cultural display or pavilion that were removed from their original cultural settings – were an opportunity for Wright to experience these different global cultures. Whilst Wright poured scorn on the Chicago World's Fair of 1893 he was in fact indebted to the Japanese Ho-o-den pavilion for inspiring his 'Prairie' architecture. International journals and magazines were another source of the wider architectural developments that Wright accessed. During this period, Wright was a recipient and critical assembler of different global cultures.

Yet, by the 1930s 'organic' architecture was expanded to embrace the whole of human society and, according to Wright, was more relevant than the two prevalent theories of organising society in the 20th century – i.e. capitalism and communism. 'Organic' architecture was destined to become a global manifesto, one that he claimed was 'everywhere and nowhere.'[18] Essentially 'organic' architecture had been removed from any cultural setting and was a denial of his earlier proclamations. Wright's fame and ambition in his final 'Legacy' period were an expansion and aggrandisement of a pre-existing global strategy, which was based upon his expansive 'organic' architecture. When travelling overseas he claimed that he only ever saw 'confirmation' of his ideas: 'as for the Incas, the Mayans, even the Japanese – all were to me but splendid confirmation,' he wrote dismissively.[19] It is within this last period as Wright bestrides the globe that he adopts the mantle of star-achitect – a global practitioner who was invited to build projects beyond America in a manner that was not related to the host country, thus promoting a homogenised global culture.

1

UNUSUAL VIEWS OF OUTSTANDING SITES

Wright called Japan the 'most romantic, artistic, nature-inspired country on earth . . . [its] art and architecture really did have organic character.'[1] Contrary to most other architects in America at the time, who traditionally sought their education in Europe, Wright's first journey outside the United States was to Japan with his wife, Catherine, and two of his former clients, the Willitses, on a mission to purchase woodblock prints. They left Vancouver by boat on 21 February 1905 and arrived in Yokohama less than a month later on 7 March. The party broke up on arrival, leaving Wright free to purchase woodblock prints and visit several tourist sites.

I arrived in Japan on 29 October 2005 to retrace Wright's journey. My itinerary was based on the book, *Fifty Views of Japan* (Wright's photographic record of his 1905 trip), in which Masami Tanigawa provides the likely route that Wright would have taken; indeed a number of hotel records were found to confirm this route.[2] The original photographs show Wright's enthusiasm for Japanese temples and with vernacular architecture, ornamental gardens and landscape.

Wright described his first view of the Japanese archipelago in March 1905, from on board the *Empress of China,* a Canadian steamer:

> Imagine, if you have not seen it, a mountainous, abrupt land, the sea everywhere apparently risen too high upon it, so that all gentle slopes to the water's edge are lost. All shore lines abrupt. It is morning. Pure golden skies are seen over far stretches of blue sea dotted in the distance by flocks of white sampan sails-white birds at rest on the blue water.[3]

Wright went to Japan seven times in total: each trip responding to a different emotional, financial, and professional need. He incorrectly noted the date of his first visit as 1906, in *An Autobiography*[4] and claimed that he went to Japan 'in pursuit of the [woodblock] print' and that he wanted to 'rest after building the Larkin building.'[5] Yet, it has been alleged that there was another motivation for the visit: as a last-ditch attempt to save his faltering marriage to Catherine.[6] Perhaps even more troubling was the fact that Wright had to borrow $5,000 from his pupil Walter Burley Griffin, to finance the trip.[7]

Japan had an uneasy relationship with the West. The first western explorers were the Portuguese Christian Missionaries in the 1540s, who were tolerated by the Muromachi Shogunate because of their firearms. However, the insular Tokugawa Shogunate were suspicious of Europeans, and by 1638 Japan became a closed country. It was in the mid-19th century, with the Meiji restoration of 1853, that many Japanese artefacts start to flow to the West giving substance to the 'Oriental' ideal. Fine Japanese artworks provided the impetus to a number of artists including the French impressionists and James Whistler, as well as Frank Lloyd Wright. In a rare piece of lucidity in *An Autobiography*, Wright acknowledged that his collection of Japanese woodblock prints were an inspiration to his architecture, writing convincingly that their aesthetic composition had genuine significance.[8] However, these first cultural exchanges between western consumers and Japanese art generated as an oppressive 'external gaze' that stifled Japan's own progress and identity.[9] The exotic allure of 'Japonisme' led to a number of artisans having to turn out reproductions of their own culture simply to satisfy Western tastes. Wright also often quoted the Chinese philosopher Lao-Tse: 'the reality of a room . . . was found in the vacant space enclosed by the roof and walls, not in the roof and walls themselves.'[10] Wright used this saying as a starting point to deconstruct the box-like spatial arrangement within Victorian homes to generate his own Prairie Houses. But Wright failed to understand that Japanese spatial concept was based on 'flatness' and his Western objectification of space based on perspective was a piece of 'cross-cultural confusion.'[11]

There was a connection between Wright's first employer, Joseph Silsbee, and his first exposure to Japanese art.[12] Wright began working for Silsbee in 1887, who was a keen collector of Japanese art and artefacts.[13] Furthermore, Silsbee was the first cousin of Ernest Fenollosa, a member of the Boston Orientalist group who had studied and taught in Japan from 1877 onwards. The group saw that the rapid Westernisation of Japan under the Meiji restoration posed a threat to its artistic legacy, and so sought to promote Japanese cultural and artistic credentials by publishing books and organising public lectures. Edward Morse wrote *Japanese Homes and their Surroundings* (1886), and his observations were reciprocated in Wright's own writing on the Prairie Houses.[14] The use of the standard planning module, the open plan, the central hearth, the concealed entry, and the absence of ornament were all ideas contained in Morse's book and later developed by Wright.[15] Reading Okakura Kakuzo's *The Book of Tea* (1906), I was surprised that the ancient rites, ceremonies, and architecture of the tea house carried so many modern resonances.[16] The asymmetric composition of the Japanese tea house, and plain aesthetic, confirmed many of Wright's early architectural ideas and his later notion of 'organic' architecture. Later in 1893, Chicago hosted the World's Fair. The Exposition was regarded as a triumph of the academic Beaux-Arts tradition, as favoured by the likes of Daniel Burnham, but Wright called it 'a fateful year in the culture of these United States.'[17] Yet, set in a prominent location in the centre of the Exposition, was the Japanese pavilion, which followed the historicist theme. The pavilion had a mixed legacy: it included the Heian (794–1185), Muromachi (1392–1593) and Edo (1615–1868) periods, all rolled into one building. It was Japan's own view of itself, a neo-Japanese representation to the West. Although the decoration was overwhelming, the underlying cruciform of the central space was of more interest to Wright, with many of the Prairie Houses possessing this spatial layout.[18]

TOKYO

Wright recorded his impressions of Japan in *An Autobiography*, providing a valuable insight into the country in this period of rapid change. He recalled his first view of Tokyo:

> This teeming, enormous area is fascinating Yedo [now Tokyo]. A vast city channelled but with wide bare earth streets swarming with humanity their undeterminable length, beaten down hard by traffic, lined both sides with blue-grey tiled roofed two storey wooden buildings. A great city that is a gigantic village.[19]

Wright was notably well prepared for the artistic adventure to the land that had intrigued him for many years: 'it all looks – just like the prints' he remarked.[20] In contrast, German modernist architect Bruno Taut arrived in 1933, and was traumatised by the chaotic architectural styles he saw in Ginza, 'the spectacle which had already offended, now positively assaulted the eye.'[21] More recently still, Rem Koolhaas noted in cynical mood: 'First Impression: the vastness and shamelessness of its ugliness . . . when beauty happens it is absolutely surprising.'[22]

A century after Wright's first impressions, I arrived at the green idyll of Narita International Airport, surrounded by rice fields, and travelled by train to Ueno, a district of Tokyo. As the train passed above the modern metropolitan city, the scale and modernity of Tokyo was a revelation: searing corporate skyscrapers were juxtaposed with intimate, two-storey family homes. Weaving in and out around the city fabric on the train, everything seemed contingent and subject to change. I could find no references to the past – was this relentless contemporary city a vision of the future, a city detached from its history?

The scolar and translator of Japanese, Edward Seidensticker, notes how the ancient city Edo, now called Tokyo, was stratified by geography and social hierarchy into a 'High City' and a 'Low City.'[23] The 'High City' was based around the ancient castle and moat, with the feudal hierarchy of the Shogunate system radiating out from the castle. Whereas the 'Low City' was a peripheral settlement nearby the estuary, where artisans and merchants lived and worked. My friend's Japanese wife had booked me into the Asia Centre Hotel; he said that a Western hotel in the 'High City' would be reassuring for my first experience of Japan. Emerging from the subway beneath the twin Ayomae towers, the Asksaka district was distinctly commercial, Americanised and dull. The hotel had a generously long lobby, but my room was small, with the bed just fitting between the window and the bathroom pod. This fibreglass pod was a strange green colour, with matching sanitary ware. Most curiously, it had a heated and self-cleaning toilet seat, with a number of graphically illustrated water settings; intrigued, I went through a number of options!

Having read so much about Frank Lloyd Wright's masterpiece, the Imperial Hotel (1923–67), I was keen to find its latest reincarnation. The third version of the Imperial Hotel (1970) is a thick four-storey base slab topped by a vertical 17-storey cruciform tower. As I walked into the polished lobby, I was approached by a porter, and directed towards a concierge where I met the manager. There was no time to stand around in the vast corporate lobby and, as groups arrived and others departed, it was loud and animated. The manager showed me a book, *The Imperial Hotel – A Legend in Photos*, which records all the important guests, including Babe Ruth and the All American Baseball Team, Marilyn Monroe and Joe DiMaggio, John Wayne and Jodie Foster.[24] He told me about the Old Imperial Bar, designed by Wright and which was still standing and to which I was escorted upstairs by a porter. The Old Imperial Bar, with its dark interior, had taken on a frontier aspect. It was only a quarter-full in the afternoon, with a group of Japanese ladies lunching and some business people drinking at the bar. The L-shaped space had the bar running down the long edge with solitary booths opposite and a seating area at the short base. It was built as Wright would have intended, with a low intimate ceiling that contained octagonal recessed lights and dark brick walls. Oya stone screens divide the space into intimate gatherings, and there were still a number of the original (uncomfortable) chairs. I recognised a wall fresco; a relic that was once in the main hotel foyer was now in this 'last-chance' saloon. I ordered a beer and a waiter brought over a couple of books about the hotel for me to look over. As I flicked through them, I felt a wave of nostalgia, and I recalled a chapter from Wright's *An Autobiography*, 'Designing against doomsday' when he described his design for the hotel to overcome a potential earthquake.[25]

When Japan's relationship with the West was reappraised after the Meiji restoration, one of the early architectural innovations to follow was the Hoterukan (1867–68) in Tsukiji district. Perfectly tautologically named – both *hoteru* and *kan* mean hotel[26] – it followed earlier examples of literally containing the Western tourists by isolating them within gates and canals from the rest of the city. However the hotel was also a means of cultural translation between eastern and western traditions. The Hoterukan had an elongated U-form, was up to 60 metres (197 feet) in length and housed more than 200 rooms over three floors. The architecture was prophetic of *giyofu* (pseudo-Western style) buildings that were based on traditional Japanese forms and construction, but given an occidental feel.[27] Other early hotels followed a similar theme, with the Italianate Rokumeikan (1883), becoming a legend of the period with its extravagant parties hosted by the ruling elite for foreign visitors, which featured Western dress and dancing. However, most of the dancing was done by the Westerners: Japanese women, if coaxed onto the floor, were reported to be 'correct but wooden.'[28] The Imperial Hotel replaced the outdated Rokumeikan, in Tokyo's High City. It was built in the Hibya district – an important commercial centre next to the Imperial Residence – and was a joint venture between the Imperial Household and leading industrialists. The first iteration of the Imperial Hotel was a three-storey timber construction in a German-meets-French Second Empire Beaux-Arts style. It was built in 1890 by Yuzuru Watanabe to include 100 guest rooms. The interior of the hotel was finished in a decidedly European style, its restaurant served Western food, and *The Times* reported in 1910 that it 'is in fact the centre of European life in Tokyo.'[29] But as Japan prospered, a second and larger version of the Imperial Hotel was required.

There are a number of intriguing theories about how Wright won the commission for the second Imperial Hotel. Wright himself claimed that he was 'called to build' the hotel,[30] while others note it was because of his connections with Japanese print collectors.[31] This is all part of Wright's self-possessed narrative, claiming that clients would appoint him due to his reputation alone – yet the truth is far from clear. The critic Arata Isozaki claims that the hotel design may have been plagiarised from Kikurato Shimoda.[32] After the inauguration of Emperor Taisho in 1912 and the resolution of internal political issues, Wright was instructed to complete the design by early 1916, and in the winter of 1917, Wright travelled once more to Japan with his female companion, Miriam Noel, to start the work on site. Wright elaborated on his brief and expounded the wider aims and themes of his Imperial Hotel design: 'The hotel is not a hotel at all in the accepted sense of the term. It is a delightful place of sojourn for travellers and a place of varied entertainment for the social functions of the life of Tokyo, the Japanese capital.'[33]

He claimed it 'was laid out as a group of buildings in a system of gardens and terraces and not as an "office building hotel" along American lines.'[34] Here, Wright was making a distinction between the corporate American hotel and his own interpretation: 'The Imperial Hotel is designed as a system of gardens . . . Japan is Garden-land.'[35] Despite this playful intent, Wright used a 'classical' axial plan for the hotel and indeed most of his institutional commissions in general. In addition, it could be claimed that the *parti* adopted for the hotel was related to many traditional Japanese temple forms, such as the Ho-o-den pavilion at the Chicago World's Fair of 1893.[36] But Isozaki relates the composition to the Western external gaze and the Beaux-Arts tradition because the spatial articulation used Western devices such as graduated perspective.[37]

The Second Imperial Hotel was very much of its time, and Wright took advantage of the scarce knowledge of modern building techniques to make one of the last major handcrafted buildings. Armed with a small army of labour, Wright devised an individual and personal form of abstract ornamentation that dominated the whole composition. There were in the order of 500 labourers working on the project, as well as 100 stone masons:

> How skilful they were! What craftsmen! How patient and clever. So instead of wasting them by vainly trying to make them come our way – we went their way. I modified many original intentions to make the most of what I now saw was naturally theirs. . .[38]

The hotel had a symmetrical H-form plan with small rooms to the outer walled part and a 'symbolic' core within the centre. The two defensive three-storey walls contained 285 guest rooms, which reflected the efficiency and compactness of the Pullman railway cars and the luxury cabins on ocean liners. Wright argued that these small rooms satisfied the needs of a 'high-class hotel on costly ground.'[39] And, rather than making the rooms a standard dimension with standard fittings, Wright succeeded in making almost each room different, in direct opposition to a rational 'office building hotel.' Between the wings of the hotel rooms, were placed the social function areas, beginning with the constrained entrance, which led to a three-storey open lobby, the seven-storey and more monumental reception rooms, a theatre and a cinema. Intersecting these formal spaces were a number of bridges and promenades that allowed guests to meet in more informal areas. In the internal organisation, Wright demonstrated his mastery of spatial manipulation, with inter-penetrating vertical spaces as well as horizontal spaces interlocking with one another.

In the 'Designing against Doomsday' chapter of *An Autobigraphy*, Wright describes in great detail anti-earthquake measures, such as the shallow foundations, and cantilevered floor design, which were in reality of limited structural benefit.[40] However, Wright's other ideas for outwitting 'the temblor' were to have a lasting effect on earthquake design. These included massing the building so that it had a very low centre of gravity, tapering its solid concrete-core wall construction, dividing the building into a number of parts, isolating the services in trenches, using lightweight copper roof cladding, and introducing a water pool for fire-fighting purposes.[41] The Imperial Hotel duly survived the Kanto Earthquake on 1 September 1923 with only minor damage, as did other modern buildings in Tokyo. Within Tokyo as a whole, however, there were 90,000 deaths and over 75 per cent of the city was destroyed.[42] A telegram purportedly sent to Wright stated: 'Following wireless received from Tokio today hotel stands undamaged as monument of your genius hundreds of homeless provided by perfectly maintained service congratulations signed Okua Impeho.'[43] The authenticity of this telegram was later questioned with no proof of the original telegram ever being sent from Japan.[44] Did Wright send the telegraph himself? Nonetheless, Wright revelled in the adulation and proof of his own 'organic' design and his divine ability to overcome natural catastrophes.

When the hotel was completed, many criticised the design, as it did not represent Japanese traditions and neither was it daringly modern. It was Wright's own view of Japan, based on 'his imagination.'[45] He claimed:

> This building – the new Imperial Hotel of Tokyo – is not designed to be a Japanese building: it is an artist's tribute to Japan, modern and universal in character.[46]

Wright had an immediate impact on the architectural scene in Japan with many students and young architects following his ideas and copying his surface decorations, but without deriving from it any deeper spatial intent. By a strange coincidence, the Showa era (1926–89) of 'enlightened peace' under the new Emperor Hirohito sought to re-define Japanese architecture in opposition to the imported Western forms. The architect, Shimoda, advocated the traditional roof on a masonry building as an example of *teikan-heigo-shiki* (crown-topped style). In addition, he attempted to reclaim the Imperial Hotel as his own; Shimoda argued that the manner of placing such a roof on stone or concrete was his own invention, and Wright's design, therefore, an appropriation.[47] The *teikan* style of the 1930s became associated with Japanese nationalism and it came to represent a dark chapter in Japanese history.[48] Wright cannot possibly be culpable for this nationalist style, yet his Imperial Hotel was an unwitting player in its sinister development. The history and the legacy of the second Imperial Hotel is thus still contested, but faced with an early global crisis of representation, Wright created an original icon – a destination that placed Tokyo, and Japan, firmly on the international architectural map.

The Imperial Hotel's quirky earthquake-resistant construction on soft mud piles was not altogether resistant to differential settlements, and during the Great Kanto Earthquake in 1923, the heavier central portion sank by 0.6 metres (23 ½ inches). By 1968 the rear of the central portion had settled by 1 metre (3 feet 3 inches), which must have made working in the hotel quite a challenge. Ogilvanna Wright visited the hotel in the late-1960s as a last ditch attempt to save the Imperial Hotel.[49] Despite an international campaign, the Imperial Hotel was demolished in 1968 and the lobby relocated to the Meiji Mura theme-park outside Nagoya. A more fitting end would have been to see the Imperial Hotel being gradually consumed by the soft mud, like an old ocean liner buckling and sinking – a ready-made modernist ruin, and a warning to all others attempting to outwit 'the temblor.'

Back at the Old Imperial Hotel bar, I nostalgically flicked through the old photographs of the hotel in Cary James's book; there is a certain romantic poignancy within the images, the hotel seemingly a ready-made ruin even in 1965. The intimate scale of the entrance was reminiscent of a country retreat, the richly textured interior was extracted from a medieval castle, and the forlorn travellers seemed to be trapped in a vast Kafka-esque brick hulk. The design seemed to me to be a hybrid combining Japanese references and Wrightian themes; and there are echoes in the plan from the original Hoterukan, the original *giyofu* lodge. As for the overbearing ornamentation, this can be seen as a reflection of Edo Castle and the Shogunate-era architecture, and it was re-configured by Wright into his own personal architectural language. Ornament was a long-standing Wrightian concern, as he sought to integrate it into the structure of the architecture. Yet, one can also detect traces of a universalist outlook to the design, and Wright is beginning to experiment with elements of an emerging global 'organic' architecture.

Arata Endo was one of Wright's assistants on the Imperial Hotel. He was a Christian and introduced Wright to a new client, Motoko Hani, a fellow Christian journalist, who was seeking to establish a new secular school in Tokyo. She saw education as the means 'to create truly free people,'[50] and these Western-style liberal values were supported by Wright, who had built

Hillside Home School (1887) in Wisconsin for his equally independent aunts. Wright sketched out the design for the main building and west wing of the school, leaving the final drafting to his assistant, Endo, with both architects signing off the drawings. The school was subsequently named Jiyu Gakuen (1921–6), which means Freedom School, and I determined to make a visit. After a short journey on the metro, I emerged at Ikebukuro station to be confronted by the never-ending Tobu / Seibu department stores, and no other identifiable landmarks. I finally recognised the Metropolitan Hotel, which allowed me to escape the vortex of consumption. Beyond the shopping mall, the scale of the city collapsed into two- or three-storey homes and, two streets later, down a very narrow lane, I found the school. The scale of the building was low and intimate, based around the children, or Wright himself, I speculated. The classically inspired spatial arrangement could be easily grasped from the street, with a recessed central communal block and two classroom wings. Uniting the composition was a dual-pitched roof that appeared very Japanese, yet Wright was inventive in using a copper covering instead of tiles – he had also reduced the pitch so that even this quintessential Japanese element was given an inventive twist.

The receptionist said that there was no tour on offer in English, but they had a few photocopied papers and an old copy of *Frank Lloyd Wright Quarterly* magazine that described the renovation of the school.[51] I followed several directional arrows, and bowed beneath the low doors to view a reconstructed classroom and an exhibition of old photos. There was another compressed entrance into the south-facing main hall, and a woman sat in the darkness offering small but delicious coffee and cakes. Beyond this point was the spatial release of the main hall. With its captivating window of abstract geometries and oblique angles, it was an enchanting space. Bathed in glorious sunshine, the natural materials and colours were exposed, and the simple volume was articulated by the generous window at one end and a stone gallery at the other. During the restoration, a mural painted by the class of 1931 had been revealed: it was based on Exodus 13 and depicted a Biblical migration. Behind the main hall and up a few steps was a dining room with a communal hearth. Dark, abstracted diamond-shaped trusses, which articulated this space with suspended light fittings, again showed Wright at his most playful. Further steps again led to a gallery with brick remnants from the Imperial Hotel and an exhibition of Wright's Japanese designs, plus projects of other architects who had been inspired by him.

Following its opening on 14 April 1921, the Jiyu Gakuen school prospered and found a number of parents who shared Hani's educational vision. By 1929, a second, much larger campus was added, and then in 1934 Endo designed a new consolidated campus for 300 students in the western suburb of Minamisawa. The original Wright school then became a graduate school and was renamed by Hani as Myonichikan – the House of Tomorrow. The school's expansion occurred despite the fact that it was not officially recognised by Japan's Educational Authority. In the nationalist climate of the 1930s the term *jiyu* (freedom) was considered to be subversive, and so Hani was asked to change it. She of course resisted. After the war, the school was viewed as a beacon of progressive democratic education and was finally given official recognition. Today, it continues to prosper with over 1,000 students. However, Wright's part of the school was threatened when the 1980s building boom in downtown Tokyo reached the suburbs. At that point, the 0.27 hectare site was valued at a staggering US$30 million.[52] In addition, the school was in poor condition and facing a potential restoration

Main window, lounge hall, Jiyu Gakuen Girls' School, Tokyo, Japan (1921) by Frank Lloyd Wright

cost of US$5 million, so a strategy was needed to conserve the building.[53] An article in the *New York Times* in February 1992 alerted the international community to the possible redevelopment of the site.[54] To preserve the school and to claim a grant for its restoration, it was designated as an 'Important Cultural Property,' and hence they are now obliged to allow visitors such as myself – plus, it was deemed that they could earn a secondary income by letting it out for conferences and weddings.

Across the road from the school was the Auditorium (1927), designed by Endo. It was openly inspired by Unity Temple (Chicago; 1905–8), with a grey textured render and a magnificent dark timber cantilevered porch. The auditorium was used to hold large school meetings, and it has a small stage, a gallery, and two ante-rooms. The dark space, with wood panelling up to the window heads and wooden seats, reminded me of a chapel vestry – was this Endo's tribute to Wright's non-conformist Welsh heritage? Beside the auditorium, the Myonichikan Publishing Buildings were also distinctly Usonian in their language. I discovered that they were in fact built by Raku Endo, the son of Arata, who had followed his father's footsteps to study at Taliesin. The whole composition therefore formed a 'Wright Court' with a school by the master, an auditorium by his assistant, and a publishing office by one of his apprentices. It is a rare concentration of 'organic' design over three generations and, overall, its effect was a muted, polite and intimate architecture.

Endo was so smitten by his mentor that he even began to follow his dress sense. He also proved to be pivotal to Wright's legacy in Japan: all of the architects who travelled to Taliesin, or practised in the Wright idiom, were connected to him. In addition to the school, Endo designed several villas in Japan that displayed his ability to continue Wright's philosophy, and were dominated by Wrightian forms, thus making them seem mere reproductions. It was interesting to note that Endo travelled to Manchuria during the Japanese occupation, and it is tantalising to imagine that Wright might have influenced an outpost of Japanese colonial architecture in China. Endo found himself unable to leave China after the end of the Second World War and became ill; he died shortly after returning to Japan in 1951. His sons, Raku and Tou, continued the family tradition in that they were schooled at Jiyu Gakuen and went on to assist their father, with Raku eventually joining the Taliesin Fellowship in 1957. As such, he was the last Japanese apprentice to work under Wright.

Later that evening I met up for dinner with my friend Aiko, whom I knew from my brief time studying architecture in Washington, D.C. We meet at

Omotesando metro station, which has a reputation for trendy shops and great modern architecture. Nearby were the international stores by global architectural practices. I enjoyed the woven façade of Tods (2003) by Toyo Ito. Its exterior was derived from overlapping tree silhouettes, and I recalled Wright observing that Japanese innate knowledge of 'organic' and nature was found in words such as *edaburi*, which means the formative arrangement of branches of a tree.[55] Ito's façade was a playful interpretation of *edaburi* as inspired from the tree-lined street it sits on. The street was very busy in the evening, with the shops still open and in the full bloom of the artificial lighting of their corporate branded architecture. We turned away from the consumer delights down a small alleyway to an intimate restaurant, my first purely Japanese encounter. Placing my shoes in a shoe repository, I then stepped up onto the dining level. Aiko had kindly spread the word about my research work, and had contacted a friend of hers, called Daichi. By good fortune, he works for an ex-Taliesin apprentice, Hachiro, and also used to work for Raku Endo. Startled by this revelation, I felt strangely close to the 'master', with only four degrees of separation between us. Daichi joined us and gave me a CD with some images of the Jiyu Gakuen School refurbishment, and he also told me of his plans to get married there. I wanted to know what contemporary architects thought of Wright, and if his architecture had Japanese traits?

Aiko: *I was surprised when I visited Meiji Mura as a schoolgirl and saw the Imperial Hotel lobby. The scale of the building was very small. I found it quite Japanese in character.*

Daichi: *Yes, the prominent roof is another Japanese feature that Wright definitely borrowed from Japan – and the scale again was low, which was quite Japanese.*

This was a validation of the recent scholarly texts on the Japanese primers that had affected Wright's architecture, and from my experience of his American work, the scale of his homes was always intimate. Although Wright's homes were also modelled on his own height of 1.72 metres (5 feet 8 inches), so they were never going to possess tall ceilings.

With their inside knowledge of Japan, I was keen to see if my proposed journey could be enhanced by taking a diversion. Aiko suggested that I try to visit Katsura Detached Palace, claiming that it was more accessible to foreigners. Katsura was the original site of Japanese modernism according to

Bruno Taut, yet his reading was more a reflection of his own ideas than the Palace itself. My friend had also recently heard that a new pavilion had been completed in Fukuoka by Toyo Ito, and it may be an example of 'organic' architecture, I made a mental note to extend my journey west.

KYOTO

The next day was Culture Day – a public holiday – and so I needed to get up early to validate my train pass at Ueno railway station and begin my westward journey. The Shinkansen (bullet train) platform was high above the street, and from there you could get a clear view across the city, although I could not recognise a single landmark. As the train pulled in a number of whistles sounded, and platform staff made some ritual moves to announce its arrival. The train stopped and a troupe of women in pink overalls and visors boarded the train to prepare it for the next journey. I dutifully waited my turn outside the unreserved non-smoking carriage and tried to sit next to a window, but ended up next to a young man who grabbed the window seat and then slept for most of the journey. As the train was readied for departure there was the usual commotion before it glided effortlessly out of the dense heart of Tokyo. Beyond were miles of never-ending urban greyness. I had guessed that my only view of Mount Fuji would be on this train, so I tried to keep awake with a keen eye on the window. The day was overcast and I was not sure that a clear sighting would be possible. Almost on cue my fellow passenger awoke and alerted me to the national landmark, and so I photographed two blurred views – of Mount Fuji beside the industrial park, and Mount Fuji over the sewage works. I hope Hokusai would have approved. My journey from Tokyo to Kyoto followed the old route of the Tokaido Road that was the subject of Ando Hiroshige famous woodblock series, *The Fifty-Three Stations of the Tokaido* (1833–4), which recorded daily life on the road. Whilst it took me three hours to cover 514 km (319 miles), it had taken up to 54 days for Hiroshige and his companions.

On his return to Chicago after his first Japanese visit, Wright organised an exhibition of Japanese prints by Hiroshige at the Art Institute of Chicago in March 1906. This was the first display of *ukiyo-e* (meaning pictures of the floating world) prints in the gallery, and the first retrospective of Hiroshige's work.[56] It was an art form that became popular during the Edo period, and popular themes include famous beauties, landscapes and heroic folktales.

Wright began collecting Japanese woodblock prints sometime around 1890, and in *An Autobiography*, he acknowledged the influence of Japanese prints on his architecture, 'Japanese prints had intrigued me and taught me much. The elimination of the insignificant, a process of simplification in art in which I was myself already engaged . . . found much collateral evidence in the print.'[57] In Wright's view 'the print lies at the bottom of all this so-called modernism.'[58] These idealised views of Japan as portrayed in the *ukiyo-e* print supported Wright's idealised view of 'organic' architecture being based upon an 'internal' and 'eternal' geometry.

Intriguingly, Wright was not only an admirer of the woodblock print, but was also a dealer in prints, so much so that by 1910, he was generating a useful income from buying and selling them.[59] The aim of his 1913 trip was thus not only to secure the Imperial Hotel commission, but also to purchase a large number of prints for the wealthy Boston based brothers William and John Spaulding. Later, whilst working on the construction of the hotel, Wright's son John noted that there was a queue of merchants waiting each day to sell prints and other artefacts to Wright.[60] In 1919, Wright thought he had secured a private print collection, for one of his clients, and sensing a financial opportunity, exported it back to the US. The prints, however, were not originals, but were 're-vamped' (i.e. old prints were re-coloured to look more valuable).[61] To placate his angry clients, Wright was forced to replace the prints with some items out of his own collection, and unfortunately by the end of the debacle, his reputation as a print collector was over. While Wright was a promoter of Orientalism by buying Japanese prints: he also was an agent of the 'external gaze' and exported cultural artefacts for his own financial gain. Yet he never saw any contradiction in that, whilst complaining about the 'lost art' of Japan, he himself was commodifing and speculating in it. Wright continued to amass prints and other artefacts from Japan, and used them as collateral to secure loans during his leaner periods in practice during the inter-war era.

After passing through the turnstiles at Kyoto Railway Station, the visible spatial order collapses. Thereafter the complexity of Japan begins: I had to negotiate three differently owned railway lines and a subway, not to mention various bus interchanges. Strangely, within the station there was a 12-storey department store, a hotel, a theatre, and a small museum. The tourist information desk was situated within the department store, where I was offered a choice of Western or traditional accommodation. I opted for a Japanese *ryokan* (guest house) with shared facilities. It was close to the centre of town, and so I could walk there from the subway station. As I left the station, however, I noticed that the urban landscape was very American, with a grid-street plan and a cluster of grey corporate buildings. Kyoto's rectilinear city plan was based in fact on the Chinese city of Xi'an, with the Imperial Palace in the middle; it was an early example of Japanese adoption of Chinese influences, or 'Japanese spirit with Chinese learning.'[62] Kyoto was Japan's capital from 795 to 1867, and its history makes it also the capital of traditional Japanese arts. My *ryokan* was situated two blocks down from the main street. The houses here were all two-storey and made out of timber or other lightweight construction, and they possessed large doors that opened out to the street. In between the houses were restaurants, cafés, schools, garages, and grocery stores. Overhead was a tangle of electricity and telephone services, secured in case of possible earthquakes. These houses were based on the traditional Japanese townhouse (*machiya*), which used to be the homes of merchants under the old feudal system. As such, they were usually placed on long thin plots with a simple façade, and the plainest spaces addressing the street. The finest rooms were located at the centre, or towards the back. Often there was a small courtyard garden. Both Wright[63] and Taut[64] had noted the typology of these houses and marvelled at their sense of animation during the day and yet their silent repose at night.

The façade of my *ryokan* consisted of one sliding door and two small windows above. I pressed the bell and was welcomed by two women. I took off my shoes and stepped up onto a tatami floor and into a large lobby with a vending machine in one corner and some left luggage in another. Attempting to help with my heavy luggage, the ladies showed me upstairs to my bedroom at the front of the house. The bed was already rolled out on the tatami floor with a flask of hot water next to it. Before leaving, my host took great care to make sure that my luggage was packed away and did not clutter.

The tatami mat first appeared in Japan about a thousand years ago and was used widely in dwellings from the 15th century onwards, such that by the time that Wright arrived it was used in all homes. The mats are arranged in a pattern that denies any possible axial connection between rooms and are commonly placed in a spiral formation.[65] Wright identified the 'native home . . . as a supreme study in the elimination – not only [of] dirt but the elimination of the insignificant.'[66] He linked this idea of cleanliness to the Shinto religion.[67] With this identification of the sacred multi-functional floor plane, Wright claimed he found 'one country where simplicity, as natural, is supreme.'[68] He continued by noting that each dwelling was 'a perfect example of the modern standardizing I had myself been working out.'[69] Wright's standardisation – or more accurately, his use of the planning module – was hence derived from the tatami mat system that defines most internal spaces in Japan. He used the module in planning each internal space, and also its relation to other rooms and the overall composition, thereby forming an innovative open-plan environment. Wright claimed, therefore, that he saw a reconfirmation of his own theories in Japan – a view that can be discredited as Wright had developed several of these ideas far earlier, when he read *Japanese Homes and their Surroundings* by Edward Morse (1886).[70]

Having found Kyoto's train station too overwhelming, the following morning I decided to stay above ground and travel by bus to my next destination: the Chion-in Gate, Temple and Belfry. The temple complex had been constructed in the 12th century by the Jodo Buddhist (Pure Land) sect, and the Temple was on a monumental scale. The thick roof construction was supported by a number of slender timber posts that defined a well-proportioned space for worship. This worshipping space was raised off the floor by a few steps, and had doors to shut out much of the light, giving the interior a dark, yet intimate, quality. Being unable to participate in the prayers inside, I looked out from the sheltered walkways onto a gravel plane where several other imposing temples, shrines and a belfry all stood, loosely connected to one another, but without any formal axis or path. A visitor's booth provided some guidance to the shrines, I even had my sketchbook stamped to confirm my pilgrim status! The complex remains remarkably unchanged after a full century and I was able to capture the same view of the temple that Wright had photographed a century earlier.

Another site that Wright had visited was the Daigo-ji Temple complex, which houses the 16th-century walled garden, Sanpoh-in. Looking at the model of the garden in the entry space, the plan reminded me of a Wright composition with a free arrangement of pavilions around a simple garden set within a perimeter wall. I wandered into the garden and was enthralled by the light pavilions, their internal spaces defined by a tatami-mat module and paper screens revealing or hiding inner courts and gardens. The overhanging roofs provided shelter for circulating between the different spaces, and pilgrims in white had gathered beneath a sacred tree. As photography

Garden of Sanpoh-in, Daigo-ji Temple, Kyoto, Japan (1905) Photograph by Frank Lloyd Wright

was prohibited, I sat down at the lower of two pavilions that directly engaged with the garden to sketch Wright's 1905 views. The garden was unchanged over the last century, except that one cypress tree had been lost. The Sanpoh-in garden is an example from the Monoyama period (1573–1615) and its restoration came about because of a chance meeting between the main priest and Japan's then regent, Toyotomi Hideyoshi. It is claimed that the first restoration took only six weeks, but in fact it took another 20 years to arrive at its final form. Apparently, Hideyoshi provided too much material, making the design difficult to resolve; the garden possesses over 700 stones, one famously cost 5,000 bushels of rice. It also has a pond with a small island and two earth bridges. Hideyoshi's patronage resulted in a 'golden era' of artistic work in Kyoto, and Wright claimed that 'all phases of art expression in the Momoyama period were organic.'[71] Then, confusingly, though citing the imperial period, he praises the artists from the later Edo (Shogunate) period Tawaraya Sotatsu, Ogata Korin, and Ogata Kenzan.[72] The seemingly

Roof pylon, Mukogawa Women's University, Koshien Hall, Osaka, Japan (1930) by Arata Endo

unplanned arrangement and affluence of the Sambo-in garden was a reaction to previous eras of austerity, and led to the Edo period stroll garden.[73] The influences of Zen, tea consumption, and indigenous beliefs were reconfigured to arrive at a 'sophisticated order', one where formal axes were removed and the composition took on a carefully unplanned aspect. The aim of the garden was hence to appear natural, where the hand of man was underplayed, and was therefore another representation of the idealised landscape.

Later that afternoon I headed for the Koshien Hotel, designed by Arata Endo (1930), which lies on the outskirts of Osaka. From the train window, I took in the dreary basin of never-ending urban sprawl as Kyoto merges into Osaka. In the distance I spotted the Akashi-Kaiko Bridge, the world's longest suspension crossing. Koshien Kaikan, the hotel's present name under the ownership of the Mukogawa Women's University, resembled Wright's 'textile block' architecture, but had a definite sense of symmetry, similar to that of the Imperial Hotel. The form was broken down into a two-storey central entry block, with two projecting four-storey wings animated by projecting canopies and terraces, textured brickwork, and traditional tiled roofs. There was a distinctive horizontal banding to the parapets, canopies, and pergola, which united the whole composition. In all, it was a lively elevation, with lots of interesting details and textures that kept the eye moving from one feature to another. In the context of 1930s Japan, the design would undoubtedly have been modern, but also easily identified as derivative of Wright's decorative style.

I was welcomed at the reception by a woman from the university who offered to be my guide. Only half the building was open for visitors, as the other side functions as the Women's University. She led me through the hotel lobby past a small fountain which was an example of the hotel's design motif, 'a magical musical hammer.' I acknowledged its beauty, and smiled. We entered the banqueting suite, which was a long open space divided into a seating area and a stage section at the far end. Rows of chairs faced the stage with side views to the garden, and there was a translucent ceiling above, reminiscent of shoji screens. The stage was ornately detailed with balls, and prisms hung from the ceiling that were finished in gold. I imagined that the Imperial Hotel's original decoration would have looked equally otherworldly – indeed, this was 'Imperial Hotel Lite.' The banqueting suite is often used for weddings, but I fear that the architecture might steal the show. On the second floor roof, over the entrance, were two futuristic pagoda towers topped with a Japanese flag. The textile-block inspired walls provided an animated relief at sunset with deep shadows, and hiding within the patterns were even more 'magical musical hammer' motifs. Returning inside we went up to the fourth floor to visit the tranquil 'Japanese' rooms that were laid out using tatami mats and had movable shoji screens. Behind the sleeping space, and down a few steps, was an enchanting space for preparing tea. We continued the tour to look at the front façade and garden. The two wings embraced the garden and were reduced in scale with each setback being topped by a hipped roof. The front garden was serene, an idealised landscape with a pool, small hill and tea pavilion. We walked to a rustic tea house along a winding path and looked back to the hotel as a reverential scene of Wrightian 'organic' architecture.

I made my way back to the station and caught a late train for Kobe. I was not expecting too much of this city, having heard of the terrible destruction wrought by the Great Hanshin-Awaji earthquake in 1995, some ten years previously. On arrival, I searched around the station for the tourist information service, and stumbled across a help desk in a department store. Although the tourist information was closed, I was kindly assisted in finding a hotel across the road. My Western-style hotel was functional and I got a room opposite a ten-pin bowling alley. Having recently been given a second chance to construct the city, I was surprised to see that its narrow alleys had been preserved, and that the road, rail, and monorail links all seemed to cut across one another in an almost arbitrary manner. It felt very dynamic and seemingly unplanned. I tried to find the temples that Wright had visited on his 1905 trip from the photographs he had taken. Unfortunately, due to the earthquake, much of Kobe had been destroyed, and so most of the temples had been badly damaged. I got some excellent maps from the tourist information and found the temple with the large Buddha easily – I wondered if the modern replica was rebuilt in fibreglass, ferro-cement, or maybe stone or whether it even mattered? The Ikuta shrine and temple were tangled in the dense city fabric, so it took a lot of questioning to find the complex. There was a festival at the temple, with a panda figure at the entry greeting small children with balloons. All the temples had been rebuilt after the earthquake, so that Wright's photographs were now a part of the site memory.

Many architectural discourses mention that temples and shrines form the key to understanding Japanese culture and architecture and by virtue of worshipping more than one god (Shinto is polytheist), it supports a plural set – or

Entry to Yamamura Villa, Kobe, Japan (1918) by Frank Lloyd Wright

a relative set – of values. The first shrines were set on a piece of unpolluted land that was roped off simply, then a tree or stone was placed within the square area where different gods (*kami*) were invited to inhabit the space. The architectural critic Charles Jencks views the inclusiveness of Japanese religion as similarly allowing traditional and modern architecture to co-exist.[74]

Outside Kobe is the Yamamura Villa (1918) that Wright designed as a second home for a local sake brewer and which was constructed by his assistant, Arata Endo. The house was later bought by a steel company and used as a guest house until 1974 when it was designated as a Cultural Landmark and renovated. My usual navigation technique involved several detours and requests for direction, and in Kobe this was made doubly tiring by having to go up and down numerous hills. The area around the villa was now built up in a suburban form with seismically resistant detached dwellings within walled enclosures with garages and private gardens. This suburban form was a development of the traditional *Buke-Zukuri* dwelling for the warrior class. The main feature of this house type was the all-enveloping high wall, with the house either situated at the centre of the plot or towards the front. Again, the least decorated and utilitarian rooms were placed closest to the street, emphasising the inward orientation of the home in preference to the street. The suburban equivalent now had an opening gate for the car, with the homes remaining aloof from the street and their neighbours.

From the images I had seen of the Yamamura House, I was excited to see how far Wright had taken his Japanese-influenced residential designs back to their origin. In 1918 Wright's house designs were in advance of contemporary Japanese dwellings. Only the Yamamura Villa survives as an example of Wright's domestic design in Japan. The villa follows the Taliesin mantra, in being '*of* the hill,'[75] stepping back with the receding contours. Overall, it rises to four stories high, yet is only two-storeys high at any point, and in plan it has a slight turn at its centre. The walls are canted and finished in a mixture of natural coloured render, with Oya stone bands and features. The Yamamura Villa was concurrent with the Barnsdall House (Hollyhock House) in Los Angeles (1918–21) and they share similarities in several elements particularly the canted walls, horizontal banding, bridging feature, and their internal decoration. The walls of the Yamamura Villa hide a reinforced concrete frame construction, which provided good seismic resistance and also

Galleried landing, second floor, Yamamura Villa, Kobe, Japan (1918) by Frank Lloyd Wright

allowed Wright to deliver his trademark spatial continuity. As I approached, a set of ornamental urns greeted me, and I entered the house beneath the first-floor breakfast room that formed a sheltered carport. At the door, an elderly Japanese man sold tickets and I picked up some slippers. On the first floor, there was the breakfast room that commanded great views on three sides, overlooking the entrance, the adjacent hill, and a prow that addressed Osaka Bay. At the back of the room was a hearth with an abstract expressionist design. There were recessed window seats and ornately detailed clerestory lights that were detailed like individual lanterns. Wright had developed an intricate design of four patinated copper squares for the house, and used them extensively to diffuse the natural light and for internal screening.

Up on the second floor was a stunning galleried landing that directly engaged with the spectacular autumn colours, and behind the landing were three Japanese-style rooms featuring tatami floor mats, retractable screens and built-in cupboards. The wall decorations and cupboards were, however, muted in comparison to Wright's typical Western rooms. I had hoped that perhaps this was Wright's tribute to Japanese architecture, but unfortunately not, as these rooms were a late addition by the client and were designed by Endo. Beyond the landing were the servant quarters, now converted into a small gift shop with a few of Wright's details turned into jewellery, key-rings, and T-shirts. In the background *Frank Lloyd Wright: A Film*[76] was playing, and every so often the voice of the 'master' could be heard promoting his own reputation. The square dining room on the third floor was a reversion back to a Western style, with a hearth by the door and a ceiling feature that gave the space a peculiar centrality of a medieval tent. It was detailed with intricate clerestory lights, integrated electrical light fittings, vertical timber prisms and horizontal dark trims – these interiors were clearly derived from the Prairie House period but with a hint of Secession boldness. The dining room opened out onto an Oya stone porch and a terrace with an expressionist arch around the first-floor chimney framing a view towards the bay. Looking back at the house with its long drawn-out form, it was reminiscent of a ship with its bow towards Osaka Bay, and the tall chimneys seeming to add two funnels to the composition.

Despite such early tastes of modernism, Japanese clients tended to be reluctant to embrace Western values and architecture whole-heartedly. From the 1920s, this meant that there were three house types, namely, *wafu-jutaku* (the Japanese-style house), *yofu-jutaku* (the Western-style house), and the so-called *wayo-kongo jutaku* (combined Western- and Japanese-style dwelling).[77] Often the brief for a private dwelling in Japan required up to three different entrances – for the occupants, guests and servants – as well as a number of public reception rooms for social events. It was also traditional for most Japanese houses to be orientated towards the south. One of the most intriguing and bizarre *wayo-kongo jutaku* houses must be the Fujiyama Mansion in Shiba, Tokyo; it had two separate façades, one a Western mock-Tudor construction with half-timbered gables, the other in a Japanese style based on a nobleman's dwelling of the late-Muromachi period. On plan, they were joined together around a western central courtyard or a Japanese *tsubo*, as a device that was used in several inter-war homes to unite the two conflicting needs of western and eastern architectural traditions.

Reflecting upon the *wayo-kongo jutaku* typology, the Yamamura Villa was hence a successful integration of two traditions without resorting to a dual identity. Was this perhaps because it had two architects, Wright and Endo? Its interiors articulate the conflict between two approaches: Prairie House versus the Japanese Dwelling. Its internal spaces are thus dissimilar. Wright's rooms are constructed around a focused perspective that is familiar and legible for Westerners, whilst Endo's Japanese sequence of rooms are flat and exist in a self-contained void. The loudness of Wright's ornamentation was tempered by the stillness and simplicity of Endo's rooms. Yet juxtaposed they offer an inventive example of cultural translation and integration. Analysis of its interior revealed that the floors were laid out according to Western feet-and-inches, whereas the height of the building was based on a Japanese module.[78] The external language throughout was Hollywood Hills meets Osaka. The Yamamura House was a trans-national house embracing both sides of the Pacific Ocean, uniting the *Buke-Yashiki* Japanese home and the California Barnsdall House. It shows that Wright was already forming a global attitude to architecture, one that could stride over the vast Pacific Ocean.

FUKUOKA

I had extended my journey west to include Fukuoka as my friend in Tokyo had told me about a new planned settlement called Island City, which has a new garden and a pavilion by Toyo Ito, known as Grin-Grin. The 40-hectare Island City site was on reclaimed land to the north of Fukuoka and was more or less L-shaped in plan. Over half the area was to be for industry, related to shipping; a quarter was for a garden; with the remaining portion for residential use. A train line connects Huis ten Bosch, the recreated Dutch town, with the new Island City – from fake town to new town. It was a short bus trip through the dormitory blocks and over a bridge to Island City and the garden festival. The new garden was meant to be the focal point for the development, with the residential zone and industrial sector to follow. The Japanese garden tradition was now replaced by zonal planning and themed experiences: fire, water and wind. A small rounded elf was the motif for the garden and it seemed to be popular with families and elderly people.

Grin-Grin was 185 metres (607 feet) long by 50 metres (164 feet) wide, and had three 'pavilions' that formed a new landscape with tilted walls, planted roofs and walkways. The pavilions were generated from a 'single surface twisting twice to form three blocks.'[79] This was certainly an inventive twist on the traditional pavilion roof, and a 'shape design (Sensitivity Analysis)' computer-aided-design method was used to modify the initial form imagined by Toyo Ito and then generate the optimum structural shape 'with the least possible bending stress and a minimum of strain energy and deformation.'[80] The ground was drawn up to the roof, with green lawn

Overlapping roof forms, Grin-Grin, Fukuoka, Japan (2005) by Toyo Ito

turning into walls, and the garden path was extended into the roof decks. This new 'borrowed landscape' seemed to be from the children's television show the *Teletubbies*,[81] I concluded. It was an inventive interpretation of an 'organic' landscape, a re-creation of nature that united the ancient garden traditions of Japan and touched on Wright's 'organic.' As ever in Japan the finished form was executed with an honest expression of materiality, precision, and great workmanship. The pavilions were busy inside with a number of exhibitions: botanical prints from the Royal Horticultural Society of London; an idealised rose wedding-garden; a hydroponic test tube garden; and, a sinister genetically engineered blue rose. There were other pavilions for refreshments and trade exhibits. The wild flower plantation was colourful, although its recent cultivation made me sceptical about its indigenous credentials. Behind the wild flowers was a miniature golf course. The Japanese garden in the 21st century certainly reflects the society's contemporary cultural concerns.

On my way out, I called into the marketing suite to enquire about the new residential zone. The context of Japanese housing raises interesting issues: timber homes in Japan usually last about 25 years, fire-resistant structured dwellings last around 35 years, and so there is a constant process of renewal in housing. Traditional Japanese housing types are being replaced by Western homes with a front and rear garden. The houses, marketed according to gross internal area, each had a different material and colour treatment. These were standard suburban Western housing units placed around meandering roads, without any redeeming feature or unique identity. There was no sense of being in Japan, or even on an island, and there was no cultural signage or place-making in evidence. Within this middle-class suburban environment, the Mitsui Home Group has developed a house based on Wright's early Prairie Arthur B. Heurtley House (Chicago; 1902).[82] So you can now purchase a Wright home and site it anywhere in Japan, thus enhancing Wright's global outreach, but compromising Wright's early proclamation that 'there should be as many kinds (styles) of houses as there are kinds (styles) of people.'[83]

NIKKO

I made full use of my Japan rail pass by making it all the way to Nikko on the eastern side of Tokyo. There was a chill in the air and at the *ryokan*,

I was given a mobile space-heater and was reminded again about 'slipper' etiquette. I switched off my heater and went to sleep in the company of some late-night chat in the next room. From the ten photographs that Wright had kept from the 1905 trip, he had shown a keen interest in waterfall sites around Nikko. It is thought that he bought some of these images, but I still decided to visit the Keggon Falls. Nikko is also well known for the Tokugawa Shogunate mausoleums, as well as the source of the Oya stone that Wright had used extensively at the Imperial Hotel.

In Nikko, the autumn colours were receding, and the clear sky had a coolness. The mausoleums erected by the Shogunate were built as a means to consolidate their military power and to gain posthumous authority by elevating their leader to the realm of a deity. The architectural expression of these mausoleums was therefore critical to support their rule and authority. Within the complex there are about five different sites, each set at a different level with a distinctive shrine or feature. The first temple was dedicated to Buddha; these were only the second Buddhist representations that I had seen in Japan, despite its lasting impact on the religion and culture of the nation. Detailed analysis of the site reveals that there was a shift away from Buddhist architectural forms towards Shinto after Togugawa Ieyasu (the first shogun) became an avatar within the Shinto creed. The scale of the shrines were smaller than the temples I had visited in Kyoto. Although based on simple forms, the shrines displayed a wealth of decoration, including the use of gold in many of the interiors. The modernist, Bruno Taut, derided the site as baroque bombast and non-authentic kitsch.[84] Yet, I consider these overblown displays of Shogun authority as a point of departure for Wright's own experimentation with decoration at the Imperial Hotel, as he sought to integrate ornament within the structure.

The landscape setting, entry and circulation around the site were to influence Wright,[85] with its abundant turns and abrupt quarter turns, coupled with gradual and steep rises in elevation. Furthermore, it was claimed that one particular site, the Taiyu-in-byo, was an early model of Wright's Unity Temple (1905–8),[86] and I was keen to view this temple at first hand. Taiyu-in-byo lay within a stone wall enclosure with one central entry, and inside the compound were a few small shrines in the court by the gate. The main shrine was in three parts beginning with worshipping space. I removed my shoes before climbing the steep stone stair and entering an enclosed intimate area. This space was defined by a tatami spiral arrangement with circular columns that marked the perimeter. Pilgrims faced a lowered covered link with the main shrine shrouded beyond. There was a definite axial arrangement with the three different spatial experiences from worship, to link, to shrine. The three spaces were all at different heights, with a few steps dropping down to the link and then up again to the shrine itself. Wright's plan of Unity Temple had a similar tri-partite plan but the spatial qualities, entry condition and means of inhabitation were not at all similar. Wright's design for the Unity Temple has an oblique entry, a refined section, and a more subtle play of volumes.

After my tour of the mausoleums, I grabbed a quick lunch and then caught a bus up the hill passing a number of half-timbered mock-Alpine gift shops. The bus journey took me up into the mountains, and the gradual ascent became many hairpin bends, and soon the valley disappeared below. At the summit was a small town on a lake with more tourist shops. The lower vantage point up to Keggon Falls was blocked off and the cable-car was not working, nevertheless, from where I stood, the size of the falls were impressive. In the evening light of the autumn, the stone took on a blue-grey hue, the water looked icy, and the receding leaf coverage provided a speckled orange pattern.

TOKYO REVISITED

Having retraced Wright's journey around the country, I finally returned to Tokyo. For the bargain price of about 2500 yen, I took a room in the transient budget community, located in the Asakusa district of the Low City. My room was truly tiny: even the tatami mats were cut down, and so I had to sleep diagonally. By the time I had settled in, made a quick call home and had a shower, it was almost midnight. Managing to find a restaurant, I ate some sushi, drank a beer and felt quite at home.

The Low City, or lowlands, were reclaimed marshes to the east of the old Edo castle next to the small rivers, tributaries and canals, and were the preserve of artisans and merchants. It was planned on a more formal system with localised grids, walled enclosures and gates. Local districts had their own distinctive characters, or trades, with the most infamous being the entertainment district of Yoshiwara with its tea houses, theatres and brothels. Such activities were recorded in the famous woodblock prints that Wright collected. In *An Autobiography*, Wright mentions visiting one of the gated communities:

> Ahead of us looms a great black gate. Directly in front a great cherry tree is in bloom, like drifted pink snow in the light of innumerable red and white lanterns. Just inside the gate came upon the Orian or Yoshiwara procession. The prints have prepared us for that. The procession is now prepared for us. . .[87]

The Low City is wonderfully diverse, and the global high-tech image of Tokyo here becomes more local and animated: a man walked the streets pulling a small trailer full of cardboard; set back from the street was a small shrine to a half-man / half-frog golden effigy; one street was full of stainless-steel kitchen wares; small old shops sold traditional kimonos; and fish restaurants advertised their live catch in their windows. The Low City was animated and captivating and so evocative of the earlier woodblock prints; in contrast, the High City was the ultimate fruition of the Meiji Restoration, a sterile assembly of 'dead forms' from the West, as Wright predicted.[88]

My time in Tokyo had now sadly come to an end, and so I headed towards Ikeburro to meet up with Daichi and his boss, the former Taliesin apprentice. I met him at exit number one and we chatted about his wedding plans at Jiyu Gakuen. His office was set in a residential block, mixed-use at its most diverse, where we were welcomed by Hachiro, who was dressed in black and looked like a professor of architecture. The office was small, and as I walked in, some more people appeared from behind corners. There was a Taliesin lamp that may well have belonged in any number of Wright's Usonian commissions: Hachiro had picked it up for $50 in the USA. I sat down at the meeting table and Daichi introduced me to everyone. I showed them a copy of *Fifty Views of Japan* with the original photographs taken by Wright in 1905, and we discussed the route he took. Hachiro and I discussed the renovation of Jiyu Gakuen, he told me that the ideas behind the school were very much in tune with Wright's own principles. The reverential address of 'Mr Wright' was adopted – not the jocular 'Wrighto-San' that Wright often used in his writing on Japan.[89] He told me that two other associates were going to call in later, and that we were going to view some slides. The slides were a combination of Hachiro's own images and several slides passed down by Raku Endo. Indeed, there were slides of Raku at a presentation and critique with Olgivanna in Taliesin West under the bright canvas roof, there were interior views of Taliesin North showing Japanese artefacts (of good quality and valuable), and a picture of Hachiro on a motorbike on a trip across America.

I asked about life in the Taliesin Fellowship – I was always curious about the Fellowship idea, it all seemed very regimented and not the place for a full and open creative milieu. The associates confirmed that it was 'tough at times,' but they enjoyed their time at Taliesin West in Arizona. They recalled fondly making shelters in the desert as part of their architectural education. I questioned them about living and working with Olgivanna – the matron of the Foundation – but I did not get much of a response, everyone was very polite. After their time in Taliesin, one associate had become an urban designer, the other worked in a commercial architectural practice, and they all agreed that Hachiro's architecture carried on the mantle of 'organic' design. Most of Hachiro's work was now focused on timber crafted homes with traditional detailing in the expanding suburbs of Tokyo. It was a special evening with the associates, full of warm memories and a lot of interest in my own journey seeking out examples of 'organic' architecture.

Wright was the first global architect to come to terms with the shrinking modern world and the early 'crisis' of globalisation. When asked in 1913 to design the Imperial Hotel, Wright developed an all-embracing work of art that integrated all of his Japanese influences from the symmetrical planning of the Ho-o-den (with a Beaux-Arts classicism) to the woodblock print and Togukawa Mausoleum at Nikko. It was Wright's hybrid vision of Japan, which was a very different view from Taut's, who dissected Japanese architecture into the authentic (Imperial) and the kitsch (Shogunate).[90] Wright used the unfashionable kitsch representation for his crowing work in Japan, and made a piece of postmodern architecture by calling on a number of historical themes and combining them using his own personal language. For me, the Yamamura Villa was also prophetic of a cultural hybrid and a nuanced response to early globalisation, with a concrete frame that accommodated the 'Prairie' and traditional Japanese spatial experiences. Wright's more progressive legacy can be seen in the recent works by Toyo Ito, such as Tods store in Omotesando, Tokyo, and Grin-Grin in Fukuoka. These projects develop abstracted natural themes and use advance computer modelling to explore new spatial and 'organic' geometries that are specific cultural responses. Altogether, there is evidence of a definite, but never simple, influence of Frank Lloyd Wright on Japanese modern architecture.

2

VANITY FAIR

Wright's first journey to Europe in 1909 was that of an as-yet-unknown architect experiencing a mid-life personal trauma, following a failed marriage to Catherine and an elopement with Mamah Cheney, the wife of a former client. During the extended journey to Europe with Mamah, he visited Paris, Berlin and Vienna, and enjoyed a longer residency in Fiesole, Italy. Wright's first journey to Europe has been portrayed by some historians as part of modern architecture's evolution, but Wright's main concern was his vanity publication – the Wasmuth Folios. In these cultural capitals, Wright experienced the ending of the old imperial values that were then being questioned by modernists working in a variety of genres. Modernist thought and expression was to reach a pinnacle just before, and immediately after, the First World War, and Wright was ideally situated in 1909–10 to be able to absorb some of this cultural unrest within northern Europe. Famously, Arthur Rimbaud claimed that: 'It is necessary to be absolutely modern.'[1] But, in establishing a singular and definitive view of the phenomena, modern architecture became overtly deterministic with a single modern expression, as promoted and defined by self-serving cultural arbiters. More interestingly, Wright sought out other cities and regions and consequently, he was even better able to question the modern 'cultural capital' zeitgeist.

PARIS

I attempted to retrace Wright's European journeys but this was difficult, as there were only patchy records of his trip in 1909 and 1910. Like Wright, I began in Paris – a city that Wright criticised on several occasions because of its academic codifications of classical architecture. I left London Waterloo for Paris on the Eurostar train on 6 July 2006 on a warm summer day. The rail connection from Britain to Europe is now taken for granted, and the journey itself passed without event. On the train, I checked Wright's *An Autobiography* to verify my route, I reflected that Wright had taken almost a year away from his American practice and he had to sell some of his precious Japanese prints to fund his elopement. Outside, the fields of Kent mutated into the plains of France with the brief interlude of the darkness of the Channel Tunnel. Paris emerged quickly enough from the plains. Yet, while the Parisian suburbs do not sprawl out as far as the wide conurbation of commonplace suburbs around London, they have other problems. There had been some recent unrest and rioting earlier that summer, when alienated groups of youths living in high-rise social housing towers had turned against the police, an obvious symbol of authority. While some claimed that the riots were due to unemployment and a lack of opportunities for the young, others argued that modern architecture was the reason for the unrest.[2] High-rise social housing, as pioneered by Le Corbusier after the Second World War offered a new mode of living with clean, light, hygienic and secure flats. But these towers became alienated from their community and lacked social cohesion, consequently it was claimed they were a factor in agitating the angry youth. Wright would have concurred that living at such close quarters with each other was 'a negation of life not an affirmation of it.'[3] Yet, it might equally have been argued that the banality of low-rise suburban existence, as advocated by Wright in his Broadacre City, could also breed discontent and resentment.

Wright and Mamah arrived in Le Havre in October 1909, from where they travelled to Berlin to meet with his publisher. Wright recorded very little about this visit to Paris; within *An Autobiography,* he mentions some 'Belated Memories,' and paints something of a lonesome figure of himself: 'the misery that came over me in a little café somewhere in Paris on the Boulevard St Michel. Caring neither to eat nor drink I was listening to the orchestra. It was the end of a rainy day in a long depressing rainy season. The Seine most of the time over its banks. Late at night.'[4] Wright laments his 'anguish . . . longing and sorrow' at leaving his family, noting that '[I] could not achieve what I had undertaken as ideal.'[5] It was yet another burst of ego and another 'trial' for him to surmount. He does not seem to have engaged with the city itself; there was no response to the wide boulevards, or the cultural ferment created by the Futurists (their first manifesto was published in *Le Figaro* in 1909), the latest architecture of the day (Auguste Perret's new reinforced-concrete apartment block), nor any chance meetings. Thus Wright seemed to dismiss the wanderings of the Parisian *flâneur* as being irrelevant to him.

Wright claimed that he always disliked Paris. Indeed, when he dreamt of old Europe, it was of Germany or Vienna – but 'Paris? Never.'[6] This of course was Wright restating his distaste for the French neoclassicist tradition from the École des Beaux-Arts that had dominated the 1893 World's Fair in Chicago, which he detested. But within *An Autobiography*, Wright revealed his admiration for Eugène Viollet-le-Duc and Victor Hugo. From Chicago's All Souls Library, Wright borrowed Viollet-le-Duc's book. *The Habitations of Man in All Ages* (1876), and also claimed that he had already read the *Dictionnaire Raisonné de l'Architecture Française* from Madison City Library.[7] He stated that the 'Raisonne was the only sensible book on architecture in the world. I got copies of it for my sons, later.'[8] John Lloyd Wright confirmed that he received a copy of *Discourses on Architecture* from his father, noting that 'Viollet-le-Duc was a teacher of what Dad now calls organic architecture as early as 1860. His influence upon my father was marked.'[9] Eugene Viollet-le-Duc was a fascinating figure – instead of enrolling at the École des Beaux-Arts to study architecture, he undertook an apprenticeship with practicing architects and as such became devoted to Gothic architecture. The common point between Viollet-le-Duc and Wright was the context of the late-19th century, when there had been an eclectic architectural scene and excessive ornament that contrasted against the emerging work of engineering pioneers who established a 'truthful expression in structures.'[10] Furthermore, Viollet-le-Duc established a clear method to produce an honest architecture, saying: 'It must be true according to the programme of requirements, and true according to the methods and means of construction.'[11] These became the rationalist primer for Wright's early thoughts on architecture.

During his early years in Chicago around 1888 when Wright was 21-years-old, he recalled that 'study classes at All Souls were busy with Victor Hugo's *Les Miserables* under the guidance of the Pastor.'[12] As well as studying this French romantic text, Wright and the other students undertook to recreate the tale in a costume drama. Wright was given the role of student leader Enjolras, which fitted in well with Wright's self-image. Wright regarded himself as the leader of the uprising in All Souls and was now ready to undertake a wider revolution in the Chicago metropolis. Furthermore, to complete the heroic vision, Wright described in detail his full French military garb, complete with sword, which he had worn at the costume drama where he had met his future first wife, Catherine.[13] However, Paris in 1909 was now the city of his mistress and it was not surprising that he was troubled by a belated memory.

It is almost inevitable that during any visit to Paris, you pass by Notre Dame Cathedral on the Île de France, it is part of a well practised tourist ritual. The Gothic splendour of its façade is visible from the adjoining plaza that is nowadays animated with tourists and skateboarders doing tricks. Inside, however, the dramatic Gothic interior retains a brooding presence. Wright was captivated by Hugo's classic text, *The Hunchback of Notre Dame*, noting that the chapter '*Ceci Tuera Cela* (This will kill that) . . . was one of the truly great things ever written on architecture.'[14] Within the text, the archdeacon proclaims: 'The book will kill the building.'[15] Hugo thus suggests two consequences of the advent of the Gutenberg Press around 1440. Firstly, that 'the press will kill the Church'[16] and that 'the book of stone, so solid and durable, would give way to the book of paper . . .' or, as he summarised, 'printing will kill architecture.'[17] Hugo lamented the course of the architecture and in the cult of the antique leading to 'this decadence we call the Renaissance . . . It was this setting sun which we take to be a dawn.'[18] It was this last remark that Wright would use himself to berate the Renaissance and the classical tradition. Thus, Wright identified himself a neo-Romantic in the tradition of Hugo. Wright concludes that with his reading of Viollet-le-Duc, Hugo and Owen Jones, 'I was grown up pretty well in architecture'.[19]

In the evening, I visited the Pompidou Centre (1972–77) by Richard Rogers and Renzo Piano: a great spectacle of populist architecture and a fun 20th-century palace, its animated façade and beach-like plaza a counterpoint to the carefully codified traditions of classical architecture. The Centre had recently held an exhibition on the work of the French–Swiss architect, Robert Mallet-Stevens, and I had come in search of the exhibition catalogue, but there were none left. A helpful assistant did, however, help me to find some other books about the architect, and explained the best route to Croix, where Mallet-Stevens had designed an modern villa and which was my next destination. Mallet-Stevens had written about Wright and it was claimed his Villa Cavrois

(Croix; 1931–2) embraced many of Wright's ideas, I wanted to investigate this early connection between Wright and French modernism.

The small town of Croix to the north of Paris had long been the base for local cotton weaving, and on the Saturday morning I arrived there, it was busy with a local fruit market that animated the centre of town. Nestled within an affluent postwar French suburb, a large hoarding announced that the Villa Cavrois was currently undergoing major restoration works with state funding. There was a lodge that protected entry to the villa, reflecting the 'progressive' mood of the 1930s when the traditional gatekeeper's lodge was replaced by a garage and house for the chauffeur. The garage had a sweeping form that responded to the car's turning circle, and an impressive cantilevered roof provided good shelter for its passengers when they stepped outside. I noted that the masonry had a similar coursing to that used by Wright in Chicago, with flush vertical mortar joints and recessed horizontal mortar joints to emphasise the horizontal aspect throughout. Mallet-Stevens had clearly provided a wonderful pavilion for the car, and he noted in that 'science creates new aesthetics . . .'[20] For Mallet-Stevens, it was a simple pavilion, but for Wright, the car would reframe the whole rural and urban landscape.

Front elevation of Villa Cavrois, Croix, France (1931–2) by Robert Mallet-Stevens

The original classically planned garden was now gone and the surrounding land sold off over the years for new suburban homes. I walked around the suburban block to try to get some views of the villa. Spotting a man on his ride-on lawnmower, I requested a view of the villa from his back garden.

The Villa Cavrois was an exuberant display of cubic volumes that broke away from the usual formality of the country villa. Instead, it had low horizontal forms with long openings, and an offset central tower. In a perceptive anecdote, the client's eldest son, Jean Carvois, recalled that Mallet-Stevens took him and the whole architectural team to Belgium and Holland to view the Palais Stoclet (1905) by Josef Hoffmann and Hilversum Town Hall (1924–31) by W. M. Dudok. Furthermore, there were clear family connections – Mallet-Stevens's uncle was Adolphe Stoclet, and the latter's own dwelling was a formative influence on his architecture. Wright, as we will see, was at the centre of this creative milieu. Cavrois also stated that a brick was taken from the Hilversum site for his new house.[21] Despite referencing these dynamic early modern precedents, the villa was set within a classical landscape of formal geometry, with a perfect circle at the rear – evocative of an early roundabout – and a long formal axis at the front. Some claim that Wright's influence on the design was demonstrated in the plan of the house layout, separating 'the domain of the couple' from the children and servants.[22] However, the form of the Villa Cavrois was essentially linear, with a long formal façade onto the garden – whereas with Wright's 'Prairie Style' designs there were always cross-axes with cruciform or L-shaped plans to break up the form. This in turn created an informal relationship with the landscape as a series of enclosed private gardens.

In his contribution to the 1925 *Wendigen* publication (discussed more fully later in this chapter), Mallet-Stevens wrote: 'Frank Lloyd Wright was one of the first to be adventurous, to break with a tradition bordering on routine, so that he could be creative, and his oeuvre is grand, rich, logical.'[23] Mallet-Stevens regarded Wright as an exponent of the 'New World,' un-burdened by European traditions and possessing a universal message: 'Wright's architecture is human, is true and will be understood and liked everywhere. Regionalism is dead; with a few exceptions, the dwelling of man is the same all over the civilised world, and its beauty must be the same.'[24] Thus, Mallet-Stevens articulated the dominant modernist view of progression towards a universal aesthetics. Despite Mallet-Stevens's advocacy, Wright remained a marginal figure in France, and Jean-Louis Cohen notes that the prevailing 'superiority complex' of Beaux-Arts made it difficult for Wright's work to penetrate France.[25]

ROTTERDAM

Despite Wright never actually having visited Holland, his work was openly disseminated there by both the rationalist De Stijl movement and the more expressionist Amsterdam School. With this in mind, I took a diversion from my journey between the old imperial capitals of Europe to visit the work of Dutch architects who had been influenced by Wright in Rotterdam, Kijkduin, Hilversum and Amsterdam. I arrived in Rotterdam in the evening and got some basic directions from the railway station to Hotel Commerce. Although the hotel was not quite the fantastic bargain I had been looking for, I was rewarded by its proximity to the school just around the corner – the Sint Franciscus College, Secondary School (1922–4) by H. Sutterland and P. G. Buskens. Even in the twilight, I could see its striking resemblance to Wright's work. It had an asymmetric composition, an animated façade of different overlapping forms, a strong horizontal aspect, a brick skin with prominent horizontal lintels above the doors and windows, and circular ornamental urns at the entry.

On the following Monday, I was finally able to gain access and be escorted around the school by a teacher who had a broad knowledge of its past. The school interior was dominated by long corridors, but the classrooms were generous, with tall ceilings and some still possessed the original windows with their expressive ironmongery. The gymnasium was intact and retained its original colour-banded tiled walls and wooden floors. Over time, some of its playing fields had been sold off for residential development and a new wing had been added, enclosing a central playground. The principal's office was adjacent to the entrance, but the most prominent corner in the school was the biological science classroom. I found this to be refreshingly Dutch and subversive, openly promoting the ideal of science ahead of any religious or school authority. The school was a very successful example of the use of Wright's 'organic' architecture within a new context and as a totally different type of building. The Wrightian approach gave the school a civic scale and a particular identity.

When Rotterdam emerged as a prosperous city in the early 20th century, it took on a progressive outlook not dissimilar to the city of Chicago. Born at the end of the 19th century Robert van't Hoff was the son of an affluent

Sint Franciscus College, Secondary School, Rotterdam, Holland (1922–4) by H. Sutterland, and P. G. Buskens

Rotterdam bacteriologist. He studied architecture at the Birmingham School of Art and the Architectural Association in London. While there he gravitated towards the bohemian lifestyle of the Camden and Bloomsbury art circles, and even got a commission to design a house and studio (1913–14) for the artist Augustus John. In 1913, van't Hoff received a copy of Wright's *Sonderfelt* volume with its introduction by Charles Ashbee, as a gift from his father.[26] As an aspiring young socialist, it was claimed that van't Hoff was impressed by Wright's statement that: '[t]he machine can no longer be removed from the world; it's here to stay and is the pioneer of democracy, which is the ultimate goal of our hopes an desires.'[27] Inspired, van't Hoff undertook a voyage to America in 1914 to visit Frank Lloyd Wright and they discussed a possible collaboration on his commission for Augustus John.[28] Nothing ever came of this proposed joint venture, but van't Hoff returned to Holland with drawings and photographs of Wright's work, and put these to good use after he received two commissions in Huis ter Heide outside Utrecht.

At Utrecht's tourist information office, they told me that the Huis ter Heide was 10 kilometres (6 miles) outside the city and directed me to take a train to

Gest and then a bus to the suburb. The region is heavily forested, with a series of large apartment blocks placed perpendicularly to the road. They reminded me of Le Corbusier's modernist vision of tall slab blocks within an unblemished landscape. But Huis ter Heide itself was a mundane private suburb. I wandered aimlessly for a while, before spotting an elderly couple whom I asked for directions. Luckily, the husband knew of van't Hoff and showed me a local guide to his work. Beside another busy dual carriageway, I glanced upon Villa Henny (1915–19), now shrouded by a thick wall of vegetation. The gate was open, so I ventured up its gravelled driveway between the high hedges. As I rounded a slow bend, I saw a white cubic modernist villa set in the middle of a wide green lawn, surrounded by trees. Its cruciform plan was easy to read, and each façade stepped forward to generate a balcony, pool, and terrace that reached out to the generous garden. Each elevation had a substantial opening, so that I could see straight through from one side to another, which was achieved by the novel use of a reinforced-concrete frame construction. As I walked around the Villa Henny, I speculated whether it had been scaled up for The Netherlands – it was set high on a plinth, and the whole mass of the villa seemed far bigger than Wright's Prairie Homes.

Van't Hoff not only designed Villa Henny, but he also helped to build it, thereby attempting to form a bond with the workmen as a clear display of his socialist beliefs. Trying to build such a complex new building during the First World War was already difficult enough, but with materials so scarce, it took five years to complete. Perhaps unsurprisingly, it left van't Hoff disillusioned with the whole process. The use of a concrete frame construction made the house a contemporary of Le Corbusier's Dom-ino House concept,[29] whereby an open frame would support a free internal plan. Wright's proposed reinforced concrete 'Fireproof House for $5000,' as published in *Ladies Home Journal* in 1907, might also have appealed to van't Hoff's inclinations. A more formal analysis would consider the Villa Henny as a combination of Wright's Coonley Playhouse (Chicago; 1912), and Andrea Palladio's Villa Capra 'La Rotonda.'[30] Thus, it was a hybrid displaying a number of Wright's 'organic' design features, yet set firmly within a European classical sensibility, particularly in terms of its site, scale and massing.

An article in a Dutch newspaper alerted Theo van Doesburg to the Villa Henny. The avant-garde grouping of De Stijl had been established in Rotterdam during the First World War and 'implicitly presented their work and ideas as an attack on the hegemony of Amsterdam.'[31] De Stijl was a very loose association of artists, poets and architects brought together in 1917 by the painter, designer, writer and propagandist, Theo van Doesburg. The movement developed out of the Arts and Crafts, art nouveau and German expressionism, and tried to embrace William Morris's idea 'that society could be transformed by art.'[32] The Villa Henny seemed to give substance to De Stijl's rhetoric as its first architectural image, although it was conceived entirely independently. Thus, Wright's work also provided an impetus for developing De Stijl's neo-Plastic theory and Wright became a source of inspiration for these rationalists.[33] J. J. P. Oud disseminated Wright's work, and claimed that his projects displayed a number of ideas that were very much in keeping with the aims of De Stijl: 'Wright detaches the masses from the whole and rearranges their composition . . . In this way Wright has created a new 'plastic' architecture. His masses slide back and forth and left and right; there are plastic effects in all directions.'[34] Wright was therefore seen to be at the forefront of modernist thought.

On my short train journey to The Hague, I failed to see the open countryside depicted by the Dutch landscape painters of the 17th century. Instead, the so-called Randstad – or the rim-city – conurbation that extends from Rotterdam to Amsterdam – was animated by varied forms of canals, forests, small towns, factories and detached homes. I was reminded of Wright's Broadacre City but, without the overall authority of the all-seeing architect, it was a partial realisation of Wright's dis-urban utopia. I caught a bus to the beach resort of Kijkduin and passed the affluent suburbs of The Hague. Kijkduin is sheltered behind a tall sea wall, with a lighthouse and small shops looking out to sea. Holland depends on these structures for its very existence and their being inhabited by small kiosks gives them an added social relevance. The Wright-inspired Meer en Bosch housing development was designed by Jan Duiker and Bernard Bijvoet (1920) and is now hidden within a larger low-rise suburb. The scheme was conceived as a picturesque summer retreat, with a curved street plan that provided shelter from the wind. The homes were truly reminiscent of Wright's Robie House (Chicago; 1908–10), with long overhanging roofs shading the strip windows beneath, stepped massing with receding upper planes, and a firm footing within the landscape. Each house embraced its plot and used readily available materials such as local brick, tile and thatch. As I walked along the street, I met a retired couple in their garden, and I took the chance to talk about their home. They said that the house was divided in two, and that they had altered it substantially to make better use of the space available. I was invited in to view its expanded central hallway and the infilled external terrace that now formed a larger living area.

My hosts told me of a house a few doors down which has not been altered and which still has a thatched roof. They made a few phone calls to arrange a visit for me. I was duly surprised and amused by the expressive thatched roof that gave this Robie-inspired house a truly distinctive 'organic' form, yet also a sense of heavy inertia in contrast to Wright's dynamic design. There were other expressionist hints, with a carefully detailed door housing a stained-glass panel, an offset letterbox and purpose-made ironmongery. The owner was elderly and sat at the end of his extended living room, close to the open terrace so that he could enjoy the warmth of the sun. The original compact plan had a traditional internal layout with a long entry hall leading to all the bedrooms, kitchen and living room. All the bedrooms looked towards the back garden, and the long living area extended into the open terrace at the end. Whilst the house referenced Wright's dynamic elevation for the Robie House, inside the layout was more traditional with a separate room for each function. Wright's daring overlapping interior spaces were obviously not that well understood then, or perhaps only the external image of the Robie House had been available at the time. It would take some time for Holland to fully understand Wright's 'Prairie Style.'

Despite his early enthusiasm for Wright, Oud's article in the 1925 *Wendigen* journal lamented a missed opportunity. Now, he claimed that Wright's legacy was 'pernicious,' and 'a less happy one,' noting that Wright's designs were produced for affluent Americans and that the proliferation of direct imitations of Wright's homes in Holland was a problem.[35] Oud acknowledged Wright's designs as being spatially innovative, but he questioned their social relevance outside suburban America. In his astute critique, Oud identified a 'cult of forms instead of an orientation towards the inner nature.'[36] He believed this had diluted the modern 'cubic' aspect within Wright's architecture. It was a telling analysis of the cult of impersonation that often occurs in architecture, and in doing so, Oud identified the emerging band of 'Wrightjes' or 'little Wrights.'[37] Assimilation of Wright's designs in Holland reached its peak in 1924 and Jan Wils was dubbed 'Frank Lloyd Wils' by his peers.[38] Yet, for any case of outward imitation, there often exists a compelling case for incremental innovation, whereby traditional residential design mutates gradually, attempting to develop modern designs. These Dutch 'Prairie Homes' represented an early form of cultural hybridisation, whereupon the image of the

External view of house, Meer en Bosch, Kijkduin, Holland (1920) by Jan Duiker and Bernard Bijvoet

American modernity was projected onto the traditional Dutch landscape of the polder lands.

HILVERSUM

I caught an evening train towards the north end of the Randstad to visit Hilversum, a small town some 30 kilometres (18 miles) south-east of Amsterdam, and which is known today as the Dutch 'Media City.' Located on Simon Stevinweg Street in its suburbs, are a number of the semi-detached houses designed by Jan Wils that again shared a similar composition with Wright's Robie House. However, in Hilversum, these dwellings were stretched and rotated; they were like the Robie, but with multiple perspectives. In 1914 Jan Wils worked for Berlage, where he acquired first-hand knowledge of Wright's work. He published a number of articles about Wright and claimed that 'contemporary' lifestyle demanded new forms of architecture, and that the Dutch landscape was suited to Wright's 'wide, low and long' architecture.[39] Wils built the Olympic Stadium (1928) in Amsterdam. It, too, acted as a tribute to Wright by extending the Prairie House idiom to a building type that Wright had never even considered. The stadium was a simple brick oval which emphasised the horizontal with a modest five-storey elevation, all offset by the tall Marathon Tower. In its brick façade were deep horizontal cuts for the entrance, offices and associated stadium facilities; other masses projected out beyond the oval to animate the whole structure. Its intimate scale derives from a bygone era of the pre-commercial sporting event. Yet, it is also claimed that the first Coca-Cola advert appeared (as part of a sponsorship deal) at the 1928 Olympic Games, another example of modernism's dependency on capitalism.[40] The impressive Marathon Tower was designed to accommodate the first Olympic flame of modern times, and Wils added to the sense of theatre by including balconies for the horn-blowers and loudspeakers to announce the winners of each event.

Back in Hilversum, the civic work by Willem Marinus Dudok was a bold inflection of Wright's architecture. Indeed, English historian, Nikolaus Pevsner, identified Willem Dudok as the most important intermediary in 'the peaceful penetration' of Wright's work in Europe.[41] He claims that Dudok took the lessons of cubic composition from Wright and developed his own signature architecture out of them. While some called Dudok's work 'middle of the road modernism,'[42] this barb acknowledged that Wright's work had become part of mainstream modernism in The Netherlands sooner than it had in any other European nation. In 1915, Dudok became the Director of Public Works in Hilversum, and his friendship with Oud may have provided his first exposure to Wright, as well as a stern warning of the perils of imitating Wright too closely.[43] Yet Dudok openly articulated his debt to Wright in 1925, 'Wright deepened my consciousness that architecture is the art of space, and not of the flat plane.'[44]

Hilversum Town Hall (1924–31) by Dudok is a truly spectacular building: its monumental scale and confidence seems to be meant for a substantial city, not a Dutch backwater. Its powerful cubic massing had a number of overlapping horizontal volumes which were offset with a thin vertical clock-tower; it recalls De Stijl, whilst the sense of dynamic form is borrowed from the Amsterdam School. The brick edifice was perhaps the feature most inspired by Wright's Larkin Administration Building (New York; 1902–6), but Dudok carefully refined the design to accommodate the numerous functions of a town hall. Its confident form was matched by remarkable interior spaces that reflected a real civic pride, with the spaces flowing from one to

External view, Town Hall, Hilversum, Holland (1924–31) by Willem Marinus Dudok

another. Stone and marble floors were used throughout, yet the walls were kept simple. One repeated detail is a vertical lighting module feature that provides indirect lighting at important wall junctions and openings, and which also reflected Wright's use of hidden lighting in many of his commissions. To the interiors Dudok displayed rich sumptuous materials and colour. This 'diluted' modernism inspired a number of British municipal buildings, Hornsey Town Hall[45] (1933–35) and Greenwich Town Hall (1938–39) being two prime examples.

AMSTERDAM

I travelled by train from Hilversum and approached Amsterdam via the harbour. A large cruise ship was docked and it made an interesting contrast with the neat rows of dwellings on the canals. Cruise ships were viewed by early modernists as the manifestation of good design with their sleek construction representing a unity between form and function, but nowadays the overblown luxury liner seems to represent kitsch consumerism. My first port of call was the Stock Exchange (1897–1903) by Hendrik Petrus

Berlage. Unfortunately, the main halls were busy with a concert and an exhibition, so I had a coffee at the Berlage Bar that looked out onto a small square full of busy tourists. The interior space of the café blended a wealth of tiled decoration and finishes to create 'a total work of art.' The Stock Exchange was conceived as 'a monument reflecting the resolute and practical spirit of Amsterdam's merchant class,'[46] and it was certainly a success in demonstrating global trading prowess at the time.

When completed in 1903, the Stock Exchange began a critical trans-Atlantic exchange, as images of the Exchange were shown at the St Louis World Fair of 1904, which Wright is known to have visited. There were similarities between the Stock Exchange and the Larkin Building; both were massive brick constructions, with a concentrated inner space and surrounding galleries.[47] In addition, the Stock Exchange façade displayed elements that were borrowed from another American, H. H. Richardson, particularly the strong plain façades and the use of Romanesque motifs.[48] Louis Sullivan, told his former draughtsman, William Purcell (a contemporary of Wright in the 'Prairie Style') to visit Berlage during his trip to Europe in 1906. Purcell noted that Berlage already knew of Sullivan and Wright, and had read an 1900 *Architectural Review* article about Wright.[49] Thereafter, Berlage himself undertook a lecture tour of America and visited Chicago in 1911, meeting up with Sullivan and Purcell whilst lecturing at the Art Institute. Unfortunately, he missed the chance to meet Wright, but took the opportunity to visit a number of his buildings in Chicago and New York. Indeed, it was Berlage's subsequent lectures back in Zurich that really consolidated Wright's reputation in Europe, rather than the Wasmuth Folios.

Out of Amsterdam came another reading of Wright's work that celebrated his expressive attributes and individual talent. The Amsterdam School movement believed the individual architect was a prophet and/or artist who could invest in building materials a spirit that transformed them into art. Both Berlage and Wright exemplified this attribute, and Wright's work was disseminated through the Amsterdam School's magazine *Wendigen*, which supported the artistic qualities of architecture rather than the technological.[50] This journal sought an international audience from the outset, and its editor, Hendricus Theodorus Wijdeveld, approached many 'likeminded artists' to contribute to the publication. It must also be noted that *Wendigen* was in itself a work of art.[51] A beautifully illustrated article on Wright was published in 1921, followed by a 1925 special edition on Wright, featuring seven specially commissioned articles by European commentators. These essays were subsequently compiled into a book called *The Life Work of the American Architect Frank Lloyd Wright* (1925).[52] Wijdeveld approached several potential contributors, but no British or Bauhaus architects chose to participate. More intriguingly, Le Corbusier did not contribute to the series, but admitted 'familiarity with some of Wright's buildings.'[53]

Berlage's article in the *Wendigen* book addressed the nature of Wright's work and its relevance to modernism beyond America. Re-reading his article today, it seems that the Berlage piece became a mantra that was repeated by many modernist historians thereafter. Berlage questioned the 'cultural' significance of Wright and his architecture, and wondered whether his work was of 'a general rather than a particular value?'[54] He believed that Wright was an individual talent and he wished that we 'honour him most as the endowed artist . . .'[55] Thus Wright was placed outside the mainstream modern thought and considered an 'artist' of particular value, but not of universal stature. Perhaps it was this critical analysis that would drive Wright to emerge from his regional practice, to become a global presence.

BERLIN

I had visited Berlin in 1995 not long after its unification when it was still an edgy, divided metropolis and the Reichstag was being wrapped in a ceremonial foil by the artists Christo and Jeanne-Claude, as if awaiting a symbolic rebirth. It was a relaxing, carefree summer for me in the Tiergarten. A kilometre to the south, Potsdamer Platz was then a wasteland, inhabited by cranes and piling rigs. On my return in 2006, it had become a brash commercial quarter, a blatant reminder that Western capitalism had defeated Eastern Block collectivism. My exploration of Berlin began at the Adlon Hotel, which was where Wright and Mamah had registered as 'Mr Lloyd Wright and wife.'[56] The subsequent exposé by the *Chicago Daily Tribune* that Wright was in fact with someone else's wife caused Wright to go undercover for the remainder of his European journey. The hotel was beside the Pariser Platz, with the symbolic Brandenburg Gate at its head, and where the main boulevard of Unter den Linden forms an important axis through the city, leading to the Schlossbrucke and the former Soviet East Berlin. The Adlon was opened in 1907 and welcomed a string of celebrity guests including Charlie Chaplin, Herbert Hoover, Josephine Baker and Marlene Dietrich. Despite surviving the Second World War, it was badly burnt during the subsequent Soviet occupation and fell into neglect, and was finally demolished in 1984. The new Adlon Hotel completes a nostalgic postmodern vision. Externally, it looks like a good copy of the original, with a traditional stone facing. Inside, its glazed central lobby has heavy columns, arched openings, rounded projecting bays, moulded wood details, a small fountain, stained glass insets, and deep chairs; probably not dissimilar to how it would have been when Wright visited, I thought. The receptionist told me that the original guest register was destroyed during the Second World War, and as a result there was no trace of Wright staying there.

In *An Autobiography,* Wright attempted to justify his publishing venture in Berlin by claiming that he was prompted by historian Kuno Francke to undertake a visit to Germany: 'I had always loved old Germany – Goethe, Schiller, Nietzsche, Bach.'[57] Yet Wright's real reason for the visit was to publish a set of folios of his work, he claimed that he had received a proposal by 'the very able publisher Wasmuth in Berlin – to publish a complete monograph of my work.'[58] Yet in fact Wright himself paid for the printing costs.[59] Furthermore, the number of Wasmuth Folios intended for European circulation was minimal. A smaller picture book, *Frank Lloyd Wright: Ausgeführte Bauten* (which Wright called *Sonderheft* (special edition), with an introduction by Charles Ashbee was produced in 1911 at a print run of 9100 copies, 3900 of which were for sale in Europe.[60] The far more extensive two-volume monograph, *Ausgeführte Bauten und Entwurfe von Frank Lloyd Wright* (1911), with Wright's introduction titled *Studies and Executed Buildings,* had a print run of 1250 – of which around 100 were available for sale in Europe.[61] Wright's alleged 'conquest' of Europe would seem entirely implausible based on such a small circulation.[62] Furthermore, Wright's ambition was to create 'a primer for a new American architecture'[63] and not European domination. Another modernist myth emerged that Wright had put on an exhibition while in Berlin to promote his work, but all that happened was that Bruno Möhring gave a lecture to a Berlin architectural club in February 1910.[64] Tantalisingly, if Wright had actually made more of an effort to promote his work in Berlin, he could have addressed all the so-called 'pioneers of modernism'[65] at a stroke, since they happened to be employed in Peter Behrens' office at that time: Walter Gropius, Le Corbusier and Mies van der Rohe.

Wright was extremely astute in realising the potential of the Wasmuth Folios: they were an opportunity for him to assert his own architectural identity in an idealised format where he could present all his built work, proposals and writing as a 'complete image.'[66] To complete his Folios, Wright assembled a temporary atelier that included a former draughtsman and his son, who resided in Florence, Italy. They carefully traced images of the completed projects, which were then transferred onto lithographs in Berlin – thus presenting a unified artistic conception for his work. He saw the folios as an opportunity to prove his artistic credentials. The *Ausgeführte Bauten und Entwurfe* was, therefore, a major artistic undertaking, with each lithograph seen as a work of art on its own merits. There was even a 'deluxe' version printed on Japanese paper, with a leather binding.[67] These folios became a commodity in their own right, as well as disseminating the architecture illustrated and described within. The possibilities of modern reproduction available to Wright were manifold but, instead, he selected an antiquated, limited print edition, which denied the potential of mass exposure. It was a mistake that he never repeated in subsequent reproductions of his work. Despite not being widely disseminated, a handful of copies did reach a number of influential architects in Europe but most of the Wasmuth Folios were burnt or damaged by water during the tragic events at Taliesin in 1914.

Next, I next visited the suburb of Potsdam to see the Einsteinturm (Einstein Tower). Potsdam had been the official residence of the Prussian kings and German kaisers, and was the site of the peace conference after the end of the Second World War. Across from the busy station plaza there is a densely forested hill, Telegrafenburg. I followed the small road, the *Albert Einstein Strasse* which led to Albert Einstein Science Park. There, I encountered a number of observatories in a variety of architectural styles, with a dominant Renaissance-inspired Astrophysics Observatory Potsdam (1876–79) being the most prominent – it seems that all architectural styles aspire to the stars! I persevered through the woods and, standing serenely in a small clearing, was this remarkable building in both its ambition and expression. The Einsteinturm had a long gestation period that began with the Theory of Relativity postulated by Albert Einstein in 1905, which established a new relationship between light, space, and time – the beginning of modern physics. The astronomer Erwin Freudlich became captivated by Einstein's subsequent General Theory, which argued that light could be bent by gravity. Freudlich had met the architect Erich Mendelsohn through mutual friends and they exchanged ideas about the observational tower throughout the First World War. In 1920, Mendelsohn began to work full-time on the project, with the aim of translating his expressionist perspective drawings into functioning architecture. The optical instruments for the telescope and coelostat were designed by Carl Zeiss and dictated the basic dimensions of the tower as well as the size and operation of the cupola. In addition, the plan was dictated by the spectrographic chamber and the need to produce two artificial light sources, one from an oven and the other, an arc source. Consequently, Mendelsohn became mainly responsible for designing a weatherproof shell and service provisions for the scientists. However, in the chaotic circumstances of postwar Germany, with its shortages of materials and hyperinflation, reinforced concrete could only be used below ground; above ground a brickwork armature was dressed with stucco. Yet the finished building was a seductive monumental form that symbolised the potential fusion of modern science and modern architecture.

When the tower was opened in 1921 it generated enormous publicity because of Einstein's popularity and its startling design. It was either lauded as a 'proper balance between individuality and function,' or criticised for its 'irrational design.'[68] Einstein himself flattered Mendelsohn when, in a one-word review of the Tower, he labelled it 'organic.'[69] Mendelsohn never designed such an overtly expressive architectural form again, and instead he developed a pared down 'dynamic functionalism' an architecture that was an 'expression of capitalism's mix of efficient production and glamorous consumption.'[70] Funded by the Mosse publishing house, Mendelsohn visited America in 1924 and travelled extensively there. He visited Wright at Taliesin, where Richard Neutra, a former employee of his, was then working. Neutra acted as a translator and mediator for the visit, toning 'down the criticism each made about each other.'[71] 'The result was highly congenial weekend, which encouraged both men's belief that they were following the right architectural path.'[72] It was a meeting that could have potentially yielded so much more than mutual admiration: Wright the self–styled American 'organic' master, and Mendelsohn who was allied to German functionalism. They seemed to have a great deal in common but their meeting notably did not propagate a wider and critical 'organic movement.'

The meeting also initiated a reappraisal of Wright in Germany, and Mendelsohn contributed an article to the 1925 *Wendigen* issue and

External view, Einsteinturm, Berlin, Germany (1921) by Erich Mendelsohn

subsequent book. In his essay, Mendelsohn emphasised Wright's break with the past and the fact that his concept 'proceeds logically in response to organic laws.'[73] Adding that 'the organization of his buildings is exemplary, pertinent, free, open, full of motion,' he called Wright a 'great artist, whom we respect.'[74] The European 'organic' movement – or 'other tradition' identified by Colin St John Wilson[75] – offers an example of a neglected history, whereby the theories that Hugo Haring developed during the 1920s, and which he continued to refine up to the 1950s, were dismissed in preference for a purely 'rational' history of modernist architecture. Haring acknowledged the need for both functional and expressive architecture and he offered nature as the main source of his inspiration.[76] Haring used 'organic' to describe the function of a Greek temple, and the responsiveness of Gothic against the formality of classicism. In addition, he claims both William Morris and Ruskin used 'organic' to describe attributes of Gothic architecture.[77] These 19th-century theories lauded the 'organic' responsiveness of Gothic against the formality and geometry of classicism. Haring elaborated on this Gothic potency alluding to the issue of national identity, which Britain and Germany had embraced in an attempt to deny classical

Mediterranean orthodoxy and to establish an 'organic' Nordic theory as an alternative.

STUTTGART, MUNICH AND OBERAMMERGAU

As I travelled south by train towards Austria, I stopped at Stuttgart. I caught a local bus that took me up into the surrounding hills, past affluent homes, and I alighted near the ideal modernist suburb of the Weissenhofsiedlung housing exhibition, built in 1927. Following the Dawes Plan of 1924, an influx of American capital stabilised the German currency and meant that state house-building could begin in earnest.[78] The Weissenhof layout responded to the hilly setting and generated its own technological landscape with Mies van der Rohe's own long apartment block providing a fixed backdrop. Whilst it was claimed that there was an open brief for each architect there was also a careful selection of architects by Mies van der Rohe in an attempt to promote like-minded 'left-wing architects.' The invited architects were all sympathetic to the rationalist *Neue Sachlichkeit* (New Objectivity) grouping that attempted to produce a new form of affordable housing that responded to new ways of living, embracing technology and exhibiting a very plain material aesthetic. Hence the more expressive architects such as Haring and Mendelsohn were rejected.[79] Most of the dwellings were intended for an 'educated middle class,'[80] that also included servants' accommodation, and was, in essence, a speculative private development.

Today there is an Information Centre and Museum in the row of Houses 28, 29, 30 by Mart Stam, with a large model of the site and an extensive bookshop with scholoarly academic studies of 'International Style' modernism. The exhibit notes that half the dwellings were lost during the Second World War, and that the remaining houses and apartments had been marginally altered. Now the site is even being 're-modernised' and previous alterations removed. Due to his fame as a pioneer of modernism, Le Corbusier was given a prominent corner site that looked down onto the city. Corbusier's designs for Houses 14 and 15 displayed great spatial and sculptural daring with a raised plinth from which pilotis elevated the living space two storeys above street level. Whilst the façade alluded to a generous villa, the reality was a rather mean plan with tight internal spaces with no practical value in terms of exploring new forms of dwelling. Nestled behind was House 13, the realisation of Le Corbusier's Maison Citrohan (1920) ideal, the original 'house as a machine for living in.'[81]

It was withdrawn from the street and hidden behind some tall trees, so that its abstracted façade was concealed. Raised on pilotis once more, the dynamic vertical plan allowed for a generous double-storey living space on the first floor, a mezzanine floor above, and bedrooms that shared the roof terrace – finally the 'house as a machine' had found a home in a city which excelled at car production.

At the opposite end of the street was House 33, by Hans Scharoun, which exhibited a number of expressionist curved forms that broke up the monotony of the cubic forms used elsewhere. Within its plan was a visual axis from the entry door to the garden that divided the ground floor plan into a front living area and a rear service zone. Upstairs the three bedrooms were set at the back of the building and they too shared an extensive terrace. The strong landscape connection would have pleased Wright. It was even claimed that Wright was an underlying influence upon most of the architects selected to build at the Weisenhoff, as all the homes exhibited open plan designs and innovative 'cubic' forms which Wright had pioneered back in Chicago. The *Die From* journal in 1927, observed that Wright 'had the necessary qualities twenty years ago. He knew the way to a new kind of living.'[82] This was a fitting riposte to those who questioned Wright's modernism in preference of Le Corbusier. I saw the Weisenhoff as a dull formal exercise in form making, a collection of white and pastel coloured cubes scattered beneath Mies van der Rohe's dominant escarpment. Apart from Scharoun's house, it was a very restricted and partial definition of modernist housing. It was also prophetic of the 'International Style' modernist with its own limited architectural vocabulary. The Weisenhoff could have been so much richer by including architects from the Nordic tradition and America such as Haring, Alvar Aalto and Wright himself. Imagine what great homes these three architects could have provided. Wright could have exported his Millard House (1923) with its Textile Block from Los Angeles to Stuttgart. Certainly it would have made the Weisenhoff more inclusive, diverse and richer in materiality and expression.

I returned to the centre of Stuttgart and caught a second bus to the Mercedes Benz factory to see the new car museum by UNStudio (2001–6). The final part of the journey, on foot, was perhaps fittingly hazardous, taking me across a number of traffic junctions and beneath the autobahn. The museum's free-form structure seeks to combine aerodynamic car design with architecture. There were antique cars outside from Wright's era, and he famously bragged about having a 1929 Mercedes sports car, a typical exhibitionist gesture just before the Great Depression. As I entered the building, it became an impressive form of brand reinforcement: the central atrium was in the form of a three-pointed star – the Mercedes Benz logo – with a lift at each pinnacle, the atrium was finished in exposed concrete that followed the subtle grey colour palette. At the ticket counter, I was given an audio guide and instructed to take a lift to the top floor, where the exhibition begins with a stuffed horse and the first carriage ever built by Daimler Benz. A downward spiral then takes you back down to the gift shop, but the procession is far more sophisticated than a simple descent. Large galleries project out beyond the spiral, inviting you to take a detour and then re-join the promenade, and there were views back towards Stuttgart from the galleries. But more telling were the views to the autobahn itself, a reminder of the physical (not to mention environmental) consequences that the car has had on our landscape and society.

Rather brazenly, the exhibition has an image of the Guggenheim Museum in New York by Wright as a part of their timeline, yet there was no recognition that the museum owes its formal planning and the organisation principle to Wright's ramped design from 1959. Wright had designed the Guggenheim as a temple to artistic continuum, and the ramp there was built by American bridge-builders. Now, in Germany, the bridge-builders had created a temple to the car. Wright would, of course, have called it splendid confirmation of his genius. Indeed he had designed a number of car-based projects with a spiral form such as the Gordon Strong Automobile Objective (1925) which was proposed as a ziggurat on top of Sugarloaf Mountain in Maryland, with a planetarium inside, and which was not only a precursor of the Guggenheim but also of the Mercedes Benz Museum.

With most of his work on the Wasmuth Folios completed by mid-summer 1910, Wright travelled to Oberammergau.[83] Using Munich as a base for my own journey to Oberammergau, I also had time to visit its Olympic Park (1972), designed by Gunter Behnisch with the assistance of Frei Otto. The undulating Olympic Park had a picturesque outlook, with winding paths leading to several stadia, which were scattered within the landscape. The design of this park was purposely anti-classical and a conscious reaction to the 1936 Berlin Olympics organised by the Third Reich.[84] The historian Blundel Jones claimed that 'spontaneity and informality were celebrated, equality and fraternity proclaimed.'[85] The Olympic swimming pool was a hybrid construction, with a number of orthogonal pavilions nestling beneath a wide tent structure, and, inside, it was busy with children enjoying the added attractions of water flues.

External view of Olympic Hall, Olympic Park, Munich, Germany (1972) by Gunter Behnisch and Frie Otto

The tent structures now looked rather dated, their plexi-glass cladding having turned a shade of brown from the sunlight and their steel supports looked chunky and overbearing. The whole site felt like a deconstructed circus, but with parts of the tent left behind after the event.

Wright had himself experimented with lightweight tent structures and they assisted in loosening his form making and lead to his 'second coming' in the Arizona desert in the late 1920s. His Ocatilla Desert Camp (1929) displayed free geometrical planning and was realised using lightweight timber and canvas. These temporary structures were vital and spontaneous, their free geometrical forms sought to combine function with lightweight ephemerality. And the Olympic Park by Behnisch reminds me of the potential offered by tension structures in creating new 'organic' forms.

At Oberammergau, Wright saw the famous *Passion Play* in the summer of 1910, an event that occurs every ten years. The town represents a quintessential alpine settlement with vernacular half-timbered housing on narrow streets set against a dramatic landscape. The town's cafes and bars were packed with opera tourists and I managed to get a ticket for the evening performance of *Aida*. The Passion Play Theatre was partially enclosed to shelter an audience of 4700, whilst the proscenium and the stage were left open to sky and the elements. The covered enclosure was based on a generic railway station design, with six iron arches supporting its roof. It was completed in 1900, and I shared the same experience as Wright did, watching classical opera in an early-modern train shed. The performance and staging were impressive, as the *Passion Play* the performance lasts seven hours and includes about 2000 actors, musicians and technicians. One of the curious contradictions with Wright was that whilst he was at the forefront of contemporary architecture, his wider cultural influences and preferences were classical/baroque and romantic. In *An Autobiography*, he referenced Bach and Beethoven[86] and he believed that 'when Beethoven made music I am sure that he sometimes saw building like mine in character.'[87] But he hardly noted any contemporary composers such as Arnold Schoenberg or the concurrent American jazz movement. It implied a rather narrow cultural exploration of modernism and its many manifestations.

VIENNA

I had made arrangements to meet Hanna, a friend's sister and, having exchanged a few texts, we met at Vienna Railway Station. Hanna was an architect and had been well briefed about my visit. She had kindly organised a mini tour of the city for me, and had even found villas designed by a former tutor who was inspired by Wright's 'organic' architecture. Haus am Nordhang and Haus unter Baumen (1968) by Ronald Rainer sat within the same long suburban plot. The three-storey dwelling (Nordhang) is at the top of the site, with a single-storey pavilion (Baumen) at the bottom, and a dense landscaped lies in between. Nordhang had a ground floor entrance and garage, an exposed reinforced-concrete frame on the first level, and a brick clad upper storey with deep timber facia. The upper storey also had wraparound corner windows, which was a typical Wright motif, but their application here was similar to the work of the Italian architect, Carlo Scarpa. Rainer was educated in Vienna and had worked in Germany and Holland. He returned to Vienna to teach at the Academy of Fine Arts, and used the following quotation taken from St Augustine to describe his approach: 'beauty is the splendour of truth.'[88] It revealed a Gothic sensibility towards space and materiality that was displayed in the two houses. While I felt that Rainer's houses did exhibit 'organic' qualities, Wright's influence was here mediated through the work of Scarpa, whose work was widely respected.

We returned to our car to visit the two houses designed by Otto Wagner. He was the most prominent architect in Vienna during the turbulent years at the end of the 19th century, had an established academic career and was appointed as director of the School of Architecture at the Vienna Academy of Fine Arts in 1893. The first dwelling, Villa Wagner (1886), was based on a formal and symmetrical neo-Palladian composition that reflected Viennese sensibilities at that time, whereas Villa II (1912) had a more abstract form, with its rear plane slipping away from the front façade, and an offset first-floor loggia at the rear. Wagner kept up to date with the latest architectural debates, and it is claimed that he had a copy of Wright's Wasmuth Folios. He showed the folios to a number of his students, and reportedly admitted: 'Gentlemen, today I have something special. This man knows more than I do.'[89] It was this kind of endorsement that Wright had sought in America yet, by happenstance, it was in Vienna that it was actually given.

Back in central Vienna, we drove around the Ringstrasse for a few junctions. It was an opulent demonstration of the wealth and power of the Austro-Hungarian Empire at its peak. In 1857, Emperor Franz Joseph undertook a complete remodelling of the city with an imposing new ring forming a boulevard for the city dwellers, whilst the city itself dispersed out into the suburbs. This might be interpreted as embracing a more democratic and egalitarian Habsburg Empire but, unfortunately, it was mainly conceived to impress upon the people the power of the monarch. However, the Ringstrasse did also represent a wider structural change related to the Enlightenment and a more secular society, in that it contained a new university, museum, theatre and opera house. The Secession was a reaction against the culture (and the architecture) of the Ringstrasse: the artists Gustav Klimt and Koloman Moser rebelled against the academic art tutelage at the Academy of Art in 1897. They were inspired by the work of the Glasgow Four (which they had seen in *The Studio* journal),[90] and published their own periodical, *Ver Sacrum,* which expressed their dissatisfaction with state-controlled 'Ringstrasse' art and the seemingly arbitrary award of art commissions.[91] Two of Wagner's most prominent students in the Secession were Joseph Maria Olbrich and Josef Hoffmann, and Wagner himself subsequently joined the movement in 1899.

Whilst visiting his publisher, Wasmuth, Wright claimed that he saw the work of Olbrich for the first time and seemed to identify with him. However, this was again a misleading statement as Wright had visited the St Louis World Fair in 1904, where Olbrich's work had been prominent.[92] The Secession Building (1898), by Olbrich, was built for their first exhibition and was to prove a defining monument for the movement. When I visited the Secession Building, it still maintained its startling presence beside a busy traffic junction, and the gilded golden dome or 'golden cabbage' as it is often called, still referenced an artistic revolt against neoclassical mediocrity. I passed beneath the Secessionist motto – 'To every age its art, to art its freedom' – into a cramped lobby that was ill-suited to mass consumerism. I purchased a ticket to view the *Beethoven Frieze* (1902) by Klimt as well as a contemporary exhibition in the main gallery. A long, narrow staircase led to the basement, where the Klimt fresco adorned a small gallery. It was an extravagant sequence that narrated a universal theme – the quest for happiness – and adopted a number of global references with classical, medieval, and Arabian myths being intertwined. The main exhibition space at ground level was articulated by a number of slender columns that defined a square gallery with two smaller rectangular side galleries. There was a muted pallet of materials with white painted walls and a simple ceiling with square glass panels to allow natural light to be distributed evenly. It was an easy space to comprehend and allowed the art to be displayed within a modern context. Authors have speculated that a number of the ideas from the Secession Building were later used in Wright's own Larkin Administration Building (1902–6) and Unity Temple (1905–8).[93] Indeed, all three buildings possessed a symmetrical plan, three main masses (entry, link and main space), a major concentrated internal space, extensive natural lighting and a plain exterior finish.

When Wright visited Vienna, it was not the early symbolic period of the Secession that he witnessed, but the later period of conservative neoclassical reaction. Wright met Josef Hoffman in 1910 and again on his return from Moscow in 1937, but there was no record of any architectural dialogue beyond mutual friendship.[94] Hoffman's celebrated Palais Stoclet (1905–10) in Brussels was a neoclassical 'modern' edifice not dissimilar to Wagner's Villa II. Various commentators have claimed that Wright was actually an American Secessionist[95] and Alison and Peter Smithson[96] believed that Wright's all-embracing conception of space, which included all furniture and fixings, was Secessionist (art nouveau) in its intent. Indeed, on his return to Chicago, Wright pronounced that his Midway Gardens (Chicago; 1913–14) went beyond the sensual 'European Art Nouveau' revealing 'the straight line . . . and the flat plane'[97] so that the whole composition became a three-dimensional cubic abstraction. Wright was thus refreshed from his European adventure and embraced a more 'modernist' form of expression.

In the evening, Hanna and I went out to the American Bar by Adolf Loos (1907). I was surprised that it was so small inside; there were already two other couples sitting in the two booths opposite the bar and, with our arrival, the room was suddenly crowded! The space is particularly sensual: the ceiling is coffered with marble, and is framed with onyx-clad beams that continue as wall pilasters to the floor; the walls are in-filled with mirrors above and mahogany panels below; and the floor is tiled. Dim lights are fitted beneath the mirrors at each pilaster, but most of the illumination comes from the bar itself. Whilst the space is cramped, the parallel mirrors below the ceiling reflect the bar to infinity. Was the bar a mediation on our urban life, I speculated – a singular existence in a sea of similarly isolated lives? Loos was a polemicist who exposed the Ringstrasse as a 'modern Potemkin' full of pleasing façades.[98] He also ridiculed the Secessionists, particularly Olbrich, with their all-embracing concept, leaving the client unable even to choose how to dress themselves.[99] Loos's renowned lecture on 'Ornament and Crime' (1910 and later published) stated that 'modern ornament has no forebears and no descendants, no past and not future,' and hence ornament was not only culturally suspect, it was wasteful and resulted in 'craft slavery.'[100] He questioned the role of the artist and the craftsmen as separate and distinct, arguing that modern industry could arrive at suitable designs without the influence of the artist or architect. Consequently, there was no need to apply any external architectural treatments to most buildings to signify their status. Wright, however, found it difficult to kick the ornamental habit, and in 1909 he presented a talk on 'Ethics of Ornament', in which he stated that ornament should be 'organic with the structure it adorns . . . at best it is an emphasis on structure.'[101] Wright followed the lead of Sullivan in attempting to forge a new American tradition that included 'organic' ornament, and Loos had been similarly influenced by Sullivan's *Ornament in Architecture* (1892).[102] All three architects agreed that the ornament of the past was a corruption of the present, yet whilst Wright attempted abstract means of ornament to represent a new set of cultural values, Loos was more progressive in exploring the innate qualities of materials to adorn his spaces.

Hanna had left a post-it marker in my guidebook against the MAK Gallery (Museum of Applied Arts) with the words: 'Visit and have a coffee?'

The MAK (1863) likes to be called 'the house on the Ring.' It is, in fact, a neo-Renaissance palace with a brick façade and stone-framed openings, with a passing resemblance to the Victoria and Albert Museum in London. Inside, there was a grand internal court with a two-storey loggia that acted as a reference point for my wanderings. On the first floor, there were exhibits from the Wiener Werkstatte, showcasing their high quality design, plus displays by Margaret Macdonald and Charles Rennie Mackintosh, again emphasising the importance of international networks in the development of art nouveau. There were architectural models by the likes of Zaha Hadid and Frank O. Gehry posing as creators of works of art, but the most interesting for me was a model of the Schindler/Chace House (1921–2) in Los Angeles by Rudolf Schindler – a house that heavily referenced Wright's work and which is now part of MAK California.

Schindler was educated in Vienna, again under Otto Wagner. He recalled that sometime after 1911, 'a librarian in Vienna handed me a portfolio – the work of Frank Lloyd Wright. Immediately I realised – here was a man who had taken hold of this new medium. Here was "space architecture".'[103] In addition, Schindler attended private lectures given by Loos. He graduated in 1912, working briefly in Vienna before securing a job in Chicago in 1914 to work for a medium-sized commercial practice. Then, in 1917, Schindler was hired by Wright to assist on the Imperial Hotel in Japan, and in 1920 he moved to California to supervise the construction of the Aline Barnsdall House (1918–21) in Los Angeles. Schindler worked for Wright up until 1923, before establishing his own practice. Richard Neutra had a similar education to Schindler and was also inspired by Wright's Folios in Vienna. He worked with Loos until he was drafted into the First World War. After the war, Neutra became Mendelsohn's assistant in Berlin before leaving for America in 1923. He found a room at Hull House in Chicago (a settlement house for European immigrants), and met Louis Sullivan, who was, by then, in ill health and died shortly thereafter. At the funeral, he met Wright and he remarked, star-struck, that 'it was like coming into the presence of a unicorn.'[104] Neutra worked for Holabird & Roche, where he recorded the new construction techniques and published them in Stuttgart in 1927 as *Wie Baut America* (*How America Builds*) (1927), which also included images from Wright's work. In addition, Neutra was employed by Wright for almost a year on the Automobile Objective scheme and in 1925 Neutra joined Schindler in California, where they briefly worked together before falling out over the Lovell House commissions. In the end, Schindler built the Lovell Beach House (1925–6) and Neutra got to do the Lovell Health House (1927). These two architects were the manifestation of Wright's influence in Europe and it was a pity that he was unable to take pride in the success of their work – instead Wright became jealous of their achievements.

Both the Lovell House commissions were extraordinarily innovative, but the Lovell Health House was to gain wider exposure, since it more fully embraced the 'International Style,' and it was included within the exhibition in New York, *The International Style: Architecture since 1922*. Wright had initially been omitted from this exhibition, but was later included in a room alongside Oud, Le Corbusier and Mies van der Rohe. However, in the accompanying catalogue, Wright was only considered to be half-modern, it claiming that his 'individualism and . . . relation to the past . . . makes them not so much creators of a new style as the last representatives of Romanticism.'[105] Wright issued a hostile riposte to the exhibition, attacking the roles of cultural arbiters and the derivative formula at the heart of the new 'style.' Tartly, he wrote: 'is architecture 'modern' because alter-egos need some formula to follow?'[106] For Wright, the underpinning of the 'style' was formulaic and consequently merely another option for an untalented eclectic architect to follow.[107] Drawing on his experiences in Japan and Brazil, Wright also questioned the validity of the term 'International Style' to different cultures and environments.[108] Wright attacked the 'social' aspect of the 'International Style,' which he equated to communism.[109] Thus, Wright saw himself as an individualist against the mass propaganda of the 'International Style,' and this was a position that was to define his architectural writings in his later years. He often recited the same old objections to international modernism, which always guaranteed him good publicity and exposure. Furthermore, at the height of Senator Joseph McCarthy's pursuit of 'un-American activities' Wright had taken it upon himself to align himself with Elizabeth Gordon of *House Beautiful* to deride 'International Style' modernism as being 'communistic.' It was a dispiriting stance, for despite an early career full of modernist ideals, Wright in the end became embroiled in populist, nationalist, jingoism. Yet these statements made for great copy for the newspapers and they ensured Wright a productive 'Legacy' period in the late 1950s.

3

EGOR'EVSK CULTURAL CLUB

Frank Lloyd Wright was famously invited in 1937 to attend the First All-Union Congress of Soviet Architects in Moscow. Only two decades before, the October Revolution in 1917 ushered in Communist rule that sought to redefine the country and society, based on Marxist principles, and all property was nationalised within days of taking office, thus enabling a completely different concept of architecture and the built environment.[1] However, the subsequent civil war with the White Army delayed any real progress in establishing a communist society. Then, during a period of relative peace, Vladimir Lenin instigated the New Economic Policy (1921–7) which founded a planned economy (essentially a combination of capitalist economy and communist politics). After Lenin's death, Joseph Stalin gained power and issued his first radical Five-Year Plan (1929–34), which set targets for rapid industrialisation based on wholesale collectivisation and the reorganisation of the rural environment and economy. Wright's visit in 1937 came after the implementation of the first Five-Year Plan, at a juncture when Stalin sought to consolidate his power. It was concurrent with the Great Terror, during which dissidents and previous supporters of Stalin were subject to purges and the whole of society was placed in a permanent state of fear.

TO RUSSIA

Wright was sympathetic to the Russian struggle, having met several displaced Russian nobility in Japan. At Taliesin Wright often watched Russian films with his Fellowship students and even engaged in sporadic correspondence with the Russian press. The Russian media saw him as an anti-capitalist ally – whilst Wright, of course, thrived on any available publicity. Wright's motives for his Russian visit are not clear, apart from his usual need for self-promotion and his talent for political naivety. He sailed on the *Queen Mary* from New York to Cherbourg, and then travelled by train to Moscow, with brief stopovers in Paris and Berlin. It is unclear if Wright visited the 1937 Paris Exposition; he certainly discussed Boris Iofan's Russian Pavilion at the Fair but did not mention the Nazi German Pavilion constructed by Albert Speer opposite it, representing the fullest aesthetic confrontation of totally opposing totalitarian regimes.[2] The architect Clough Williams-Ellis – who had visited Russia in the 1920s, represented Britain at the Soviet Congress, and recalls a chance meeting on the epic train journey:

> I had taken my seat in the dining-car of the Moscow express when the waiter brought along a couple to sit opposite me. I bowed and said 'Good evening' at a venture, and got the same back in very slightly Americanised English. I said I was on my way to the Moscow architectural and planning conference. The man said, 'You are an architect then? So am I.' 'Your name?' I asked. 'Frank Lloyd Wright.' 'Ah,' I said, 'how kind of chance thus to turn a legend into present reality,' or some such civility, acknowledging his fame as I knew would be expected.'[3]

Wright's good humour did not last the whole journey. Williams-Ellis noted an acrimonious and complex[4] border crossing that he described more fully: '[M]y companion flatly refused to open anything at all and went off into the most uncontrolled fit (or show) of anger that I have ever beheld in a grown man.'[5] Wright was persuaded by his wife, Olgivanna, who spoke Russian, to open at least some of his precious belongings and they continued on to Moscow. However, on arriving in Moscow on 21 June 1937, he was given the welcome that he expected: 'sure enough, there was a large reception committee especially to do him honour as one of the leading lights of their current architectural revolution. Thus acclaimed, he thawed delightedly into smiles and hand-waving,' – and remarking later the same day, 'these are the people, theirs is the future!'.[6]

I too travelled by train, in my case, setting off from London, changing trains in Brussels and Cologne, and arriving in Moscow on 21 June 2007, exactly 70 years later. During the first night, the train stopped in the middle of Germany and a new passenger joined my sleeper cabin. In the morning, my German-speaking fellow passenger introduced himself as Ivan and, despite our inability to find a common language, we got on well and exchanged the odd couplet of information aided by our mobile phones. The vast level landscape of Eastern Europe passed by at a slow pace – it was like a custodial stay, but with moving scenery – the early sun became afternoon showers, and we rumbled on along plains of wheat fields, distant forests and wide rivers. At the border with Russia, a guard passed around some forms that were in Cyrillic. Ivan had, by then, won over my confidence and helped me fill out the form. An indifferent female border guard came in and looked over my documents and took my passport away. I had to press her to return my passport in exchange for my completed forms. After the border guards, local women came with blue plastic bags, full of local delicacies. Ivan bought half a chicken, but I made do with some gluttonous pancakes and beer. However, the high point of the day – if not the whole journey – was the changing of the train bogies (trucks). The train went into a long shed and was broken up into its carriages; we were then lifted up off the rails by four jacks, and some men in orange boiler suits began replacing the western-gauge bogies with eastern-gauge wheels for the onward journey.

In the evening, I decided to explore the dining car. It was a long walk through the jolting carriages with some hazards; and as I stepped gingerly from one carriage to another there was no guarding, and in the air was the pungent smell of urine. The rolling stock reminded me of Cold War espionage and spy thrillers – I imagined a malevolent figure appearing from a carriage at any moment with an impenetrable pair of glasses. This grittiness continued into the smoke-filled dining carriage interior, which was clad throughout in timber-effect brown Formica. There were limited options for food, so I ventured to have a sandwich; a slice of black rye bread with three slices of salami made for a tasty dinner. Still, the dining car had proven a bit of a disappointment, with limited food, too much smoke and, as I had romantically envisioned, no chance meeting with an architectural superstar. On waking the next morning, however, I was outside Moscow, Ivan had left in the night and the train was busy. The guard put on his best uniform, complete with a smart cap, and gave me broad smile as I departed the train.

MOSCOW

As a keen tourist, I could not wait to explore the city and to see Red Square for myself. I am old enough to recall the displays of Soviet military might during the height of the Cold War. My recollections were of the Brezhnev and Reagan eras, the last stand off before the advent of Perestroika under Mikhail Gorbachev in the 1980s. I entered Red Square through the Resurrection Gate, a 1995 replica of the original ceremonial gate first constructed in 1538 and later rebuilt in 1680 that had formed part of a procession route used by the Tsars. In 1931, the gate was demolished by Stalin to allow better access for military hardware for his own processions through to Red Square. Rising gently before me, the Square was busy with many Muscovites taking in the evening air. I spotted a wedding party excitedly taking photographs around the Kremlin towers, military cadets celebrating their passing out, whilst their senior colleagues lounged casually around Lenin's tomb. The mood within the square was light-hearted, and there were curious tourists like me taking in the eclectic scene. Straight ahead was the picture-postcard image of St Basil's Cathedral with its anarchic multi-coloured onion-dome towers; to the right was the cubist inspired Lenin's Mausoleum (Alexey Shchusev, 1924–30) in front of the assertive Kremlin; to the left the old GUM state department store (Alexander Pomerantsev, 1890–93), modelled on 17th-century Russian architecture, yet with a distinctive classical symmetry, and now a haven of designer goods. Red Square represented the conflicting identities of contemporary Russia; romantic, modern, controlling and consumerist.

I was impressed by the Kremlin's scale and authority; its daunting walls and fortified onion-capped towers, complete with rotating red Soviet stars, were a constant reference throughout my visit. When I attempted to gain entry, the gates closed as I approached and thick-set paratroopers in grey fatigues formed an impregnable physical barrier. Why should this be? Behind them, I could see a few limousines pull up and a group of wedding guests gathered with a troupe of dancing girls. It was slightly comical scene, and I had to adjust my perceptions of what was contained within the impenetrable Kremlin walls.

I walked towards the river to get a glimpse of the re-assembled Cathedral of Christ the Redeemer (1995–2000). The white marble cathedral was gloriously sited on the northern bank of the Moskva River and elevated on a substantial plinth which, on closer inspection, turned out to be an administrative building and car park. It was about 5pm and the edifice was closed for business; the gigantic bronzed doors were shut and pedestrian barriers surrounded the church. The Cathedral of Christ the Redeemer was another replica of the original, possessing new onion domes that glistened with the new patina of gold, although the yellow-orange tint made me doubt the sincerity of the oligarchs who had paid for the new cladding. The detailing of the bronze frieze above the doorways looked authentic, yet it all seemed strangely unconvincing. The 69-year absence since its demolition by Stalin in 1931 and its reconstruction had removed any sense of the cathedral's authority. It was now a tribute to Russia's new capitalists – sweet revenge over Stalin's failed intention to erect the Palace of the Soviets.

When Wright arrived in Moscow, it was in the midst of a major urban renewal campaign dictated by Stalin, with the medieval two-storey timber city being replaced by a programme of beautification. Wright marvelled at this new construction work within the city, noting the destruction of several churches without any regret. 'Their works were even more wonderful. Old churches were going up in air, dynamited to make way for wide avenues for the new Moscow. Moscow was being made ready for five million citizens.'[7]

As the reinstated capital of the Soviet Revolution, Moscow had become the subject of debates concerning what should be the most suitable manifestation of a Soviet city – the rhetoric, planning and image of Moscow had to be carefully aligned. In 1932, there was a competition with seven invited entries to replan Moscow and accommodate a population of five million by restating its Soviet identity. Many of the schemes reflected the radical debates that had thrived in the 1920s, with Nikolai Ladovski proposing a Parabola City, Moisei Ginzburg advocating a disurbanist scheme, and Le Corbusier's proposing redevelopment including tall towers on an orthogonal grid structure.[8] As ever, the competition proved inconclusive, giving the impression of a progressive engagement, but failing to agree a winner. In the end, the competition was decided by a meeting of the Central Committee, with Stalin proclaiming: 'We accept neither the view of those who reject the very principle of 'the city' and who urge us to convert Moscow into a huge village, nor of those extreme urbanists who wish to create a city on the capitalist model, with its excessive density of population.'[9] The General Plan for Moscow was duly unveiled in July 1935 and, under it, the city was to be limited in size and reconstruction based on 'unity and harmony of architectural composition,' or rather the City Beautiful had come to Moscow.[10] Concentric boulevards and a new central axis were consolidated around the centre of power, the Kremlin. It was essentially a Potemkin city of façades which hid the old slums behind, a reaffirmation of the radial planning that had dominated Moscow's history under the Tsars.[11] The plan reflected Stalin's view of a perfect society derived from the centralisation of government, the isolation of social groups, and a visually pleasing aesthetic.[12] In addition, the city centre was to be remade to become the setting for mass public gatherings and propaganda displays.[13]

Wright commented on the process in the *Architectural Record* in 1937, proclaiming that the plans were 'far ahead of any city planning I have seen elsewhere' – he even acknowledged that there was a 'splendid opportunity' within a Moscow freed from private property and sentimentality.[14] Yet the idea of the centralised city was already dated in Wright's opinion: 'Are you on the right road when you prepare Moscow to take five million country people, instead of sending Moscow out to the five million?'[15] Wright was, of course, advocating his own dispersed Broadacre City template, but he was there ten years too late to have any actual effect on Russian urban planning.

During his 1937 visit, Wright viewed a number of the constructivist buildings. He saw the newly completed Proletarski Palace of Culture (1937) by the brothers Leonid and Victor Vesnin and noted the 'good design' of the auditorium, but moaned about the lack of Russian 'spirit and character' within the modernist edifice.[16] In addition, Wright visited the Barvikha Sanatorium (1934) by Iofan, noting the trans-Atlantic liner 'luxury' of the rooms in a 'very well-designed and very well-built structure.'[17] However, Wright was not altogether convinced by constructivist architecture and was wary of their intellectual approach. His comments were, if anything, almost a justification for socialist realism, as he complained:

> [T]he modern buildings were hard and coarse, unsympathetic and badly proportioned. This would apply to all but a score of them with

> perfect justice. I don't wonder the Russian people reacted to them as they did, rejecting them in favor of the old classic order. The so called modern buildings must have been hateful to the mystic emotion, the passion of the people of Russia.[18]

It was strange that Wright was so hostile to Russian modernists as a number of them had cited his 'Prairie Style' as an inspiration to their own architecture. Within the constructivist grouping, there were a number of instances of Wright's influence, with Ginzburg having gained knowledge of the 1910 Wasmuth Folios whilst studying architecture in Milan – and the Lokshin House (1917) in Evpatoria, Crimea had resonances to the Frank Thomas House (Chicago; 1901) and Heurtley House (Chicago; 1902).[19] The Lokshin House certainly exhibited a formal symmetrical composition, with a hipped roof profile, triple central windows, ornamental urns, and semi-circular entry arch.[20] In addition, a house built in 1912 by Panteleimon Golosov near St Petersburg was based on the Warren Hickox House in Illinois (1900); the latter two had been published by Wasmuth.[21] Other acknowledgments of Wright's work were derived from the *Wendigen* publication of 1925, prompting Lazar El Lissitzky to assert him as 'America's only architect, who dared to discard all textbook precepts and to create a new type of dwelling, which has revealed him as the father of contemporary architecture.'[22] Furthermore, Ginzburg in 1926 considered Wright an 'American farmer-pioneer' and admired the Robie House for possessing 'an entirely new plan, simple, open, suffused in air and light, and developing freely in space.'[23] The farmer as pioneer certainly captured a certain 'folksy' aspect of Wright's residential work and his later life at Taliesin. It must be noted that the Russians had a good critical understanding of Wright's work, and clearly identified with the idea of farmers as pioneers.

I used the Moscow Metro to visit some of the constructivist architectural sites and these journeys were a memorable part of my visit. Above ground, the Metro stations had a confused identity, either progressively modernist or classically inspired. Yet beyond the turnstiles, I entered a magical world of bustling entrances, dark tunnels and underground marble palaces. Long timber escalators descended deep below ground with such dim lighting that I could barely see the end of the stair. Each platform had a consistent and brilliant plan: you enter the platform at one end, change in the middle, and exit at the far end. To offset this rationalism, the stations were eclectically decorated below ground with either grand palatial or early modern styles. The former was proliferated with marble columns and arches, and truly ostentatious chandeliers. It was certainly a celebration of proletarian culture – even Wright was impressed. Whilst dismissing the falsity of luxury,[24] he stated that 'the Moscow subway is a succession of well-planned palatial stations . . . that makes the New York subway look like a sewer.'[25]

The Narkomfin Building (Ginzburg, 1928–30) was a constructivist block of flats that sat beneath one of Stalin's sentinel towers, the Vosstaniya Apartments (Mikhail Posokhin and Ashot Mndoyants, 1950–54). Indeed, most of the constructivist buildings seemed to be nestled below one of the seven Stalin towers. The complex is set back from the street behind a small park, with mature trees that shield the full extent of its current physical deterioration into a romantic modern ruin. The sand-coloured rendered façade was flaking away and its steel reinforcement was visible. Still, it was daringly modern, with a long horizontal form possessing strips of glazing and balconies to the park elevation and dynamic semi-circular balconies at the gable end. The ground-floor pilotis had been infilled, the original constructivist ideals grounded by the grim reality of Russian pragmatism. Narkomfin was an example of a social condenser, based on a non-hierarchical collectivist aim to liberate women from domesticity so as to boost industrial production. Consequently, Narkomfin reflected this collective identity with two distinct elements: the dwelling block and the communal centre. The dwelling block was distributed over six storeys with an open and closed deck-access on the second and fourth floors. It possessed an innovative set of apartment types, including the first duplex units ever constructed in Russia. And, on the top storey was an individual flat for Nikolay Miliutin, the famous Soviet social planner, thus while the new society professed to be egalitarian, some planners were clearly more equal than others. The communal block had a modernist cubic mass with expansive glazing to reflect the international modernism aesthetic. It contained a sports hall at the lower level, with communal dining, reading and recreational rooms at the upper level, and summer dining spaces on the roof.[26] There was a lingering sense of nostalgia around the complex; a lost social ideal, a defeated communal aspiration and a neglected artefact.

On my way back to the Metro, I took a photograph of the Vosstaniya high-rise block, only for a passer-by to stand in front of my camera. He was full of admiration for the tower and proclaimed in English, 'Stalin

Balcony to Narkomfin Housing Complex, Moscow (1929) by Moisei Ginzberg

good!' The contrast between Narkomfin and Vosstaniya was stark – they represented two very different ideas of a communist society and architecture although only 25 years separate the completion of both apartment blocks. The tower was an assertion of Stalin's power and an overbearing presence that radiated from beyond the Kremlin to the expanding city. With its dominating mass and classical symmetry it was an oppressive presence, and even the statues that adorned the high-rise were an expression of the strength of the state. Inhabited by the ruling elite, the tower was there to consolidate Stalin's power. Despite claiming to represent the proletariat with its 'social realism,' it was merely a pleasing aesthetic that hid a dominant state.

FIRST ALL-UNION CONGRESS OF SOVIET ARCHITECTS

The Congress was held in the House of Columns by Matvey Kazakov (1784), a neoclassicial edifice in the so-called 'Empire Style.' The building had a mixed history, it was built as 'clubhouse' for the Moscow Assembly

Detail of Vosstaniya apartments, Moscow (1950–54) by Mikhail Posokhin and Ashot Mndoyants

of Nobility under the Tsars and then, during the Soviet period, it was used for state funerals and Stalin's infamous show trials. It had an imposing scale with a symmetrical front façade, an elevated columned portico, and highly regulated openings. The central courtyard was filled in by Kazakov to form a hall that is framed by 28 Corinthian columns. I managed to locate a side entrance that was open, but it only had an unmanned ticket booth with leaflets that promised a full programme of eclectic entertainment – ranging from classical music to heavy metal.

During the first Five-Year Plan (1929–34), Russia engaged a number of foreign experts to assist with its aim of rapid industrialisation. Within this context of engagement, Wright's opinions were sought out by the Russian media, and letters were exchanged with *Pravda* and *Architecture of the USSR*. *Pravda*, the official Soviet newspaper, had approached Wright in 1932 to ask for his comments regarding architecture after the Wall Street Crash, to which Wright retorted: 'Capital will only spend money to make money.'[27] The following year, *Pravda* again approached him to speak about the effects of the Great Depression on US academia; a strange question to ask Wright, given that he had just established his (non-academic) Taliesin Fellowship. Regardless, Wright equated intellectuals with capitalists and said there had been no change in either institution, noting the 'Capitalistic system is a gambling game.'[28] With the establishment of the single Union of Soviet Architects to replace the diverse groupings of the 1920s, David Arkin became the editor of the official journal, *Architecture of the USSR*. In 1934 Arkin published some 'Notes about American Architecture' and noted Wright as being a 'prominent and eccentric spokesman of contemporary architectural thought.'[29] Furthermore, in describing the 'Prairie Style' as an American 'attempt at folk appearance,' it was a telling analysis of Russian views on Wright's aesthetics.[30] Wright's provocative responses were not always published, but they ensured he was worthy of an invitation to the First All-Union Congress.

I was surprised how brief Wright's address to Congress had actually been – considering that he was the most prominent international architect in attendance and how anodyne were its contents – perhaps a reflection of the paranoia and fear that gripped the conference at the height of Stalin's purges. There were three main themes within Wright's address: technology, aesthetics and new societies.[31] Technology was an apolitical subject that Wright could easily discuss without causing offence, and so he began the

Mr and Mrs Iofan and Frank Lloyd Wright at the Society of Relations Banquet, Moscow (1937). The architect Boris Iofan was a prominent modernist architect in the 1920s and early 1930s but later became a leading exponent of Stalinist architecture.

address by acknowledging that the first flight between Russia and America had recently been completed by a Russian aviator – and he used this to call for a cultural link between the two 'new' nations, arguing that Russia offered 'great hope for the world.'[32] Wright observed that the 'rapid growth in science, industrial technology, and mechanical means.'[33] had only resulted in the skyscraper, which Wright admonished:

> Our highly acclaimed architectural achievement is the skyscraper. But what does it really represent? The skyscraper is no more and no less than a victory for engineering and the defeat of architecture. This rising, steel framework of a skyscraper is generally hidden behind a thin facing of stone blocks imitating feudal towers. Skyscrapers are stunning, but they are false and artificial, like the economic structure that gave rise to their emergence in dull congested urban areas.[34]

This open attack on the ultimate symbol of capitalism, the skyscraper, generated a bout of spontaneous applause. Closely related to his attack on the skyscraper was Wright's attack on aesthetics. Again he equated the American experience of his youth with Sullivan in Chicago: 'We too were faced with a choice – either crawl back into the shell of an old culture, or barely go forward and create our own social order?'[35] Wright observed a similar tendency in contemporary Moscow: 'In some of your buildings, constructed to serve the people, I noticed architectural motifs created in the old days by the aristocracy's culture . . . It is difficult to overcome the palatial style.'[36] This was, of course, a veiled attack on some of the recently completed metro stations and the Palace of Soviets competition. Wright proclaimed:

> The tendency towards grandomania when prevailed upon in one place, sometimes becomes apparent in another – and where it is least expected. Aspirations for such magnificence at times become popular because it becomes apparent that there is difficulty in finding another, more refined expression of life in architecture.[37]

Wright's assertion of 'grandomania' was an astute observation of Stalin's taste in architecture, in which scale was utilised to make oppressive architectural statements. In front of the eclectic Moskva Hotel, Wright noted that 'mere size seems to captivate the Russians as it seduced us earlier.'[38]

In his speech, Wright then went on to dismiss the 'left and right wing' approaches to architecture – the 'left wing' were modernist from central Europe and the 'right wing' were neoclassicists.[39] For Wright, both approaches were unsatisfactory.[40] Wright believed that the only true expression of the people was 'organic' architecture: '[t]he correct path to the creation of organic architecture consists of the scientific organization of building activity and animating it with a genuine spirit of humanity.'[41] Wright was interested in the potential of a new society that was not founded on capitalism, and he was part of wider debate during the Great Depression, and so he lamented that '[p]rivate property ownership makes correct planning impossible.'[42] Hence, the possibilities of the Soviet system after the October Revolution offered a more rigorous ideal and 'correct planning ideas' without the need to deal with private landowners. So Wright envisioned:

> [o]rganic architecture will not only express such ideas of a new free life but also ensure, in the USSR, the possibility of living one's life better than anywhere else. Ideas of Soviet Russian organic architecture will spread to those other countries on the continent.[43]

Wright then called for a new Soviet society coupled with 'organic' architecture that could form an expansive and global movement but, of course, he was naively out of touch with the developments following the October Revolution. The popular myth in the 1920s of a worldwide revolution had, by the 1930s, been replaced by the reality that Russia was likely to be the dominant communist country.

Following the First All-Union Congress, the *Architectural Record* published two articles in October 1937 by the two American delegates, Frank Lloyd Wright and Simon Breines. Wright's was a reflective piece on recent Soviet architecture and town planning, the Palace of the Soviets competition, and included anecdotes of various meetings with Soviet architects.[44] Breines's article was a more insightful summary of the actual conference proceedings, noting the diversity of the USSR with delegates drawn from 26 different nations and including both architects and workers' representatives.[45] Breines noted the dominance of the neoclassical idiom,[46] the aim of Congress was 'a new mastery of the classical heritage,'[47] others called it 'viciously anti-modern.'[48]

MAGNITOGORSK

I extended my trip to visit the Ural Mountains as the planned settlement of Magnitogorsk was celebrating 75 years of existence. The city had been the subject of a design competition in 1930 that sought to define a new 'Soviet City' beyond the old established towns. Magnitogorsk was to reflect the Stalinist concept of an ideal settlement, and its location was determined by national and regional needs for efficiency and growth[49] – well, that was the theory. In the case of Magnitogorsk, this was also closely aligned with military strategy, given that the Soviets believed that a second metallurgical base was required to complement the Donets Basin in the Ukraine, and that it should be as far away as possible from the main European powers.[50] There was also a compelling regional justification as the Urals contained some of the largest iron ore deposits in the world. Yet it required a direct source of energy to make steel. A 2000 kilometre-long (1242 miles) railway line was therefore built to link the iron ore in the Urals with the coal mines in the Kuznersk basin in Siberia.[51] Such a staggering undertaking required considerable political will and forced labour to harness Russia's geological wealth. The expansion of Slavic influence in these so-called 'backward' regions was a further justification for this internal colonialisation of Russia.[52] For Stalin, the self-styled 'Man of Steel,' Magnitogorsk was a vivid symbol of Soviet Russia's rapid industrialisation.

I was somewhat apprehensive about taking an internal flight, but the journey was comfortable enough, and I was accompanied by several young fellow passengers. Some were tennis protégés with large bags full of rackets and seated next to me was another Ivan, this time a student who was travelling home to see family. He talked about the wonderful forests and lakes around the Urals. At Chelyabinsk Airport, we waited around the few seats in the large hangar for our luggage to arrive. When I went to the taxi booth and asked about getting a ride to the bus station for my onward journey, the attendant enlisted a translator from one of the young passengers and, after organising my carriage, I collected my bags and got into a rather cramped Lada taxi with a large driver and an even larger fellow passenger. At the bus station, the taxi driver went straight to the front of a long queue at the ticket booth and made the necessary enquiries for me, writing down a list of times and prices for the bus. I nodded and asked optimistically for an express bus, which resulted in more shouting and negotiating. Eventually, however, I got a ticket, tipped the kindly taxi driver and waited for my bus. After a long wait, a weary looking bus arrived and we headed off into the Urals, with the ethnically diverse group of passengers reflecting its place at the crossroads between Europe and Asia. The bus broke down twice, and on each occasion, the driver disappeared underneath the bus with some spanners.

I was surprised at the vast verdant landscape that unfolded before me and I certainly felt an affinity with the feature-less landscape; it was similar to the American countryside that I had experienced on my earlier road trip from Taliesin North to Taliesin West in 2000. The bus journey effectively straddled the border between Europe and Asia (the Ural Mountains traditionally signifying the end of Europe) and the nearby town of Yekaterinburg was the official frontier between the two continents. The Urals rolled on, and the driver put on a video of some Russian slapstick comedy to entertain us. After meandering through the impressive panorama towards Magnitogorsk, the bus seemed to have been caught in a time-warp as it entered a dark city, dominated by its steelworks and the empty, magnetic mountain. I was reminded of an industrial town from the Victorian era, with its array of tall chimneys belching out plumes of black and orange smoke. Immediately, I noticed that the town was divided by the river, with

Petrol station in the Urals, Russia

industry concentrated on one side whilst the residential and civic areas were located on the other.

There was only one hotel listed in my guidebook, and so I took a taxi to Valentino's. The hotel had very long dark corridors and curious stairs hidden behind corners. To relieve my nervousness I switched on the television for some solace and recognised the overtly dramatic music of *Who Wants to be Millionaire?* (I wondered if here it might be called 'Who wants to be an Oligarch?') Even more amusing was the next programme, *The Simpsons* dubbed in Russian – a real transcultural confrontation and hilarious at the same time. Feeling hungry, I checked my map and there seemed to be a choice of two main streets, Lenin or Marx – a philosophical conundrum that I decided to cut short by opting for Marx.

Beyond Moscow, the ideal Soviet settlement sought to mitigate the division between town and country. Friedrich Engels had identified in *Anti-Dühring* (1878), a method of promoting social equality: 'The abolition of the division between town and country.'[53] These sentiments were repeated by Lenin as he viewed the uneven distribution of wealth between the town and the country to be an example of all that was wrong with capitalism:

'rural neglect, isolation from the world and barbarism, as well as of the unnatural accumulation of gigantic masses of people in large towns.'[54] At the time of the October Revolution, only one-sixth of the Russian population were resident in cities, and so the majority of the nation consisted of mainly illiterate rural peasants – consequently, addressing rural poverty was a pressing need. Stalin's initial Five-Year Plan explicitly stated the need for rapid industrialisation and the state sought to provide 'for the construction of 200 new industrial towns and 1000 new agricultural ones.'[55] The plan was packed with targets for achieving socialism with explicit timeframes and backed up by tables, charts and graphs: '[s]ocialism was the goal, planning was the method.'[56] Scientific planning by the Soviet regime was to replace the arbitrary methods of capitalism.

The nationwide competition for the design of Magnitogorsk closed in March 1930, but it was somewhat retrospective, as work on building the city had already begun by 1929. The sociologist Mikhail Okhitovich advocated a 'disurban' solution to urban planning in his lectures and articles, which responded to the call by Marx and Engels to eradicate the difference between town and country. Furthermore, Okhitovich embraced the technological revolution in transport and energy transmission to eliminate the need for the city to be founded on land: instead, it would be a city on the move and in a constant state of flux.[57] Inspired, the Russian designers, Ivan Leonidov and Muliutin, developed their 'linear city' idea for Magnitogorsk with parallel zones for infrastructure (railways, roads), cultural and recreational facilities, residential strips, a park and market zones.[58] The linear city design used seductive graphics and texts to describe a city that would be fully integrated into its landscape, with parallel 25 kilometre (15½ miles) open-ended strips to allow for future expansion. The mixed residential core was to be integrated within a green zone that included facilities for children, and the civic and administrative functions were distributed throughout the plan.[59]

Despite these ambitious plans for the new city of Magnitogorsk, the winning design by Chenichev was a relatively conservative scheme based on a compact model of urban settlement – similar to the 1932 plan for Moscow. Work had begun on constructing the plant in 1929, but it was only in March 1930 that McKee and Co. of Cleveland, Ohio, were appointed to design the steelworks. The stated aim was to match the largest integrated plant of the time in Gary, Indiana: 'catch and overtake' was the party's slogan.[60]

In *An Autobiography*, Wright expanded on his ideas for a new society and reflected on his Russian adventure and the work of the disurbanists:

> Russians, make good use of your ground for the new Russia! Can the Soviets not see that electricity, machines, automobiles, radio, television – the architecture of splendid highways and spacious, far flung Agriculture can make the old form of the city (centralisation) not only useless, but harmful to the future? . . . I would much like the young architects of the USSR to see, and some day they may see, Broadacre City – the city that is everywhere and nowhere.[61]

It is surprising that both the Russians and Wright had considered the same process and arrived at similar solutions, but in two very different ways. The centralised one-party state in the Soviet Russia and its application of a top-down ideology contrasted dramatically with an American condition, underpinned by individual democratic rights and a weaker federal government. The intellectual basis for Wright's urban manifesto was firmly situated in his own experience and engagement with the city. During the Great Depression of the 1930s many intellectuals in the US began to propose solutions that were often extremely radical. They debated the ills of capitalism that had alienated the poor and resulted in low wages coupled with high rents. Cities themselves were likewise seen as concentrating the problems of capitalism. Whilst the solutions proposed were innovative, pragmatic and incremental.

The prototypical American capitalist Henry Ford was a practical reformer who also advocated breaking up the city, stating in 1919: 'We shall solve the City problem by leaving the City.'[62] For Ford, the ideal American life was agrarian: 'I am a farmer . . . I want to see every acre of the earth's surface covered with little farms, with happy, contented people living on them.'[63] Ford promoted two separate but related schemes for decentralisation – Muscle Shoals in Tennessee, and Village Industries in Michigan. The Muscle Shoals proposal was a regional concept to harness the power from the Tennessee River to produce nitrate fertilizer, irrigation for farming, and hydro-electric power. Whereas the Village Industries were of a much smaller scale, built between 1918 and 1941, to 'enhance rural life' by offering rural resettlement coupled with small-scale local industries. The concept was closely related to those of the Russian anarchist and communist, Peter

Kropotkin, as contained within *Fields, Factories and Workshops*.[64] Henry Ford remained a personal inspiration for Wright, and he called Ford a man of 'common sense' particularly for his wish to decentralise the city and the factory.[65]

This culture of pragmatic and incremental engagement formed the cornerstone of Wright's understanding of urban communities and social reform. At the start of his career in suburban residential design, he became concerned about the encroaching consumer culture, the narrow focus of the architectural profession, and the poor design of small community ventures.[66] Wright advocated simpler homogenised residential designs that could break the cycle of individualism and consumerism which he believed had turned the suburbs into an unruly aesthetic battlefield – thus, the 'Prairie Style' can be viewed in a broader sense as seeking to harmonise public and private spheres.[67] Wright's first communal scheme of the period was the Roberts Block Master Plan (1896) in the emerging suburb of Oak Park, and he proposed a central communal space and housing 22 lots around it. For the City Club of Chicago Land Development Competition (1913), Wright designed an ideal suburb that was segregated according to class and income: the housing types were stratified with the 'better class' Quadruple Blocks dominating the centre. The apartment blocks were segregated according to gender, and the workmen housing were located at the periphery. A variety of social functions were woven into the scheme such as schools, markets, a library, power plant, fire department and non-sectarian temple. Yet, with no apparent transport infrastructure (other than roads), no industry, and no police station, it was a middle class wonderland.[68]

Wright consolidated these ideas and gave them architectural form in his polemical Kahn Lectures in 1930, which were summarised within the book *The Disappearing City* (1932). Within this text, Wright questioned the economic basis of the city and its three main economic artificialities: rent for land, rent for money, and the apparatus of capitalism[69] – the artificial economies of capitalist cities. Wright identified five agencies to develop a decentralised and democratic society: these were electrification, the internal combustion engine, mechanical systems of refrigeration, new materials and mass production by the machine.[70] It is astonishing how similar his ideas were to those of the Russian disurbanists. He noted: 'It is the nature of universal electrification that the city is nowhere and everywhere.'[71] Wright turned himself into a technological visionary, declaring that 'tele-transmissions of sight and sound' would remove the need to travel to the city.'[72] Furthermore, car ownership had expanded dramatically in America during the 1920s and 30s, there was a 20-fold increase in ownership between 1917 and 1930, with one car per household by the early 1930s, and even two cars per every five people in California. Within this context Wright became less of a visionary and more the pragmatist and a 'trend planner.'[73] He claimed that the new method of organising the city was the motor car:

> [b]y means of the motor car and the collateral inventions that are here with it, the horizon of the individual has immeasurably widened. It is significant that not only have space values entirely changed with the new standard: It is more important that the new sense of spacing based upon the man in his motor car is now at work upon the man himself . . . After all he is the city? So the city is going where and as he goes . . .[74]

Wright proclaimed that this new settlement was based on the freedom for the individual to escape the centripetal city and was a means of generating a new indigenous architecture. 'We are going to call this city for the individual the Broadacre City because it is based upon a minimum of an acre to the family.'[75] Wright believed in the 'experiment' within America which had yet to realise its full potential in his eyes, and indeed he believed the freedom of democracy and Broadacre City were joined together in his proposal.[76] Whilst the 1935 Broadacre plan was 'socially diverse' and inclusive, it lacked any 'practical strategy for implementation.'[77] Wright therefore hawked his Broadacre City to any dictator willing to listen – in addition to Stalin, he sent his son to see Mussolini in 1935. Another paradox was leadership in Broadacre City itself, but Wright saw himself – the architect – as 'the logical interpreter, perhaps the only one who can show us the way is an organic modern architecture.'[78] It reveals that Wright's vision of democracy was almost Stalinist in practice.

Yet this juxtaposition was to become tangible, by a most remarkable turn of historical events – when Stalin's own daughter became a resident of the Taliesin Fellowship. The story began when Olgivanna's daughter, Svetlana Peters, died in a car crash in 1946. Many years later, Olgivanna heard the news that Stalin's daughter, Svetlana Alliluyeva, had defected to America in 1967. Olgivanna invited her to visit Taliesin, believing that there was a mystical connection between the two Svetlanas, and that one could replace the other.[79] When no reply came back, Olgivanna pestered Svetlana with letters and telephone calls, until she relented and visited Taliesin West in 1970. Such was the force of Olgivanna's will, that she arranged the marriage between Svetlana and Wesley Peters, the chief apprentice and her former son-in-law, within three weeks of meeting one another. Predictably, the marriage did not last, due to Olgivanna's constant interference, but the second Svetlana Peters delivered the most damming commentary on the Fellowship, when she equated Olgivanna with the absolute power of her father. She lamented: 'why had I come to this weird place, where everything reminded me [of] what I have run away from? This primitive communism under a dictator.'[80]

Back in Magnitogorsk, I awoke to a dreary overcast and rainy morning as I left the Valentino Hotel and walked to the Metal Workers Square – and towards what I thought would be the centre of town. I followed Marx's road again, with Stalin's road following a parallel path. From my research, I carried a number of images of the various 'highlights' of the city so that I could show the pictures to someone if I got lost. It was a harsh environment for a pedestrian beside six lanes of road traffic and two central tram lines, lined by anonymous six-storey apartment blocks to the west and factories to the east over the river. This was part of the 1960s Khrushchev-era standardised linear super-blocks that formed the Pravobereshnij-Rayon plan, and it looked a bleak existence. The linear form was reminiscent of the original concept for the city, but the modern aspect of the linear blocks was tedious and overpowering. After an hour of monotony, the urban form revealed a large vacant plaza that possessed a low civic building, plus a dramatic war memorial at the river's edge. This memorial to the Great Patriotic War (1941–5) was a giant iron sculpture of two foundry men holding a sword above their heads. But at the foot of one foundry man someone had left an empty beer bottle, while over the river the steelworks were discharging plumes of black and red smoke. It was far from heroic.

I continued on towards the Metal Workers Square, and came across the Stalinist housing blocks on Leninsky Rayon from the 1950s. These over-scaled Beaux-Arts inspired perimeter blocks, however, formed impressive squares and quadrants, as if displaced from 19th-century Paris to a planned modern city on the very edge of Europe. At street level, there were some cafés, hairdressers, mobile phone shops and other small ventures. Above ground, each apartment had a balcony that had been infilled with plastic

View along central axis of Karl Marx Prospect, Magnitogorsk, Russia

sheeting to make the space more usable. Inside the perimeter blocks, there were playgrounds, parked cars, and some areas left overgrown with grass. The Metal Workers Square was truly vast, with the wide neoclassical façade of Magnitogorsk University as its focal point and a broad tree-lined highway leading down to the river. The scale was breathtaking, and its severe outlook reminded me of the Communist era: I could well imagine the road and square full of military hardware and marching soldiers. Beside the square were small cafés for the students, a modern post office and a neoclassical opera house. I called into the post office to get some stamps and directions for the original Socgorod district and Pobedy Square. The woman did not recognise the map I showed to her, nor indeed the main image of Pobedy Square. She asked some of her customers for some advice, soon the whole post office was looking at my image and getting into an animated debate. She gestured towards a minibus stand outside and wrote down the number 22.

When it arrived, the number 22 minibus was a true collective, with the passengers pooling together their money to hand over to a child who grinned manically in the front seat. A wide-eyed driver was hunched over the steering wheel and concentrated intently on the road ahead, accelerating too hard and braking too quickly. I realised it was best not to distract him. We raced towards the river, crossed a low bridge and then climbed up a hill at great speed. At the top was Pobedy Square, the original city centre from the 1930s. The square was more intimate with carefully modulated façades, although the central green area was neglected with an old T-34 tank raised on a plinth. At the back of the square, I recognised the neoclassical Palace of Culture. I ventured inside the lobby, which was clad in marble with photographs showing a number of talent competitions that now take place at the palace. The egalitarian Soviet cultural palace had been upstaged by *Russia's Got Talent.*

Behind an informal market were some of Ernst May's apartment blocks for the Socogord housing in the 1930s. At the Soviet government's behest, Ernst May, the German modernist architect responsible for the planning of 1920s Neue Frankfurt, was invited to Russia. It was common practice during the first Five-Year Plan for Russia to seek assistance from foreign experts, and May's highly accomplished 'brigade' arrived in 1930 to work on a number of designs, including Magnitogorsk. May visited the site in 1930 and 1931 and realised that the steelworks were already well under construction and also the hilly topography of the site did not make the linear city concept feasible. Consequently, May located the housing to the south-west of the plant, but this expedient solution had disastrous consequences, as the prevailing winds carried all the smoke from the plant to the apartments. The residents were nevertheless grateful to be given an apartment in the Soviet City area of Magnitogorsk, later named the Kirov district, as the majority of the workers were still living in timber barracks.

John Scott, the son of a communist academic, Scott Nearing, wrote a captivating narrative describing the construction of the steelworks. Enthralled by the events and developments in Soviet Russia, Scott reflected: '[s]omething seemed to be wrong with America. I began to read extensively about the Soviet Union, and gradually came to the conclusion that the Bolsheviks had found answers to at least some of the questions Americans were asking each other.'[81] Scott recorded day-to-day life in Magnitogorsk, and in a typically Marxist manner he tabulated the daily steelwork performance, the number of skilled and unskilled workers on site, and the monthly food allowance for a rigger.[82] Comparing it to the original proclamations in the 1934 Congress of the Communist Party of the Soviet Union, Scott claimed that the steelworks and the city were only ever 45 per cent fulfilled.[83] During the construction phase from 1928 to 1932, the population of Magnitogorsk was estimated at a quarter of a million, and Scott notes that about 25 per cent were there by 'compulsion' and two-thirds of the labour was unskilled.[84] By 1938, with a population of 220,000, the city was stratified into a number of districts: 15 per cent lived in the Kirov district, 2 per cent were in the Berekzi, 8 per cent in individual houses, 50 per cent in timber barracks and the remaining 25 per cent in the Zemlyanki – i.e. improvised mud huts inhabited by the Bashirs, Tartars, and Kirghizi peoples.[85]

Nowadays, May's apartments are almost derelict, yet the intention remains tantalising: spacious, well-designed flats with green spaces between. Some of the blocks still had residents, while others were decrepit, adding to the romantic modernist myth. I climbed another small hill to get a vantage point. I passed a number of weathered timber buildings in the Berekzi district, which Scott recognised as 'copied almost exactly from American architectural catalogues' and this resulted in it looking like 'Mount Vernon, New York, or Germantown, Pennsylvania.'[86] The displaced 'American suburb' was now fully adopted into its Russian context. In summary, the 1930 frontier industrial city of Magnitogorsk contained: idealised modernist super-blocks by May, a transplanted American suburb, timber barracks and a host of informal settlements – maybe not the ideal Soviet City but a pluralistic settlement nonetheless. Looking down from my viewpoint, I saw beneath me Stalin's vision of the steelworks with its blast furnaces, tall chimneys and plumes of smoke. The magnetic mountain was now a huge crater with the parasitical factories around its base feeding off its very last deposits, since iron ore is now brought in from elsewhere.

Scott recounts that the brutal Stalinist purges came to Magnitogorsk in 1937 'with great force. Thousands were arrested, incarcerated for months, finally exiled.'[87] Returning from a holiday in America in 1938, Scott found he was denied entry to the factory and advised to stay at home; he later travelled to Moscow and waited for three years to gain an exit visa for his Russian family. Magnitogorsk was closed to foreign visitors in 1937 and was only later reopened in the Perestroika era.

I returned to Pobedy Square and walked down the hill towards the steelworks. At its entrance there is now a giant figure of Lenin welcoming the workers (the original statue of Stalin having been removed in the 1960s). There were also some amazing reliefs surrounding the façade of the factory, as if the Christian Orthodox iconostasis were updated for the Communist era. On display were heroic steel workers enjoying their proud communal life within the dispersed city. However, at the other end of the car park by the tram station, I noticed that some of the steelworkers were already drunk. Further on, towards the river, there were some older factories as well as remnants of Albert Kahn's pared down Beaux-Arts façades, and enormous factory sheds that seemed to extend for the whole length of the city. I caught a noisy tram back into town, which was full of steel workers leaving the industrial east side behind to go home to their families on the west side.

The scale of Magnitogorsk ultimately defeated the planned Soviet City, as the political propaganda of constructing the largest steelworks in the world overwhelmed the compact settlement downwind of the plant. However, the resulting linear-city-by-default embraces its present condition and the long parallel strips of plant, river, and residencies all recall Leonidov's aspirations. Despite concentrating its housing on the other side of the river, pollution remains a pressing problem for the city. Magnitogorsk is in the top 25 of the world's most polluted cities, as noted by the Blacksmith Institute, and only 28 per cent of infants within the city are considered to be healthy.[88] The river has the potential of uniting the city.[89] It could indeed form part of an ecological cleansing for the city, similar to other cities in the American 'rust belt,' thus forming another cultural link back to its original inspiration in Gary, Indiana. During my visit, I noticed some short walks along the river bank and that a mosque had been built within this green buffer zone. Along the depressing linear avenues dedicated to Marx and Lenin, informal markets appear at night at the traffic intersections, and often the ground-floor apartments of the blocks support small enterprises; these informal improvements add to the city's vitality and are a sustainable means of developing the city. The disurbanists claimed that modern technology would be the means of achieving a linear city, yet the conditions of Russia were never as affluent as in Western counties, so widespread car ownership was never realised. Indeed, it was perhaps discouraged as the internal passport system introduced by Stalin sought to curtail any freedom for the road traveller. The grand aims of the disurbanists and Wright's Broadacre City were therefore never implemented in full. They claimed to provide a more equitable and natural alternative to the traditional city, yet were both compromised in the end by centrifugal forces – whether the commodified capitalist urbanism of the US, or the centralised planned city of the Soviets.

EGOR'EVSK

Returning to Moscow, I spent the afternoon in the Shchusev Museum of Architecture. It was inside a neoclassical palace and I entered via a courtyard at the rear; the tradesman's entrance, I surmised. It had a trendy modern café and some bric-a-brac of classical stone mouldings. On the first floor, the formal suites contained contemporary architectural exhibits of some new towers that were being planned for the city. I browsed through the books on sale in the shop, and happened to spot an elevation that looked astonishingly similar to Wright's Robie House. Taken aback, I decided to search for this former trade union club in the Moscow suburbs. The following morning I found myself unable to get a taxi for a reasonable fare, and so instead I caught the 1 o'clock train from Moscow to the outlying town of Egor'evsk. The train ambled out of the station, the dense city soon petered out and we travelled through an endless pine forest. The journey was agonisingly slow and dull and even station names became mere milestones: 34km, then 38km, 73km and so on.

Following the Bolshevik triumph in 1917, a whole range of Workers Clubs, Village Clubs and People's Houses became an important part of the propagating of the 'new socialist culture.'[90] Within two years of the Russian Revolution, over 7000 of these clubs had been established, and the XIIth Party Congress stated their purpose explicitly as 'centres for mass propaganda and the development of creativity among the working class'[91] – a definition that was both sinister and awakening at the same time. It is claimed that the idea for these clubs came from the political clubs founded in America after the Civil War, but with a single-party state in Russia, the clubs instead became an important form of political dissemination.[92] Typically the brief for these clubs was ambitious and based on the first Workers' Palaces, therefore requiring a number of auditoria, lecture halls, study and leisure areas, gymnasia, self-service restaurants and playing fields. Gradually, the neoclassical designs were replaced by a more experimental approach, with intimate staging and local performers. Common to all the emergent clubs after 1925 was the use of a modernist architectural language.

The expansion of the so-called Trade Union Clubs around Moscow was directed by a body known as the Moscow Region Council of Trade Unions, which sought to propagate its influence by constructing cultural institutions. In 1927, a Moscow plenum adopted a plan to build 78 union clubs over a three-year period, of which 28 were to be built by the Textile Trade Unions.[93] The aforementioned town of Egor'evsk has a population of 68,000 and has been a well-known centre for the manufacturing textiles since the 1820s. It is predominately a two-storey town with masonry buildings finished in render, although there are some older timber houses and two recently renovated churches. I walked up a gradual rise, and between a war memorial and small park, I recognised the Konin Palace of Culture (1927–9) as designed by Vladimir Shchuko. He was considered an 'inventive eclectic,'[94] as he was adept at changing the style of any building to suit a particular client or demand. He had a neoclassical (a.k.a. Stalinist) style for state commissions, whilst able to adopt a more progressive modern or constructivist approach for smaller commissions. Under the Tzars, he had designed the classical Russian Pavilion for the International Exhibition in Rome (1911).

So, the Konin Palace of Culture in Egor'evsk for the Textile Trade Union offered an opportunity for Shchuko to test out the new aesthetic. The Konin Club was made up of two distinct functions: a workers' club with a discreet entry off the street and function rooms distributed over three stories facing the street and the park. There was also a major auditorium for 1500 people with a separate side entry from the war memorial park, which stepped up from the street façade to the tall stage tower at the back of the site. Somewhat predictably, the Konin Club was nothing like the slavish copy of the Robie House that I had expected from the book I had seen. The club still had a number of Wrightian features, though, including a horizontal aspect, long bands of casement windows, glazed corner details and even a shallow pitched roof. The low-pitched metal roof responded to the 'Prairie Style' aesthetic but, again, it did not achieve anywhere near the same dynamic effect. Indeed, it seemed to come more from a local vernacular tradition. The Konin Club has been newly restored and painted and I ventured inside to find a few children and their parents circulating around a small lobby space and cloakrooms. The large empty hall was an undifferentiated generic space with a grid of concrete columns, and it could be used for a variety of purposes. Down the corridor there was a newly decorated, well-stocked self-service café that looked out onto the park. I shared its impersonal space with another couple. Each of the spaces in the Konin Club were similarly remote and static; there was no overlap of function or rooms, the plan had an overtly formal composition.

Feature Corner, Konin Palace of Culture, Egor'evsk, Russia (1927–9) by Vladimir Shchuko

Within Egor'evsk, the Konin Club sits on an equal footing with the two main churches, as the brief required, and it does so by using a distinctive architectural language, thereby propagating a Communist agenda. The Cultural Clubs for the proletariat were all conceived to 'reflect the epoch of cultural revolution.' Yet, the proletariat was always an abstract idea – a single mass of people whose wants were never clearly defined – and from the Proletkult movement to VOPRA, different organisations claimed to be able to represent their needs and to proclaim standard solutions. Whilst the modern movement offered a number of exciting solutions for Cultural Clubs by Konstantin Melnikov and the Vesnin brothers, the later manifestations were neoclassical objects dispersed across the Soviet Union. All these Cultural Clubs were a manifestation of 'culture from above,' symbolising an oppressive Soviet regime that sought to maintain its own power by cultural manipulation. It was interesting to consider that the Konin Club could have been a subversive design, based on the American democratic values espoused by Wright. And it is tantalising to consider that the Konin Club could indeed have begun a 'revolution' from below based on pragmatic and incremental change.

Wright was a 'useful hostage' for the Soviet regime[95] – or, put more honestly, he was an unwitting apologist for Stalin. Yet he was not alone in this error. Other disgruntled modernists such as Bruno Taut, Hannes Meyer and André Lurçat took their concerns about the European modern movement with them to Russia. All of these modernists and their willingness to embrace the Communist Party line were of great propaganda value for Stalin, both internationally and within the Soviet Union. Wright's true motives for his visit were never clear. Some speculate that Wright wanted to propel himself onto the international scene as a man of ideas and consequence,[96] others argue that Wright believed that Stalin would respond to his vision of a new society by considering Broadacre City and the Taliesin Fellowship to be ideal models. What is also interesting is that the trend continues to this day, most globally renowned architects travel the world in the hope of realising their ideas and they are willing to work for any tyrant to realise their designs.

4

WHATEVER HAPPENED TO FRANK LLOYD WRIGHT?

In *An Autobiography*, Frank Lloyd Wright claims that his mother was responsible for generating his love of architecture, giving him Froebel educational toys and hanging pictures of English cathedrals from 'Old England' in his bedroom.[1] These romanticised details of his childhood were just the beginning of a life-long tendency to reinvent and deceive by making things seem so pre-destined. Despite the rather implausible placing of English Gothic cathedrals by a Welsh mother from a non-conformist Unitarian background, it does link to Wright's predisposition towards the English Gothic, and an acknowledgement that the Gothic Revival of the 19th century was a crucial influence on his architectural thought and practice. In addition, Wright closely followed ideological and architectural developments in Britain and, in 1901, he presented 'The Art and Craft of the Machine' at Hull House, Chicago; a truly modern interpretation of the ideas of John Ruskin and William Morris.

BEXLEYHEATH

Arts and Crafts was a concurrent movement on both sides of the Atlantic, so Wright would have been able to engage with the latest thinking, and the contemporary architecture and trans-Atlantic journals would have kept him fully informed. I decided to start the English leg of my journey by visiting the cradle of the movement, only a half-hour train ride from London Bridge, the suburb of Bexleyheath, Kent. As a modern day commuter, I took my folding bicycle with me to make negotiating the suburb a bit easier. Alighting at my destination I cycled from the busy main street towards an expanse of 1930s semi-detached properties that were grouped according to their external finishes: some had a painted rendered finish, while others displayed a mock Tudor aspect – a tribute to a fabled medieval era, and perhaps also to William Morris as their medievalist neighbour. I passed by a Georgian terrace painted white, and there, nestled within the trees, was the prototypical country vicarage, built for William Morris, one of the most significant cultural figures of the age.

The Red House (1859) designed by William Morris's friend Philip Webb, is now owned by the National Trust. Morris himself was a keen antiquarian and so established the Society for the Protection of Ancient Buildings (1877), a precursor to the National Trust (1895). I speculated whether Morris would have approved of preserving his own unique interpretation of the 19th-century medieval revivalism? I had previously telephoned to make a booking for a guided tour since this was the only way that I could view the interior. The tourist entrance is now at the back of the house, via the kitchen and the former servants' quarters – there is no front door formality nowadays. I was welcomed by an elderly lady who hid my bike under a table. I was reminded not to take any photographs inside, but I was permitted to take as many as I wished of the exterior. The house occupies the south-east corner of the large site and is L-shaped in plan. The formal entry from the north leads into a spacious hallway, stair and corridors running alongside the garden, off which lie separate rooms facing the orchard. Each elevation is asymmetrical, with its own unique outlook. The most captivating aspects are the east and south elevations, which embrace a small private garden that has a well in the foreground, offering a hint of self-sufficiency and a source of wisdom. I particularly enjoyed the modest circular windows to the first-floor studio to the south; they were a progressive statement of a more modern future, and reminded me of the constructivist *Izvestia* newspaper building (Grigory Barkhin; 1927) in Moscow.

The tour guide was keen to reinforce the more romantic Pre-Raphaelite vision of the house:

> Whilst Morris may have professed to be a socialist, it was not what he was really famous for . . . Here, in the hall, you will see the decorated door with a beautiful stained-glass window. During the early years after the house was completed, Morris would gather all friends and have their meals in the hall as a recreation of medieval traditions.

It was a tour for the aesthetes among us, and the guide went into great detail about the fixtures and the fittings, the hidden wall frescoes and re-painted doors. The Red House was intended as a realisation of the ideal suburb that Morris later proclaimed in *News from Nowhere* (1890), but instead of being surrounded by fields and orchards, it was now contained in a never-ending sprawl of two-storeyed monotony. Morris lived at the house only for a fairly short period before moving to Kelmscott Manor in Oxfordshire, where his printing works were based.

Despite the success of the Red House in articulating a progressive Arts and Crafts architecture, Morris moved increasingly away from architecture and took full control of his craft business in 1875, establishing Morris and Co. Thereafter he devoted his time mainly to design, writing and political action. In 1883, he began to read the work of Karl Marx and soon became a committed socialist and public persona to advance Marxist beliefs. Using Marx's masterpiece, *Das Kapital* (1867), Morris studied the transition of the late medieval period from a feudal society to a capitalist society.[2] The relative prosperity of the working man during the medieval period led Morris to proclaim that the old craft guilds were an early model of an egalitarian society, powerful enough to resist the church and feudal lords.[3] Within these guilds, Morris imagined a free collaboration between members, no division of labour, and no accumulation of capital.[4] By 1889, Morris declared himself a 'Communist' and his famous work, *News from Nowhere,* contained his utopian vision of a planned centralised city with a civic core surrounded by Guild Halls and parks, and extending out to an ideal suburb. Within this utopian vision, two themes became intertwined, that of the benign leader, a kind of Arthurian figure, and the peasant republic based on the idea of social justice.[5]

Morris was able to combine an essentially aesthetic discourse about the Gothic style with a social analysis of the Industrial Revolution. Yet he was also regressive in wishing to return to the old guilds and ignored the potential of the machine, so the mantle of progressive modern thought crossed the Atlantic from Britain and to America and the architecture of Louis Sullivan and Frank Lloyd Wright. It had been Wright's prominent uncle, the Unitarian preacher Jenkin Lloyd Jones, who introduced him to social concerns in Chicago. Wright duly followed his uncle to Hull House, a settlement house established by Jane Addams and Ellen Gates Starr that was modelled on Toynbee Hall, in east London. In 1901, Wright first outlined his vision of an American architecture in his lecture at Hull House entitled 'The Art and Craft of the Machine'. In this, Wright broke with Ruskin and Morris and set out a plausible American pragmatic attitude towards industrialisation, manufacture and architecture. The lecture acknowledged, that 'all artists love and honor William Morris,' and Wright described Morris as the 'great socialist' and Ruskin the 'great moralist.'[6] Similarly, Wright spoke of the medieval period as a time when 'all the intellectual forces of the people converged to one point – architecture.'[7] supporting Victor Hugo in proclaiming that 'printing will destroy architecture.'[8] Wright equated the death of medieval architecture by the printing press to the dispatching of fine art by the machine. But, instead of being pessimistic, Wright saw an opportunity to revitalise architecture by harnessing the machine.

Wright believed that the use of machines could result in a new approach to materials and to aesthetics, observing that Morris was an advocate of 'simplicity' himself.[9] In a typical reflection of the pragmatic and progressive philosophies within Hull House, Wright advocated a 'society for mutual education' that would be able to harness the machine, and he specifically called for the artist to engage with the manufacturers to develop new approaches.[10] This engagement with modern manufacturing was intended as a direct step away from the regressive instincts of Morris and the medieval guilds that he idolised. Wright saw the machine as defining a new art and new egalitarian society:

> the medium of artistic expression itself has broadened and changed . . . [with] the Machine . . . [a] tool which frees human labor, lengthens and broadens the life of the simplest man, thereby the basis of the Democracy upon which we insist.[11]

CHIPPING CAMPDEN

The English architect Charles Ashbee first met Wright at Hull House in 1900, during a lecture tour in Chicago in 1900 to raise funds for the National Trust. The two eager and earnest young architects became good friends, with Ashbee admiring 'Wright's flamboyant personal style and debonair good looks, a common taste for Whitman and rhetoric.'[12] On Ashbee's last day in Chicago, Wright took him on a tour of Oak Park, whereupon Ashbee proclaimed that Wright was 'far and away the ablest man in our line of work that I have come across in Chicago, perhaps in America.'[13] The two architects shared similar passions for the Arts and Crafts and, as such, debated the role of the machine. Despite clearly being indebted to the Arts and Crafts movement and the 'English Free Style' in developing the 'Prairie Style', Wright was as 'scathing in his criticism of the English Arts and Crafts as sentimental.'[14]

When Wright first visited Britain in September 1909, he was as a fugitive who had deserted his wife and six children, and was too socially embarrassed to look up his old friend Charles Ashbee. But when he returned to England alone a year later, he felt able to make arrangements to visit Ashbee at Chipping Camden, Gloucestershire. Ashbee had been educated privately and at Cambridge, and as a resident and participant at Toynbee Hall, he mused on the juxtaposing of the upper and lower classes: 'everyone was invited and everyone comes . . . [but] . . . everybody always does the wrong thing.'[15] Despite his background and class-conscious observation, Ashbee went on to become a leading activist. In 1888, he opened the Guild and School of Handicraft on Commercial Street in east London, seeking to resurrect a medieval guild as urged by William Morris in his writings and lectures. The guild attempted to integrate work, education and leisure. Invoking the camaraderie of a Cambridge college, they undertook theatre productions, played cricket matches, and had communal outings to the countryside.

As the guild expanded, it moved to a new premises in the East End of London, but there was always a romantic view that the country was better suited for a craft endeavour. This popular view was supported by social reformers such as General Booth and Ebenezer Howard, who advocated a reversal of urban concentration, and by Jessie Collings, who called for a peasant ownership through the 'Back to the Land' movement.[16] So, Ashbee moved his guild from the East End of London to the rural utopia of Chipping Campden in the Cotswolds, a town that had prospered during height of the wool trade in the 18th century, but had declined thereafter. The 50 guildsmen and their families moved from London in 1902 and the community prospered, so much so that there were 71 guildsmen by the end of the year.

The work within the guild was produced under one roof and organised around Ashbee, with a hierarchy in the division of labour. Ashbee was the designer, foremen distributed and supervised the work, and teams of craftsmen worked long hours under strict rules.[17] However, it appeared that the Guild was far from fulfilling the egalitarian craft-based values expressed by Morris, and even machines were used to supplement the craft work and despite the hard work, the guild recorded its first financial loss in 1905, and although a more commercial reorganisation was attempted to try to stop the rot, it was formally terminated in 1908. Ashbee had realised by then that 'the central problem was that of making quality goods by hand, in the face of effective competition from producers using machines.'[18] However, Ashbee did not even consider that locating the guild in a rural setting might have been a flawed premise.

I visited the Old Silk Mill on Sheep Street in Chipping Campden, which had been the home of the Guild of Handicraft – now simply called The Guild. The historic three-storey mill was used originally for weaving silk to make ribbons, which were then sold in Coventry and Birmingham. In fact, its large window openings and open floors made the internal space flexible enough for many uses. Today the mill contains several artistic outlets, with an art gallery on the ground floor, a jewellery studio on the first floor, and the Hart family jewellers on the second floor. Will Hart and his brother George had joined the Handicraft Guild in 1902 and remained in Chipping Campden after its liquidation. Indeed the Hart studio itself looked rather unchanged, and they are still manufacturing reproductions of Ashbee's work. I asked to look at their visitors' book, and one of the jewellers helped me to find Wright, telling me that he was still very popular with American tourists. Frank Lloyd Wright's signature was there on an entry marked '10 September 1910', it being predated by his sister, Maginel Wright, who had visited the colony in 1907. Chipping Campden has fully embraced the guild into its very fabric, with a nearby exhibition at Court Barn curated by Ashbee's biographer, Alan Crawford, and showcasing nine designers who have thrived within the rural setting. At the Robert Welch cutlery shop, I bought some extra teaspoons to replace those that have disappeared in my dishwasher. The assistant informed me that while the design studio remains in Campden, production has now moved from Sheffield to South Korea, a familiar lament that Ashbee would have understood. The modern setting for a craftwork guild embraces a global labour market and commodity flows, rather than the quaint teachings of Ruskin and Morris.

In 1950, on another trip to England, Wright returned to the Cotswolds with Robert Furneaux Jordan, the Principal at the Architectural Association School. Although Wright did not record his thoughts, Jordan remarked: 'It is the feeling for the organic and the romantic, I think, that explains his ecstatic response to the English Cotswolds . . . it was the stonewalls of the sheeplands, the barns, the simpler cottages and smallest churches that excited him – these and the humanised English landscape.'[19] There was no mention of Ashbee and his visit to the guild in 1910, and when confronted with an early manor house, Wright commented: 'there's medievalism, my boy, dead on your chest.'[20] I am not sure if the last remark is an endorsement of the Cotswolds or not – needless to say that the inhabited landscape of the Cotswolds and its vernacular architecture would have been of most interest to Wright. It would have appealed to his own 'folk' persona and it also refers back to his love of Italian vernacular architecture and, by extension, to his 'organic' creed. There is also an uncanny resemblance between the natural honey coloured stone of the Cotswolds and that of Taliesin North, Wisconsin, but the architectures are so different that while Wright probably appreciated the picturesque Cotswolds he was certainly too modern to reference its buildings.

BROADACRE CITY AT THE RIBA

The Great Depression in America during the 1930s brought about a more liberal political regime under the banner of the New Deal, and marked the end of the boom years of the 1920s. After his election, President Franklin Roosevelt inaugurated a recovery directed First New Deal in 1932 and a reformist Second New Deal in 1936. One fundamental change initiated in the First New Deal was a redefinition of the 'social contract' within America, where individual self reliance was now backed up with the government offering protection against the vagaries of the market.[21] New agencies were developed to transform the infrastructure of America, such as Farm Security Administration (FSA), that sought to initiate new homesteads and community experiments across America.[22] In addition to addressing urban unemployment and potential unrest, there was an impetus for a return to the land movement as articulated by Ralph Borsodi in his books *This Ugly Civilization* (1929) and *Flight from the City* (1933), which condemned urban malaise and corruption within the industrialised city.[23] The publication of these books could not have been more timely, and Roosevelt endorsed urban resettlement in the hope of alleviating urban poverty and allowing people to grow their own produce.[24]

Wright was less affected by the Great Depression than most other architects, mainly because his output had already been so minimal during the 1920s. After his return from Japan in 1922, he worked briefly in Los Angeles until 1924. He began the 1930s by engaging in several alternative practices: he presented the Kahn Lectures at Princeton in 1930, where he outlined his Broadacre City vision; he published his *An Autobiography* (1932) and set up the Taliesin Fellowship in the same year. Wright now portrayed himself as a visionary of decentralisation, and a follower of the 'anarchic' strain of the early town planners, such as Peter Kropotkin and Ebenezer Howard. Wright's Broadacre City was anti-establishment and anti-capitalist and was part of an all-embracing 'Usonian' vision, America remade according to his ideas. Reflecting the radical zeitgeist of the period, he proposed three new rights for the American citizen: a new form of social credit, an acre of land to dwell on, and the repeal of all patents.[25] The notion of free currency was widely debated as a radical means of reforming capitalism, the nationalisation of land responded to Wright's agrarian background and was a means of propagating rapid decentralisation, and finally the repeal of all private patents would allow the free exchange of ideas without commercial exploitation. Wright would constantly claim that his utopian Broadacre City was the manifestation of 'democracy', enabling the individual to live an 'organic' life, yet within Broadacre the central authority was the elected architect. This contradiction was also present in Morris and Wright's suburban manifesto, the benign leader and the peasant republic below. Yet, within the climate of the 1930s, Broadacre City was remarkable for its vison, scale and architectural unity, a whole nation remade as 'Usonia' and in Wright's image. It was, in essence, Wright's own mini New Deal.

Wright was thus caught up in the spirit of the New Deal, if not in the actual process. To address housing reform, the Federal Housing Administration

(FHA) in 1934 offered guaranteed mortgage loans for banks – a traditional American approach to housing by using the private sector.[26] This reform also reflected the American attitude towards social housing: that only the single family house was seen as fostering 'American values.'[27] Responding to these reforms, Wright returned again to the issue of the 'house of moderate cost,' which he claimed was 'not only America's major architectural problem but the problem most difficult for her major architects.'[28] This was Wright's third attempt to solve the problem, following the Prairie House for $5000 and the American System-Bulit Ready-Cut Housing (1911–17). He claimed that the problem was mainly aesthetic, in that 'our people do not really know how to live, imagining that their idiosyncrasies to be their tastes, their prejudices to be their predilections and their ignorance to be virtue where any beauty of living is concerned.'[29] Consequently, the first 'Usonian' House for Herbert Jacobs (1936–7) was a statement of the simple life, according to Wright's interpretation, of course. It had an L-shaped plan containing a large open-plan living and dining area, a small kitchen, and a separate wing for the bedrooms. Wright included several innovations such as underfloor heating, lightweight construction, integral carport and built-in furniture. The resulting house was unquestionably functional, modern and indeed superb architecture – but it did not allow the owner many freedoms to be able to live according to their needs. Wright declared that the Usonian House could be built for a 'moderate cost' of $5500, (around £55,700 nowadays) which did at least indicate some measure of social democracy.[30]

In the inter-war period Wright's work was widely disseminated in Britain, with a number of books and articles that attempted to unravel his 'organic' architecture. Within these publications, there was widespread admiration of Wright's architecture, but there was likewise some confusion about his 'organic' philosophy. Commentators such as Philip Morton Shand could not equate the striking modern architecture with Wright's written prophesies.[31] In contrast, another reading of Wright came from the historian John Gloag. He visited America in 1934 and, having visited Wright, he became smitten by the whole Taliesin Fellowship and subsequently became a staunch promoter.[32] Yet, this merely showed that Wright was so brilliantly adept at boosting his own personality that it overshadowed his architecture. As Harry Seckel noted: 'He adores adoration. Disciples are a necessary part of his existence. In short, he is an architectural Isadora Duncan.'[33] Thus, in the 1930s, Wright was not only a colourful character who had survived numerous trials and tribulations, but he was also adept at making it all seem like his destiny.

The American journal *Architectural Forum* dedicated an entire issue to Wright in January 1938 which not only contained all his latest work, but was also designed and edited by Wright.[34] With his growing international reputation and critical adulation, it was perhaps not surprising that Wright was invited to occupy the Sir George Watson Chair on behalf of the Sulgrave Manor, an Anglo-American Institution. As part of this honour, Wright was required to give a number of public lectures. Wright left Spring Green, Wisconsin, on 19 April 1939 and sailed across the Atlantic on the *SS Europa,* arriving in Portsmouth on 30 April. He had a packed agenda for a man of nearly 72.[35]

The first of the four evening lectures at the RIBA were held at the newly completed Jarvis Lecture Hall. Each evening, the hall was full and many commentators remarked that the event was more of a 'happening' than a learned architectural discourse. Wright relied on his easy-going American manner and obtuse language to illuminate and confuse at the same time. During the first evening, Wright began as a true American democrat by admonishing the 'imposing formality' of the chairman, stating that he was not going to deliver a lecture: 'Not knowing very well what formal lectures are, however, having never attended any in my lifetime.'[36] This set the tone for a series of informal talks in which Wright restated his distaste for neoclassical architecture and most contemporary architecture alike, while never clearly explaining his 'organic' credo. Wright opened the evening confidently with 'a minority report: an informal Declaration of Independence,' which involved a 'spiritual' call for 'organic' architecture that was independent from neoclassical precedent and 'International Style' aesthetic.[37] He acknowledged his British ancestry and his fate in having been raised in the 'tall grass' of a romantic American idyll. According to Wright, an indigenous American architecture had begun and developed under Sullivan, up until the 'great orchestration' of neoclassical architecture in the 1893 Chicago World's Fair.[38] Thereafter, American architecture became merely a business, supported by academics who propagated a neoclassical education and architectural companies that produced 'pseudo classical' imitations.[39] He offered 'organic' architecture as being modern, free from tradition and embracing the idea that form and function are one.[40] Wright dismissed European modernist architecture as a mere style – a new form of decoration – his so-called '58

Variety', with their 'superficial simplicity making plain surfaces and flat roofs an aesthetic.'[41] It was a staggering insult to the modernists within the audience: their work was reduced to a mere addition to the 57 varieties cited on the humble Heinz Baked Beans tin!

The second evening began with a short film about life at Taliesin in Wisconsin and its drafting room. Wright proclaimed himself as 'a worker in from the field.'[42] He praised the domestic and 'homely aspect' of older English architecture that had been achieved 'in spite of [the] Renaissance,'[43] which implied that Wright was familiar with 'English Free Style', which underpinned the Arts and Crafts movement. However, Wright did not extend his admiration to the English country manor, terming Georgio-colonial architecture a 'Renaissance of the renaissance of the Renaissance'[44] – which he called an imposition on the landscape that was 'monarchic and not democratic.'[45] It was a republican rebuke from Wright, attacking both the monarchy and British colonial architecture and, hence, an assault on the British establishment. Wright identified an alternative democratic 'organic' approach that expressed a feeling for human form and the quality of life that was to be gained by inhabiting them, which included: old Japanese buildings, Egyptian temples, and Gothic cathedrals.[46] Wright called for an architecture that was 'a little nearer to the ground, more *of* life and not so much *on* it.'[47] This was as close as Wright came to defining his idea of 'organic' architecture.

Another short film introduced Wright's third evening, this time illuminating his two homes that spanned the continent from the temperate Taliesin North to Taliesin West in the Arizona desert. Wright described his architectural community in terms of apprentices working on the land and in the studio, building new desert settlements and working on new commissions. Wright presented the first 'Usonian' design, for the Jacobs House (1936) in Madison, Wisconsin, and he set out how modern science offered the potential for a new sense of spaciousness on a human scale through 'the motor-car, telephone, telegraph, the radio and television, flying.'[48]

During the subsequent questioning, Wright was accused of orchestrating 'a back to the land' movement, one questioner noting that many families live happily in tight quarters – like sailors – and that this environment nurtured 'respect [for] each other's requirements.[49] The same questioner described the communal life of a typical working-class Cockney as a 'battleship existence' and said that people were 'perfectly happy in such conditions.'[50] The ship was a common reference for the modernist ideal, as a metaphor to promote a new modern life that was far removed from traditional values and building forms. Wright dismissed the enforced 'drudgery' that was being put forward: '[the] existence the speaker describes is, however, to me a negation of life rather than any affirmation of it. I deplore the circumstances in which such lives must be spent. It is just that kind of thing that the modern movement and life itself go up against.'[51] Wright continued: 'I feel, however, that to be humane we must stand for the philosophy of freedom rather than for any philosophy of battleship sacrifice whatever, because what has the fighting Cockney soldier achieved in life, so far, by his fighting except *the need for more Cockney soldiers?*'[52] This was a seminal confrontation between the European modernists, with their tendency towards dense urbanism, and Wright's vision of a dispersed 'organic' Broadacre typology.[53] What was most telling about this exchange was the patronising assumptions made by the avant-garde British modernist, who could not articulate any social progress for the 'Cockney' other than to provide more efficient housing. Wright at least sought to break the cycle of urban poverty by advocating a different existence based on the 'freedom' of a car and an acre of land in the countryside.

When questioned again about the loss of community in a decentralised city, Wright declared that the needs of community change over time, and increased freedom would produce different means of forming a community.[54] Indeed this was a prophetic statement considering the emergence of our contemporary virtual communities that transcend city and national boundaries. Wright elaborated on his globalised 'organic' architecture and Broadacre:

> the country is coming to the citizen instead of the citizen going to the country. I do not wish to 'disperse' any city; decentralization is not dispersal – this is wrong . . . it is reintegration . . . the great implements science has put into the hands of humanity are themselves carving out this new city that is to be everywhere and nowhere.'[55]

On the fourth evening, Wright opened with another short film on the Taliesin Fellowship: architects were shown toiling on his 200-acre farm, painting barns in Cherokee Red, and rebuilding a burst dam.[56] The film was shown so that Wright could introduce his latest schemes: Fallingwater in Bear Run, Pennsylvania, where the building was very much part of the site;[57] the Hanna House in California, with its hexagonal planning module, claiming that 'the hexagon is better suited to human movement that the rectangle';[58] and the vast Wingspread House, in Racine, Wisconsin, with its long plan containing 'wings' for children, servants and a swimming pool. Finally, the Johnson Wax Building, again in Racine, was shown during construction, with Wright telling how he undertook different tests to prove its structural soundness, and, of course, by implication his own genius. 'I regard it as not only a thoroughly modern piece of work, but more nearly exemplifying the ideal of an organic architecture than any other I have built.'[59] With such a dizzying array of architectural delights, it was hardly surprising that many people in the audience questioned Wright's relevance to Britain. Once more, he attempted to set out his vision:

> Perhaps what you have seen on the screen has given you a little idea of this new way of building about which I have been talking; this feeling for a building as something out of the ground for the life lived in it, a building conditioned by the nature of materials and the purpose of the thing done, as something actually having a fresh integrity – not theory but practice.[60]

In *An Autobiography,* when discussing his 1939 visit, Wright recalls '[we] found the old place delightful. English homeliness and quaint ugliness. As English as anything in Pickwick.'[61] Thus, England remained for him a Dickensian world, and elsewhere he spoke of his view of London as 'full of pathetic charm and a lively antiquarian interest.'[62] For Wright, 'Architectural London is senile. London is senile.'[63] The implication was that it should be treated the same as an elderly relative – ameliorated and mitigated, and preserved within a great park. Wright's 1939 visit was reviewed positively, with the *Architect's Journal* noting that the 'sermons' were a release from 'stylistic constipation.'[64] The *RIBA Journal* was equally enthralled by Wright's visit, saying that it had left London's 'architectural world a bit dazed' after the 'big bang' – but the *Journal* also noted that 'doubts [were] left unresolved.'[65] However, it was Patrick Abercrombie who was perhaps most truly dissatisfied. He had expected 'a closely argued philosophy' – no less than a Wagnerian recital of *Das Rheingold!*[66] It was not surprising that he was disappointed by Wright's 'fragments of doctrine (often, of course, contradictory)', adding tartly that the 'prophet-preacher had clearly made no preparation for his sermons.'[67] Abercrombie went on to equate Broadacre City with a 'Marxian future' as well, noting sarcastically that the houses that Wright typically built for millionaires would be available to all.[68]

In some respect Wright in 1939 was advocating a more progressive ideal of social justice and mobility, but one that was ultimately too difficult to comprehend by the class-conscious and countryside-obsessed British audience. In the talks, there was something radical in Wright's sentiments: with the recurring themes of democracy and belief in science, the sessions were aimed to look to the future, which for most British people was more of worry than a cause for optimism in the lead up to conflict in Europe. Wright's 'organic' architecture was strongly promoted as not just 'a theory but practice.'[69] And yet, the RIBA talks merely reinforced the common belief that Wright could only design for an affluent class in America. The pioneering work of the Jacobs House was lost in the bluster of Broadacre City with the dictatorial architect coming across as a supreme planner and organiser of life itself. These lectures were a manifestation of the problem Frank Lloyd Wright had communicating his ideas in Britain, with a conservative architectural establishment unwilling to suspend their own beliefs in order to comprehend an 'organic' architecture.

GOLD

Following the Sulgrave Lecture series in May 1939, the Second World War began in September. A year later, in October 1940, the RIBA began the process of nominating a candidate for its annual RIBA Royal Gold Medal. The award had been bestowed throughout the duration of the First World War and it was felt that it should continue during this current conflict. It was an unwritten rule that following two nominations for British architects, the subsequent third year should consider an overseas candidate. There were nine nominations, of which only two were foreign (Wright being one) – the other seven were British, of which four were academics. It was speculated that Wright had been put forward because Britain sought to engage America in the Second World War.[70]

Duly awarded the 1941 Royal Gold Medal, Wright was contacted to check that he would accept the award, prior to being recommended to the King, in order to avoid embarrassment of a public refusal. In a typically dramatic account, Wright stated that, 'while listening to the New Year's Eve broadcast at Taliesin West, 1941, that same winter I learned that among the

King's birthday honours of that year, His Majesty's Royal Gold Medal for Architecture had been bestowed upon me.'[71] By all accounts, Wright was delighted at the recognition, and he believed that it was 'evidence of the great change taking place in the currents of thought in the modern world,'[72] and the award finally conferred in November of that year generated the much sought publicity and propaganda in the American and British press.

Three weeks after the announcement of the RIBA Gold Medal, Wright was invited by the London *News Chronicle* to write a 1500-word article about rebuilding bomb-damaged London. Wright took this as opportunity to restate his pacifist credentials and antipathy towards the concept of the British Empire. His article for the *News Chronicle* began by Wright stating that as a result of the war, 'the Empire may die, but English domination will survive to triumph.'[73] In the same article, Wright articulated his ideas for a new society based on social justice and the ideal settlement and 'organic' architecture: 'Base capital broad upon the ground, not with apex on the ground . . . The physical body of the democratic city today would have no centre but would have many centres all well correlated, the height of the buildings increasing as the perimeter of activity was approached.'[74]

Wright regarded the war as an opportunity to remake Britain in an image of 'Usonia' and America – a reaffirmation of his earlier RIBA talks and his global agenda. Furthermore, in a short passage that illuminated Wright's thoughts on democracy and the city, he even referred to traffic congestion! For Wright, they were the same theory: a free democratic society was the equivalent of a free-flowing traffic junction. It also illustrates Wright's somewhat naive belief that the problems of the city were just those of the traffic engineer. His views were articulated in an image that accompanied the article showing the Houses of Parliament beside a car park and a motorway intersection. The image was startling and unsettling – the home of British democracy and the motor car united, the city no longer divided by class but united in a car-based democracy.

Talks by Gold medal award-winners continue to be held at the RIBA and, on 13 February 2008, I attended Edward (known as Ted) Cullinan's Royal Gold Medal address. The Institute is a good site for honouring the great and the good, with two tomb-like walls engraved with the names of past masters bearing down on any visitor at the entrance, including that of Wright. The foyer of the RIBA was busy with architects indulging in an affectionate 1960s retrospection. I rushed to the Jarvis Auditorium to get a good seat and sat down to read the citation by the RIBA President, Sunand Prasad. He noted the 'humanist' thread that has influenced Cullinan's work, one that connects William Morris and the Arts and Crafts movement, through to the Californian works of Schindler and Neutra. In a commemoration booklet, an interview with Tony Chapman was recorded and Cullinan reflected on his architectural influences:

> Oh, for my generation, it's not difficult because it's Le Corbusier, but I also love the work, the architecture and the method of building of Schindler in California – I think he was a really marvellous architect. And early Frank Lloyd Wright made the great invention of the 20th century in the Prairie House – absolutely astonishing – his later work is more show-off for the sake of showing off, but it's pretty good too.[75]

Prasad set the tone for the evening when he said that the news of Cullinan's success was greeted by genuine warmth within the profession, and a heckler shouted: 'About time!' Cullinan was born in 1931 and he cited three inspirational buildings that were completed that year: Hillvesrum Town Hall by Willem Marinus Dudok (1931), Villa Savoye by Le Corbusier (1931) and the Chrysler building by William Van Alen (1931). Cullinan focused on Dudok's Town Hall façade and noted its cubic composition as the cultural zeitgeist of cubism and jazz. Cullinan studied at Cambridge University, and he noted that the curriculum was mostly based on traditional Arts and Crafts theories. His education then took him to Berkeley in California, where he had first-hand experience of visiting Schindler's Lovell Beach House and he also admitted to being an admirer of Richard Neutra. Both these practitioners were, of course, former apprentices to Wright. Slides from Cullinan's early work also revealed his admiration of Wright himself – his home in Camden Mews (1964) was a mix of Wright tectonics, Japanese carpentry, and self-built philosophy. The Olivetti office buildings (1972) addressed Wright's idea of 'organic' form and material, and their interiors looked very much like a 'Usonian' design, with natural wood in abundance. During an informal question session, everyone was reverential – certainly not the anarchic questioning that Wright answered in 1939. Following a prompt from the audience, Cullinan recollected his brief meeting with Wright at Berkeley, when an elderly Wright almost stumbled and extended his arm out for support: 'it felt like a blessing!', Cullinan recalled.[76]

MILTON KEYNES

Wright's ideas for a democratic and just society were the cornerstone of his Broadacre City proposal and came to be realised in part in the postwar New Towns. The New Towns were conceived as satellite settlements outside the old cities of London, Birmingham, Manchester and Glasgow to alleviate overcrowding by a process of orderly suburbanisation. Another phenomenon in the aftermath of the Second World War was the Cold War and a shared paranoia of nuclear Armageddon. Even as early as 1941, Wright, in his article to the *News Chronicle*, had stated that 'the bomb overhead points to' the necessity to decentralise London.[77] So the New Towns satisfied the need for dispersion into smaller, well connected towns and to lessen the potential for a catastrophic nuclear attack.

Milton Keynes was conceived in 1962 and came into existence in 1967. It was an overtly Anglo-American concept that sought to balance American liberal commercialism with the British welfare state.[78] The New Town attempted to make itself a vision of the future by combing American urban planning within a British context. The architectural practice Llewelyn-Davies were appointed to do the design, and to assist them, they employed a number of urban specialists from both America and Britain. Milton Keynes was to become the urban manifestation of one particular American sociologist consultant, social forecaster and futurist – Melvin Webber, a professor at Berkeley University. Webber saw two themes that were transforming cities: the motor car and communications technology.[79] He combined these to produce a future vision of the city and of society. He proclaimed a 'vision of the city which is an open matrix for selection, by the individual, of opportunities for social contact, recreation, education and the rest.'[80] It is surprising just how similar Webber's ideas were to Wright's, as the latter had stated in 1935, that the three major inventions to support Broadacre were the motor car, electrical intercommunication and machine-shop production.[81]

Webber's vision of a 'loose-fit systems planning and libertarian social idealism' at Milton Keynes was manifested by a comprehensive road network, based on an American planning model, and a 50/50 split between housing built for rent and for ownership.[82] The design of the road network was a comical tale whereby the original rational American grid-iron pattern was pacified by the British picturesque tradition so as to produce a 'wiggly grid.' In addition, an integrated method of traffic control using sequenced traffic lights was surrendered to a plague of roundabouts – a lasting legacy to the Milton Keynes identity. The housing design struggled to be integrated within the overarching road network, with some architects burrowing their design within a green buffer zone, thus removing themselves from the primary means of community, the road. Nevertheless most of the housing was progressive, employing several innovative architectural practices. They designed new homes that adopted many American suburban themes that Wright had experimented with in his 'Usonian' Homes, such as lightweight construction, integrated garages and open-plan living spaces to display all their new consumer goods.

I visited Milton Keynes for a day out with my family in 2007, at the point when the town was celebrating 40 years of existence. We travelled up the M1 from London – which was incidentally 50 years old that year as well – another lasting legacy of Britain's love affair with the car. Turning off at Junction 14 we aimed for Milton Keynes city centre and weaved our way through the 'wiggly-grid' via countless roundabouts. The town was not easy to spot, and displayed a variety of dispersed forms. We passed a few generic warehouses, an expanse of green fields where a Buddhist shrine was the only landmark, and copious dense planting hiding homes from the road, before finally arriving at a large car park beside a John Lewis department store. It was my wife Amanda's first experience of a New Town, and she was totally disorientated by the lack of any landmark. 'Where's the church and the high street?' she asked, heading off in search of a map in Midsummer Boulevard. After carefully reading the map, and noting a few familiar retail outlets, we were able to plan our route around the shopping mall. At a coffee shop, we met a resident who told us that the swimming pool, snow dome and theatre were all located nearby and it was impressive that the town had so much to offer. A counterpoint to the shopping mall was provided by an open-air market outside, inhabiting a lost corner beneath a road bridge and traffic junction. Here, the spaces were more intimate and the goods were unbranded. A number of new attractions have been added to Milton Keynes to give it a more diverse architectural language. At the small and bright pink MK Gallery, there was an exhibition of art, *Circa 1967*, as if an attempt to recapture a common memory. Outside the gallery was another attempt at defining a city suffering from a mid-life crisis. The London architects dRRM had designed a cross-laminated timber tower. The logic of the tower was obvious – if you are going to build a new town you should at least be able to see what you've created! It was also a criticism of the planned dispersed settlement and, as such, drew on several historical precedents, such as the Victorian clock tower, Gothic steeple or medieval keep. It was another architectural device attempting to make Milton Keynes a 'proper' city, albeit only as a temporary solution. It was also great fun to climb for my three-year old son, but the views at the top were predictably underwhelming, with any urban form being lost within in a forest of greenery and roads.

BRYNMAWR

Wright's fourth visit to London was at the invitation of the Architectural Association in 1950 and, once again, he lived up to his star billing. He was now confronted by the fully fledged British Welfare State and its modernist manifestation – the '58th variety' that Wright had attacked back in 1939 was now the dominant cultural and architectural force. The Welfare State emerged in Britain out of a response to the inequalities and legacies of the industrialised city. The effects of the economic downturn in the 1930s did not produce any dramatic New Deal response in Britain: instead it was only after the Second World War that the Welfare State emerged.

Following the award of Wright's Gold Medal from the American Institute of Architecture (AIA) in 1949, Robert Furneaux Jordan, sent a cable the next day saying that 500 students demanded that Wright should visit London.[83] For Wright, another fawning invitation from the 'old country' was well received and he attended as guest of honour at the Prize Giving Ceremony at the AA in July 1950. At a dinner organised in his honour, Jordan gave a polite introductory speech, while Wright responded by complaining about the British establishment and, in particular, a tiresome encounter with an 'honorary title' on the *RMA Queen Mary*. Wright again spoke of London and British society as antiquated and subservient: 'I come over here and I find all this establishment, and what impresses me in your London is this feature and fact of establishment . . . I think that if I had been born here in London, you would never have heard of an 'organic' architecture.'[84] He said that he admired the tenacity of the British during the Second World War, and then speculated about his influence in Britain – only to conclude that in the realm of replanning London, his ideas were ignored: 'If I had been successful, wherever a bomb hit you, you would have planted grass. Instead of that, you have rebuilt London wherever there has been damage, and wherever a hole has been punched in your establishment. You cannot let go of that establishment.'[85] For Wright, Britain remained a self-contained place dominated by class and the establishment. Wright declared his view that 'organic' society 'does not lie in the direction of socialism or in the direction of communism or in the direction of any ism or any ist or any ite,' but only in the realm of 'organic' architecture.[86]

At the Annual Prize Giving Ceremony on 14 July, Jordan's introduction tried to draw on similarities between the AA and the Taliesin Fellowship. He remarked that they shared a 'love of architecture,' there were non-hierarchical fellowships between students and teachers (in theory anyway), and they professed an urge to 'make things, build things with their own hands and their own sweat as with their own brains.'[87] Wright's response was predictably hostile. He questioned the role of the Prize Giving Ceremony, claiming that the judges will dismiss the best and the worst and the prize will be given to the 'average of an average.'[88] Putting a dampener on the whole day for the recipients, Wright went on to dismiss architectural education as 'handing out tickets to little boys to sit around for four years studying and reading about architecture.'[89] Further, he claimed that it was inherently elitist and 'a nice occupation for a gentleman, and the favoured sons of fortune'.[90] To conclude his attack, Wright called for the profession to be 'buried . . . and the field left open to youngsters who are willing to make sacrifices that are essential to practise architecture.'[91] Wright made sure that the students realised that the real prize on offer that day was an audience with the great Frank Lloyd Wright!

In a BBC radio talk, Jordan summarised Wright in Britain by curiously equating him with William Morris.[92] The hint was that both men were more easily digested as artists and that their political motivations were interesting, but secondary. Jordan also made mention of Wright meeting Leslie Martin at the site of the Royal Festival Hall.[93] While reviewing the drawings and a model for this project, Wright stated that the auditorium was not the right shape: 'it won't work; it's got to be in the section of a trumpet.'[94] After making a reference to the Auditorium Building, Chicago, Wright eventually calmed down and acknowledged that it would be a 'very great building,' and that he would like a box for the opening night.[95] Jordan also described a tantalising view of Wright on his first visit to Wales when he visited the Brynmawr Rubber Factory under construction: 'His excitement returned when he got back to reality and to our welfare state at

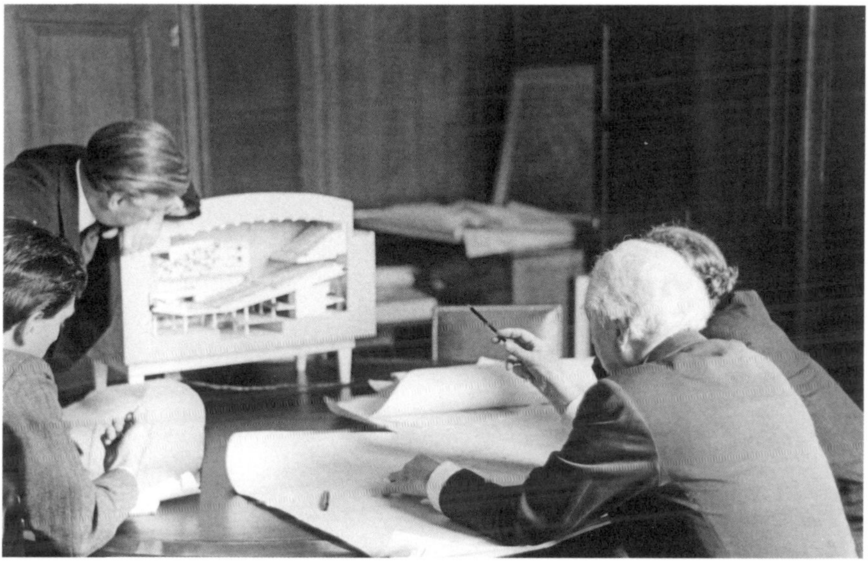

Robert H. Matthew (left) showing Frank Lloyd Wright (centre) and Leslie Martin (partially obscured on the right) a model of the interior of the Royal Festival Hall, London, England (1951)

work; he went to see his ancestral Wales and in Wales, an industrial development area . . . it was his own decentralisation at work, getting men out of dead cities.'[96]

Brynmawr had been conceived as a means to regenerate a Welsh town that had declined with the closure of coal mines and the economic downturn of the 1930s. The Barlow Report in 1940 had responded to regional decline beyond London and the South East, and the subsequent Distribution of Industry Act in 1945 sought to promote industry beyond south-east England.[97] The project was sponsored by the Board of Trade and the tenant for the Brynmawr Rubber Factory was the affluent Lord James Forrester, proprietor of Enfield Cables, who was engaged in philanthropy and had even resided at Toynbee Hall in 1931. The factory was designed by the left-wing collective, Architects Co-operative Partnership, and embraced a multi-disciplinary team of engineers and specialists with the engineer Ove Arup providing a pivotal role in realising the construction of the nine-domed production hall. Brynmawr was highly articulated, with each stage of the rubber making process given a distinctive architectural appearance. The egalitarian demands of Forrester and the Welfare State were met by providing a single entry point for both management and worker, a long entry ramp led to a common front door and a class-levelling clock. The design was a brilliant example of contemporary European modernism, but even the organic shell structures did not impress Wright. Instead he 'expressed horror at the misuse of concrete' and suggested a Warren girder that should have been made from steel.[98] Furthermore, Jordan neglected to mention that Wright had stopped to urinate against the emerging building – clearly the modern Welsh Welfare State was not as Wright expected.

When the factory opened there were hardly any orders for rubber to fulfil its potential. Furthermore, there was no strategy in place to sell the rubber or to produce it efficiently – it was therefore no surprise that in 1952, after just one year of operation (at less than half capacity), Enfield Cables pulled out of the endeavour. Dunlop took up the lease a year later and the factory supplied vinyl flooring for other Welfare State ventures, such as National Health hospitals and higher education colleges. Brynmawr's dependence on

Factory for Brynmawr Rubber Company, Brynmawr, Gwent, Wales (1951) by Architects Co-Partnership

a single product line was, however, to prove disastrous and, following a downturn in demand in the mid-1970s, the plant was finally shut down in 1982. Various attempts to resurrect the factory were unsuccessful and a campaign to preserve it proved futile – the whole structure was pulled down in 2001. The failure of another utopian scheme transplanted to the countryside bore a similarity to the Handicraft Guild in Chipping Campden.

I visited Brynmawr to see what remained of the rubber factory. Turning off the motorway onto a winding road to the head of a valley, I found Brynmawr set within a barren landscape of undulating hills. The town was a conglomerate of empty factory sheds, depressed high streets, barren housing estates and a new retail park. A road network linked all the disparate parts, but it did not add up to a coherent whole. I noted that there was a local museum within the old Carnegie Library. At the museum, I was welcomed and offered a cup of tea while I waited for the curator. The museum was dominated by a permanent exhibition of Brynmawr Furniture Makers (1931–40). The pieces exhibited a simple style of carpentry, expressing the quality of the wood. The Furniture Makers were the most successful part of a group of small-scale communal collectives that had been established by the Quakers who had settled in the valley in the 1920s. The Brynmawr Bootmakers co-operative was another short-lived enterprise.

The curator was proud of the success of the Furniture Workshops, and she was disappointed when I asked about the rubber works instead. She searched for a cardboard box beneath a long table that was cluttered with Victorian nick nacks. Within the box there were cuttings from the *Architectural Review* magazine, and local articles about the imminent demise of the factory from the 1980s, but there was no mention of Wright. The last remnant of the Brynmawr Rubber Factory was the loading shed. It had a bold elliptical concrete expressionist roof form that referenced the works of Felix Candela from Mexico and Oscar Niemeyer from Brazil. But it was now a derelict shed, full of empty beer bottles and rubbish. Rummaging around the wreckage, I felt as if the whole roof might collapse, and no one would really care. On the site of the former rubber works was the Lakeside retail park with its dominant Asda supermarket. Eating lunch at a corner table overlooking the reservoir, I lamented that the heroic modernism of postwar Britain was now replaced by generic consumerism, the latest utopia to be imposed on Brynmawr.

Entrance to Frog Orchard House beneath overhanging eaves, Ilmington, England (1959) by Robert Harvey

CHIPPING CAMPDEN REVISITED

Present in the audience at Wright's AA talk in 1950 was a young English architect, Robert Harvey, who had travelled from the Cotswolds to hear Wright speak. A mere 10 kilometres (6 miles) away from Ashbee's guild at Chipping Campden was the small village of Ilmington, where the work of Robert Harvey came to be concentrated. I had written a number of letters to the owners of houses Harvey had designed in the 1960s and 70s to introduce myself and my research and to request to visit their properties. During my visit to Ilmington, I was fortunate to come across the post lady, and so I asked for directions to Frog Orchard House, and showed her a few images of the homes that were illustrated in an article on postwar houses that I was interested in.[99] The post lady proved to be an invaluable contact, informing me that the owner of Frog Orchard House, Ilmington, (1959) would be in her garden and no doubt would be available for a chat. As I approached that house by car, I was struck by how uncannily true it was to the Wright idiom, with its dominant roof form, deep overhanging eaves, the use of natural horizontal banded stone tied to the earth and long bands of horizontal casement windows. I could almost have been in Oak Park. The house was carefully sited, engaging directly with the orchard and a southern aspect, and the garage acted as an enclosing arm drawing the visitor in, yet protecting the occupants. The owner was kind enough to discuss the house and its architecture with me. She was the second or third owner and thought it a beautiful and brilliantly designed property, and she explained how the roof was designed so that the sun always reached the end of the living room in winter, and always stopped at the window sill in summer. Despite the external appearance of the house, however, its internal spaces were divided into a formal arrangement and did not feature the flow of space that was such an essential characteristic of Wright's homes.

Robert Harvey was born in 1919 in Coventry and studied at Birmingham Art School. He claimed that he saw an article on Wright in the 1930s and was 'shocked' at the photographs of Midway Gardens.[100] Harvey began to read Wright's books and even corresponded briefly with him at Taliesin in 1942, after which he travelled to see Wright speak at the AA in July

Stonecrop, Ilmington, England (1965) by Robert Harvey

1950. Stonecrop was the house that Harvey built for himself in 1965, just up the hill from Ilmington. I left my car at the roadside and walked down a narrow lane to its location, and there beneath me was the enveloping roof of Stonecrop cut from the hillside. As I proceeded down the hill, a small courtyard came into view, but the projecting eaves kept the features of the house in permanent shade. The stone outcrop was dressed with a masonry wall possessing alternating horizontal bands of deeper and shallower stone courses. In the centre was a small water cascade that dropped into a triangular pool with a wide stone urn beside – a small shrine to 'organic' architecture. It was a hideaway that Wright and Ashbee would have understood and enjoyed, while also an intelligent adoption of Wright's Taliesin mantra: 'no house should ever be *on* the hill . . . It should be *of* the hill.'[101] Below the overhanging roof, the entrance was difficult to find, hidden and set back from the façade. I was welcomed by the owner into a small lobby and on the wall was a small wooden frieze inspired by Wright, a souvenir from an earlier visit to Oak Park. We turned and went down a few steps towards the re-fitted kitchen. Beside it was the dining room, with its wide band of glazing that revealed a panoramic view over a wide expanse of middle England. At the dining table we talked about the house. She explained that they had only just recently brought the property, saying that the estate agent called the property the Marmite house – you either loved it or hated it! I could not help thinking that the same could be said of 'organic' architecture.

The owner explained that the house was centred around 'a heating core' that included the kitchen oven, the new boiler, and the fireplace – an expansion upon Wright's traditional hearth-and-inglenook arrangement. Behind the dining room and down a few steps was the main living space, possessing views to the external courtyard on one side and to the open countryside on the other. This time the 'heating core' housed a proper Wrightian hearth, a mixture of a severe abstract pattern and rustic vernacular. Equally impressive was the expressive roof geometry that was animated by polygonal clerestory lights and skylights. From the living space we walked up a precarious staircase that had no handrail, to the master bedroom. There again the flowing fractured geometry was evident in a triangular Juliet balcony that overlooked the living room. Above the main bed was an eye-level window that framed the wide aspect. These were certainly the most expressive spatial sequences that I had seen in Harvey's work. The central core had now mutated into a private en-suite bathroom. Behind the bedroom, and in a separate wing above the old studio, were the children's bedrooms with their exposed roof trusses and high-level skylights. These spaces had been created by Harvey for his own children by dividing his double-height studio into a playroom and bedrooms. It was a truly remarkable house by an architect who clearly understood Wright's philosophy on architecture and was able to make a great addition to an emerging 'organic' tradition in Britain.

In Coventry there were a further four properties by Harvey in affluent southern suburbs. Number 112 and 114 Kenilworth Road were homes built for Harvey's two brothers, sharing a common boundary wall. Yet a few generations down the line, one half of the family had sought to sell their house for development, while the other side of the family had their neighbour's house spot-listed. Listing properties in Britain is a method of conserving building that are of historical significance, and can curtail future development. Many of Harvey's properties have been identified by the Twentieth Century Society as 'at risk' of development, and I met the conservation officer in Coventry who was concerned about Harvey's legacy. Ironically, Harvey himself was against listing his homes.

A short distance from there was Southwinds (1965) in Cryfield Grange Road, Coventry. It is an astonishing construction, a long horizontal timber house suspended over two stone drums, with a carport beneath, at once legible and incredible. This was Robert Harvey meets Craig Elwood, Coventry meets California. The house was then in a state of transition, with the present owners undertaking repairs, whilst also looking to sell the property on, or to sell a plot within the front garden (although objected to by the Twentieth Century Society). I parked my car in the carport and entered the eastern drum, consisting of an extended lobby with a circular stair. On the first floor level, I entered the lounge/dining room, with the kitchen behind. The kitchen still has its original American 'range' and the present owners speculated that the house was designed for an American rocket scientist – it all sounded very glamorous. The bedrooms were off a long corridor that spanned the length of the bridge. Each had an en-suite bathroom, and the last surprise was descending a stair into a circular swimming pool within the western pier. This was a house that certainly shared the 1960s belief in the 'white heat' of technology. Despite the daring construction of Southwinds, Harvey found it difficult to work with the planning authorities within the rural environment after 1974, and so the career of the greatest exponent of English 'Usonian' dwellings came to a premature end.

Garden elevation, Southwinds, Coventry, England (1965) by Robert Harvey

PORTMEIRION

Wright's final visit to Britain, in 1956, combined a second homecoming to Wales, this time to receive an Honorary Degree at Bangor University. The citation for his honorary degree 'hailed him as 'The Founding Father of Modern Architecture.'[102] During this visit to Wales, Wright visited his old friend, Clough Williams-Ellis. They had met on the Berlin to Moscow train attending the First All-Union Congress of Soviet Architects. Williams-Ellis recalls his apprehension before Wright's visit; 'Dare I let him loose [on Portmeirion]?'[103] Yet, to his surprise, Wright 'took it all without a blink, seeming instantly to see the point of all my wilful pleasantries – the calculated naiveties, eye-traps, forced and faked perspectives, heretical constructions, unorthodox colour mixtures, general architectural levity and all the rest of it.'[104]

Williams-Ellis created Portmeirion in 1926 as a 'holiday village.' He purchased the mansion of 'Aber Ia' with its extensive garden and cottages in 1925, and then converted the house and stables into a hotel. The design for the holiday village was borrowed from the Italian town of Portofino on the

Italian Riviera, where Williams-Ellis – like many modern Grand Tourists – had marvelled at its coastal setting and vernacular architecture. Williams-Ellis sought the same cultural references and so created Portmeirion as a self-made Grand Tour within Wales. Portmeirion also sought to be an example and to advance Williams-Ellis's populist agenda of visually pleasing architecture but it was essentially an example of aesthetic consumption. His holiday village prospered among the liberal, literary and left-leaning metropolitan intellectuals. Williams-Ellis's wife Amabel and her family, the Stracheys, were prominent socialists, and their guests included George Bernard Shaw, Bertrand Russell and Nöel Coward. The successes of the initial holiday village led to 15 more buildings being added by 1939, contributing to an 'exclusive sort of Shangri-la.'[105]

Portmeirion in North Wales is woven into my childhood. We had family day-trips there, usually during the summer holidays and I recall the intimate lanes, the unusually bright houses and the open pools. The mixture of exotic motifs, an Italianate church tower, Gothic pavilion, classical colonnades and a gold Buddha was always curious to me – it gave the place an other-worldly feel. Yet after a couple of hours of exploring the miniature town with my brother and eating ice cream, we would eventually escape the tourists to the sandy beach below. Later on, I saw the village immortalised in the television series, *The Prisoner.*[106] It provided a great narrative for the ultimate planned community with its stifling leader – was it modelled on Williams-Ellis or perhaps Wright himself? I enjoyed the paranoia of the film too, and the impenetrable plot that seemingly goes nowhere; it was film that best captured the made-up setting. A utopia that had a malevolent leader and a suppressed populous, demarcated by numbers.

Portmeirion was the Italian Riviera remade by Williams-Ellis, and similarly the Welsh myth of Taliesin was re-imagined by Wright in the American Midwest – two architects pursuing escapist fantasies. Wright used his Welsh roots selectively to revive his architectural career in the 1910s, and to add substance to the 'organic' mantra in the 1930s. Taliesin was, of course, the name that Frank Lloyd Wright used to identify his two homes in Wisconsin and Arizona. In *An Autobiography,* Wright stated; 'Taliesin was the name of a Welsh poet, a druid-bard who sang to Wales the glories of fine art.'[107] Consequently, he reimagined Taliesin North (1911) as a metaphor that embraced its setting, so that he claimed that Taliesin was '*of* the hill.'[108] Brendan Gill claims that Wright discovered the name in 'a trashy cabinet drama' by

Richard Hovey (1896).[109] The implicit suggestion was that Wright was in fact a cultural lightweight who was trying to give himself an aura of respectability. Yet, Taliesin West (1938) was a very different conception, part of a white American internal colonialisation of the desert, it was very much in line with his expansive 'organic' architecture in the 1930s. Another celebrated Welsh couplet was claimed by Wright as the family motto – '*y gwir yn erbyn y byd*,' translated as 'Truth against the World.'[110] It forms part of the Unitarian and the invented Eisteddfod mantra, which Wright recalled in *An Autobiography*.[111] Thus, Truth against the World became part of Wright's rhetoric, and it represented his architecture from the 1930s.[112] For Wright, the essence of American democracy was represented by his vision of a truthful 'organic' architecture, which existed in opposition to the remainder of the world and its architecture.[113] It was an isolationist position that came to dominate Wright's thinking, almost a position of paranoia.

According to Williams-Ellis, Wright was an avid sightseer and visited the local castles, yet there is no record of Wright ever visiting his ancestral home in mid-Wales where the Lloyd Jones clan had originated. Ironically, the ancestral home has a large stone plaque to Jenkin Lloyd Jones and not Wright – he may have been a great architect, but that is clearly not good enough in Wales! At the end of Wright's trip to Portmeirion Williams-Ellis drove Wright to his train, after making a short diversion to visit the office of leading North Wales architect, Sidney Colwyn Foulkes, to give Wright the opportunity of viewing some Welsh social housing. Colwyn Foulkes had himself considered the Welsh setting of architecture and there was 'the Welsh tradition of building into hillsides. These early Welsh cottages snuggle into the hillside as naturally as a birds nest.'[114] It was such a modest statement compared to Wright's bombastic claim that a house 'should be *of* the hill.'[115] Likewise, Colwyn Foulkes's architecture was understated. His scheme for Cae Bricks, Beaumaris, Anglesey (1948–54), accepts the contours of its site, with terraces that are integrated into the hill and open out to the town below, with small squares to provide additional interest. Furthermore, the individual homes are each articulated by a coloured lime wash, a response to the town's own idiosyncrasy and a simple means of adding individual identity. By all accounts, Wright was impressed, and claimed that there was 'Nothing like this in America,' – he also noted that his chief recollection of Wales was its 'integrity.'[116]

Wright caught a late train back to London and there he was entertained by the editor of the *Architectural Journal* at the Bride of Denmark, which was considered to be the private gin palace of the Architectural Press.[117] There Wright held forth to a small distinguished audience of modernists that included Ove Arup, Maxwell Fry and Jane Drew. Robinson noted that 'his personality dominated – or should I say hypnotised – the room.'[118] Wright was preaching to the converted, or at least to the familiar – gone were the days of antagonism of 1939. Wright was performing right on cue, and, in fact, he left for a television appearance after the short trip. More telling was the fact that there were no longer any students or younger members within the audience in the Bride of Denmark. Despite their interest in American culture, none of the contemporary architectural and artistic groupings, the Independent Group and the Brutalist, attended the gathering. Indeed, Alison and Peter Smithson later brilliantly summed up their impression of Wright as belonging to a 'craft tradition,' and by implication he was already out-dated compared to the raw materiality of Brutalism.[119] However, Peter Reyner Banham, the leading spokesman of the Independent Group and Brutalism, was to became a Wright advocate and had contributed to a wider cultural understanding of his work, particularly his rebirth at Taliesin West in the Arizona desert.

CREEK VEAN

A number of other buildings that reflected Wright's 'organic' architecture have been identified by Elain Harwood in her book, *England: A Guide to Post-War Listed Buildings*.[120] I visited most of the properties that she identified and each displayed a thorough understanding of Wright's principles without, however, ever adopting the 'organic' idiom of Robert Harvey and Robert Townsend, another 'organic' practitioner working around Bath. At Past Field (1960) by Patrick Gwynne, the original owners were still resident and described how Gwynne had explained to them the principle of a low horizontal form was the most suitable to their open site: 'putting a tall building in the landscape would be similar to putting a pea on plate – it would not rest on the site.'[121] This analysis was of course reminiscent of Wright's remark that houses should be more 'nearer to the ground . . . [and not] *on* it.'[122] Turn, Middle Turn and Turn End (1964–7) by Peter Aldington, all had an intimate scale and integrated landscape throughout the design, and their 'rambling quality' led Harwood to suggest that it resembled a British Taliesin – except that it was finished in white render and its discontinuous form hinted to the European 'other tradition' of Aalto than to Wright's 'organic' ideas.[123] Clayton House (1965–6), by Peter Aldington and John Craig, possessed an L-shaped plan that enclosed the entry courtyard, a plan form that was similar to Wright's 'Usonian homes.'[124] In addition, the garden elevation with its deep timber banding and the overhanging eaves were evidence of Wright's influence.[125] Anderton House (1970–72), again by Aldington and Craig, used an enveloping roof structure with deep eaves, allowed a free plan and engaged directly with the surrounding landscape, and Aldington cites Wright's text on *The Natural House* as a justification for his proposal.[126] Long Wall (1963), by Philip Dawson and Peter Foggo, was a direct descendent of Fallingwater, a small weekend retreat that was only two hours' drive from London. It was a house designed to experience the tranquillity and simplicity of the countryside in a carefully crafted space – which combined Wright's open plan, ground bearing horizontality, projecting eaves, and Japanese joinery.

Creek Vean (1964–7) in Cornwall, by Team 4, was the first house to be built by the emerging talents of Norman Foster and Wendy Cheeseman, Richard and Su Rogers. It was built for Su Rogers's parents, the Brumwells. I was fortunate to secure an invitation to view the property, which I combined with a camper van holiday to Cornwall. Creek Vean was a modern insertion on the periphery of Feock, and I recognised its stark featureless blockwork wall, set back from the road's edge. I crossed a short bridge over a shallow moat and viewed the Pil Creek estuary below, framed by the two building masses. The glass entrance door was recessed and well hidden from the road. The owner met me there and we proceeded down the steps that led between the living and sleeping blocks to the garden, with its panorama of the estuary opening up before us. I was very impressed by the quality of the blockwork, that even after all these years of exposure, it looked clean and bright. It was certainly reminiscent of Wright's Textile Block homes in Los Angeles from the 1920s. At the northern end of the house, we looked back towards the gallery and began to dissect the end elevation. The owner told me that Rogers always wanted the section of the building to be expressed in its elevations, which was particularly noticeable in the end view, with the long eastern wall anchored to the hillside, the glazed gallery exposed and the bedrooms looking south towards the estuary.

The garden had been extensively remodelled and was well presented. It was offset by the abstract geometry of the house, and this became more apparent as we walked around, with the solidity of the walls playing off

View from garden, Creek Vean, Cornwall, England (1963–6) by Team 4

the lightness of the glass openings. The owner pointed out that, inside, the house is simple and legible. A split staircase led to the upper living room, which opened out to the estuary, although we speculated that the house could have been rotated to the east slightly, so as to better capture the Fal River beyond. The lower staircase led down to the kitchen and dining room. There, the original stainless steel island unit, with its rounded ends, was still being well used, although the appliances had been updated. The gallery behind the kitchen had a glazed roof and served as the circulation corridor for the bedrooms, and each bedroom had a sliding door that could be left open during the day so that it became part of the fun.

Famously, Norman Foster and Richard Rogers both won scholarships to Yale University in 1961, where they were taught by Paul Rudolph, Serge Chermayeff, James Stirling and Vincent Scully. It was Scully, according to Rogers 'who opened up Frank Lloyd Wright's work . . . Wright was my first god . . . Wright's work has to be seen, experienced as space, to be understood. It was pretty revelatory . . . [Wright] was very real and immediate.'[127] Furthermore, Rogers noted that 'Wright . . . was an unashamed maker of form: he carried no illusions about functionalism.'[128] Likewise for Foster, Scully's presentation and interpretation of Wright's work was apparently 'so compelling . . . that on one short, between-terms break, he, together with Carl Abbott and Richard and Su Rogers, squeezed into Abbott's Volkswagen Beetle and visited nearly every Wright building in the Midwest.'[129]

As designers of Creek Vean, the Team explored a number of Wright themes, such as the flowing open plan and interpenetrating spaces. Yet, the geometrical and planning module rigour of Wright was not present in the house: Team 4 were more free and responded more intimately to its setting. I would even contend that the Eames House (1949) by Charles and Ray Eames with Eero Saarinen, with its split two-building form, is another and far more direct inspiration for the plan. The blockwork anchors the house within the landscape, a move of which Wright would have approved, along with the building's intimate relationship with its site. Wright attempted to invest additional meaning into his Textile Block homes, but Team 4 preferred a simpler narrative for the block, without Wright's rhetoric.

Taken together, I believe that all these homes articulate many 'organic' qualities. They were built for relatively modest clients – typically middle-class homes, they were carefully sited in the landscape, exploited open-plan living areas, used natural materials and reflected Wright's own ideas of social democracy as contained within his Usonian houses. In the 1950s, the dismissal of Wright by the Brutalists was premature, in that many other architects sought to exploit the use of natural materiality without the rhetorical language of Brutalism. In particular, Wright's Usonian houses were a source of inspiration, and his designs for the middle-income family were embraced by an array of clients and architects working across Britain. These are modest homes in every sense of the word, beginning with informed clients and architects that responded in the same way to Wright's 'organic' idiom. Furthermore, they sat outside the dogma of the welfare state, and their architecture could not have been more different in terms of their subtle siting, open plan designs, materiality, attention to detail or expression of individual character.

5

WHEN FRANK MET FRANCESCO

Wright visited Italy twice, firstly in 1910 and then in 1951, under very different circumstances. During his first visit, he was a self-styled 'rebel' who had eloped with the wife of a former client, whilst his second journey was as a star-architect, consolidating his global reach and promoting American capitalist values. Wright was a passionate critic of the Renaissance, yet in 1910 he had chosen to visit and reside Florence, the birthplace of the movement. The liberal social attitude in Florence at the time gave Wright and Mamah solace from a disapproving public, and it allowed Wright to fulfil his own architectural self-education. As a way to evaluate Wright's relationship with Italian architecture, and to recapture an earlier road trip in 2000 across America with Wright, I decided to take a 'Grand Tour' with Wright from London to Rome, using Wright's favorite means of travel – the car. The original Grand Tours were pioneered by Inigo Jones in 1613–14 and certainly for those interested in architecture it became established as a ritual pilgrimage. The act of travelling has long been an inherent part of inspiring and constructing architecture and Inigo Jones's Grand Tour brought Renaissance architecture to Britain. Wright was, likewise, inspired by his 1910 journey to Italy to reflect on its vernacular architecture to generate his own 'organic' mantra. I recreated this journey to bring these two architectural tourists together and to consider how their experiences generated new architecture.

A GRAND TOUR

Inigo Jones was at the forefront of the Grand Tour phenomenon and travelled to Italy twice around 1598 and from 1613 to 1614. The purpose and date of his first visit are uncertain, but we know he purchased a copy of *I Quattro Libri dell' Architettura* by Palladio (1570), which he annotated on the fly-leaf as 'Venice 1601' and [recorded] a price of two ducats.[1] Jones was a Renaissance man of many talents – in theatre design, architecture, painting and sculpture – and he was known to be a great traveller.[2] Consequently, he was invited to accompany the Earl and Countess of Arundel to Italy under the pretext of escorting the newly wedded princess Elizabeth and her husband, the Elector Palatine Frederick V, back to Heidelberg.[3] Starting in Whitechapel, London, on 10 April 1613, the party travelled to Margate, crossed the English Channel to Flushing in the Netherlands, and then proceeded along a route through the Protestant cities of Belgium, Holland and Germany. They arrived in Heidelberg on 7 June 1613 and stayed the course of the three-week wedding celebrations, after which Jones and the Arundels travelled on to Italy, arriving in Milan on 11 July 1613. They spent a number of months in northern Italy and entered Venice in September 1613. After visiting and carefully analysing the Palladian villas and churches in Venice and Vicenza, Jones and the Arundels continued on their journey to Florence, Rome and Naples, thereby establishing the four major destinations of the Grand Tour. They arrived in Rome in January 1614, and Arundel gained a licence to excavate one of the ancient sites and to keep any statues he found.[4] In doing so, he established a troubling British tradition for cultural appropriation and souvenir hunting. The returned booty was placed in Arundel House (on the current site of the British Museum), where his extensive private collection was gradually consolidated into a museum.

The Napoleonic Wars (1803–15) effectively signalled the end of the aristocratic Grand Tour and, instead, there developed a wider cultural engagement with other ancient cultures within Greece, Egypt and the Middle East as part of the expansion of the British imperialist mindset. A more democratic Grand Tour was to re-emerge in the late 19th century as a result of Romanticism, whereby the Tour became a form of self-exploration and discovery.[5] Furthermore, the trans-European railway network meant that a wider demographic of tourists could now afford the journey, with travel agents such as Thomas Cook offering guided tours that included transport and accommodation.[6] It marked the onset of mass tourism, with its guided itineraries, postcards and copious souvenirs.

Within this context, and some 395 years after Inigo Jones's final journey to Italy, on 6 October 2008 I set off from North London to Italy, planning to complete my own 'Grand Tour' in just 12 days by car. The car and the open road were famously Frank Lloyd Wright's favourite means of travel. In *An Autobiography* he would often wax lyrical about his journeys across the American continent: '[the] great highway is becoming, and rapidly, the horizontal line of a new Freedom extending from ocean to ocean.'[7] I too longed for the open road, blasting through Europe on a personal tour of self-discovery to Italy. It was a dry autumnal day with light cloud as I drove to Dover for an ordinary ferry crossing to Calais; this contrasted with the three days that Jones had to wait for good weather in 1613, and the dangerous channel crossing he had to endure thereafter. As northern France mutated into Belgium, I was caught in a 'middle landscape' between the heavy grey sky and the green fields around, modulated by long deep ditches lined with tall trees, and the terrain inhabited by small farms with red-tiled roofs. I crossed into Holland without stopping the car once, and was immediately caught up in the massive urban sprawl of Utrecht, followed by an industrialised coastline with its large chemical works and dockyards – signs and reflections of a global shipping hub. Rotterdam soon loomed in the twilight and so I exited the A16 for the city centre, and, after a few circuits around a never ending one-way system, I managed to find a hotel. The heavy bombing of the city during the Second World War has erased any trace of the Rotterdam that Jones would have seen, but there was plenty of architecture inspired by Wright, and I visited Sint Franciscus College, Secondary School (1922–4) once more (see page 56).

After lunch, I headed off for Germany, where the driving was much more intense due to the narrow car lanes and the undulating landscape. The early autobahns were never graded, and simply followed the contours of the land – after a few hundred kilometres, it made me feel quite sick. I broke up the monotony of the journey by stopping off at a number of service stations to consume toasted cheese and ham sandwiches and coffee, a diet that sustained me from London to Venice. For Frank Lloyd Wright the 'gas station' represented the ultimate form of architecture for the new car-based population, as he noted in *An Autobiography*:

> The roadside service station may be – in embryo – the future city-service-distribution. Each station may well grow into a well-designed convenient neighbourhood distribution centre naturally developing as meeting place, restaurant, restroom, or whatever else will be needed as decentralisation process and integration succeeds. Already, hundreds of thousands occupy the best places in the towns or, more significantly, pretty well outside of the towns.[8]

The 'gas station' was therefore a crucial part of Broadacre City, and his identification of these service stations as a form of 'generic space' was prophetic. In *The Disappearing City* (1932), Wright talked in transcendental terms about the new definition of space in relation to the car, in the sense that for the traveller the 'horizon widens as he goes.'[9] Wright proclaimed the car driver as the new citizen: 'After all, he is the city? So the city is going where and as he goes,'[10] thus removing the traditional concepts of place and fixed culture. He advocated a city founded on trans-locality – a complete denial of the hitherto traditional concepts of 'architecture, place

Standard Overhead Service Station (1932), model by Frank Lloyd Wright

and culture.' Yet, images of the 'gas stations' designed by Wright reflect his 'Usonian' architecture and, presumably, he believed all service stations should look like this in the future.

At the *Axxe* service station near Koblenz, Germany, I telephoned ahead to book a hotel room in Heidelberg and rested with a bland cup of coffee and a plain pastry. From my window seat, I saw the leaves were changing colour in a nearby forest, whereas the interior was indifferent to the seasons with its static booths with plastic covered chairs and fake wood tables. The service station is an example of the generic spaces that have been generated under late-capitalism and is a condition of 'supermodernity' (a 'non-place') without context, historical connection and identity.[11] Yet, in opposition to these 'non-places', it is claimed that there are 'anthropological places' which are the sites where there is a 'cultural identity and memory, binding its inhabitants to the history of the locale.'[12] I wonder which of these would best describes Wright's 'organic' architecture? On the one hand, anthropological spaces can create 'organically social' relationships because residents inhabit a defined cultural area and they know each other.[13] This seems to be a very quaint historical construct for 21st-century living, and Wright himself used a regionally defined space during his 'Prairie Style' period. Whilst on the other hand, Wright's 'Usonian' and 'Legacy' epochs were an example of 'non-place' generic spaces as exemplified in his eulogy to the service station. Wright offered an early understanding of globalisation, acknowledging that culture is no longer tied to a single location, but is interconnected within a fluid global network. Furthermore, the idea of a fixed history and identity that is only present in 'anthropological' places was also questionable, since history and culture are always informed by its connection to, and relationship with, other places and is mediated through the act of travelling.

As I turned off the motorway to visit Heidelberg, I could hear Wright preaching in my ear: the only need to stop one's car in Broadacre City would be to 'view the ruin' of the former city centre as a tourist.[14] Entering Heidelberg in the evening was a magical experience, with the city lost in the darkness of dim street lighting, yet revealing a preserved medieval city inhabited by students and tourists, all seeming to enjoy living within this Romantic 'ruin.' In the morning, I climbed up a narrow lane that had been excavated from the red sandstone escarpment, to great views over the compact old town, as well as the sprawling modern printing works and suburbia beyond. There was a sequence of secondary gates leading to the dramatic north elevation of the

Friedrischsbau (1601–07), a late Renaissance palace that would have only just been completed when Inigo Jones arrived in 1613. The Great Terrace in front of it was busy with tourists taking photographs. Within the medieval fort was the main courtyard, which revealed a mixture of Renaissance styles and scales. Beyond that was the Englischer Bau (1612–19) built by Elector Palatine Frederick V for his new English bride. Frederick V was leader of the Protestant League, and his alliance with the powerful British monarchy was intended to consolidate and advance his ambitions. The neo-Palladian design of the Englischer Bau symbolised this new trans-European alliance, and was consciously meant as a progression from the regional High Renaissance style of the Friedrischsbau. Its severe classical form led to a tourist myth, which attributes its design to Jones, but no proof of this exists.[15] Similarly, it is claimed that the arched entry to the garden was designed and built by Inigo Jones in a single evening as part of the elaborate wedding celebrations, an even more unlikely claim, as the arch clearly displays a number of overtly baroque overtones. The brutal Thirty Years' War broke out in 1618 and when Heidelberg was attacked in 1620, the whole castle was gutted. The Friedrischsbau and other buildings were gradually repaired, but the Englischer Bau remained a ruin, and a reminder of a lost neo-Palladian Protestant dynasty that once extended from Heidelberg to Britain.

Later that day, I crossed the border into Switzerland and, after a brief stop to exchange money to pay for the toll, I drove through Basel and entered Switzerland's dramatic interior, with the Alps looming on the horizon. I experienced a condensed version of Switzerland, with imposing Alpine mountains and torturous tunnels all viewed at high speed. During Inigo Jones's time, all travellers had to walk across a number of dangerous obstacles, including the ominously named Devil's Bridge.[16] At the southern end of Switzerland, Lugano was situated on a large lake of the same name within the Canton of Ticino. It is a very affluent city, and a new casino on the lakeside today consolidates its reputation as the Monte Carlo of Switzerland. It was also within the Canton of Ticino that the work of Tita Carloni, a 'neo-Wrightian,' was based.[17] Carloni was born in 1931 and educated locally in Lugano. He graduated in architecture from Zurich in 1954 and opened his own practice the next year. Carloni was influenced by Bruno Zevi's *Towards an Organic Architecture* and researched Wright's work using journals and books, consequently aligning himself in the postwar period of 'cultural ferment' with Wright – in opposition to the native, but French speaking, Le Corbusier.[18] Carloni reflected Wright's widespread influence as one of the 'modern masters', and he attempted to use Wright's 'organic' mantra as a means of mediating a new cultural identity. Carloni stated: '[We] naively set ourselves the objective of an 'organic' Ticino, in which the values of modern culture were to be interwoven in a natural way with local tradition.'[19] His early work adopted many of the principles of Wrightian architecture, considering the site as an inspiration and only using local materials. His first house, the Balmelli House (1957) embraced its sloping site to create an innovative sequence of spaces that were articulated using local stone and timber, and its façade expressed a subtle play of geometry. The subsequent Carloni House (1957) in Pregassona near Lugano, was another example of the use of local stone. This time, it was very reminiscent of Wright's work at Taliesin West, combining the stone with natural wood in a dramatic, geometrical manner. It was certainly a worthy tribute and local manifestation of Wright's global presence during this period.

Carloni's architecture has been considered as a regional reaction against a universal / global architecture: a movement known as Critical Regionalism.[20] The 'placeness' of architecture contains a number of historical ideas that were first explored within Romantic and Picturesque art and architecture, emphasising the use of regional design elements as a means of confronting a dominant universalist order.[21] This commitment to place also recalls the work of Martin Heidegger and his notion that each site contains its own *genius loci*. It is interesting to consider if Wright's architecture possesses a regional dimension when taken beyond America. Within Ticino, the new 'regional' tradition advocated by Carloni was, in fact, a mutation of Wright's global 'organic' architecture, and a dissolution of local character, and it was yet another manifestation of the global aspect to Wright's work. In addition, it is interesting to speculate whether the local adoption of Wright reflected a cultural engagement with America, or a means of defining the political aspirations of Ticino within the Swiss Federation. The official language in Ticino is Italian, and the promotion of Wright's work by Zevi may well have represented a cultural aspiration to connect with the 'mother country,' as well as reflecting the geographical connection with the Ticino River flowing from the Alps to the Po River.

After spending a night in Ticino, I was back on the road and descending from the Alps before I entering Italy, encountering the vast plains surrounding Milan. I circumnavigated the city using the intimidating six-lane motorway – beyond, the countryside seemed idyllic, with its vineyards and the silhouettes of small hill settlements. Venice, however, beckoned and, on 9 October 2008, I crossed the causeway to the island city.

VENICE

Venice's period of splendid isolation was terminated by the Austrians in 1846, when they built a causeway for the railway line, and it was further connected in 1931 by Benito Mussolini, when he completed the accompanying road crossing. These bridges dissolved the last remnants of the old Republic and diluted the Venetian character.[22] A friend had found a spare room for me to rent for a few days in Venice on Guidecca island, and I arranged to meet Nicola at the modern bus station, Piazzale Roma. On the ferry ride to Guidecca I chatted with Nicola, she was researching Chinese literature, and spoke the language fluently. I was impressed by her tales of her time in China learning and practising the language, I ventured that she had inherited the spirit of Marco Polo. We disembarked at Guidecca, and Nicola reminded me of the correct orientation of the ferry points – we walked along the quayside and then turned right at the AC Milan supporters' bar. We proceeded down a narrow alleyway to the end and lurched in the darkness towards an old door. Nicola put her arm through a broken window in the door and opened it from the inside. My apartment, on the second floor, was a long, narrow layout with one space running into the next. It was not very private, but it was fun nonetheless. In the morning, I opened my window to look out onto the lagoon, with sailing boats moored away from the bustle of modern day Venice.

It was in Venice in 1951 that Frank Lloyd Wright gained the greatest adulation during his time in Italy, courtesy of the Venice School of Architecture and its director, Guiseppe Samona, its main design professor, Carlo Scarpa, and the historian, Bruno Zevi. They were all advocates of Wright's ideas and promoters of 'organic' architecture. Zevi accompanied Wright during his 1951 visit to Florence, Venice and Rome, and his recollections provide an intoxicating tale of Wright's triumphant welcome:

> When Wright walked in the calli or through the piazzette, or when he travelled by gondola, Venetians of all social strata recognized, greeted and applauded him. Wright was surprised and happy – such recognition had never happened to him before.[23]

Carlo Scarpa (left), Frank Lloyd Wright and students in Venice, Italy (1951)

I began my visit by searching for the site of the Masieri Memorial, an unrealised project that Wright had begun in 1952. The memorial site was buried deep in the city fabric, but after many twists and turns and requests for directions, I found a forlorn-looking metal door and, optimistically, pressed an electronic buzzer. The door opened and I entered a narrow alley with a distinctive semi-circular ceiling motif guiding me to another more highly crafted, metal door with inlaid stone and small circular openings. The building now belongs to the Venice University School of Architecture, and although there was a conference taking place that morning, the administrator was friendly and offered to show me around in the afternoon.

Angelo Masieri had been living in a house on this site, which had belonged to his family for some decades, while he studied architecture in the 1940s. It is claimed that Masieri asked Wright to design a house and studio for the site when they met in 1951.[24] However, the following year, whilst travelling to meet Wright to discuss the project in more detail, Masieri was killed in a road accident. His widow, Savina, wrote to Wright, inviting him to design a memorial building on the site – either as an apartment block or a hostel for 16 to 20 students.[25] Wright elected to design a hostel, and sent a sketch elevation and plan in 1953 to Savina. The plan showed the building pulled back from both boundaries, generating a path along one edge that led directly to the canal, and a thin lightwell along the other side against the Palazzo Balbi, thus breaking the continuous façade along the canal. The ground floor was to house a central library space with dining facilities to the rear and, beside the side entry door, Wright had resurrected his touchstone from his 'Prairie Style' years – the symbolic hearth. Whilst the library was to be orientated to the south to engage directly with the Grand Canal, there was little evidence in Wright's plans as to how it would actually function: there were no bookshelves, for instance, and only four desks placed against one wall. The double-height space was articulated with a mezzanine floor for four student dormitories with their windows facing the Palazzo Balbi separating wall, plus one corner dormitory looking onto the canal. On the first, second and third floors the layout for the student dormitory plans and central hearth were repeated, and there was a generous common sitting room that again engaged with the canal.

In his 1953 elevation, Wright adopted a classical and academic 'a-a-b-b-b-a-a' seven-bay rhythm[26] with five balconies on the ground and first floors, diminishing to three balconies on the second floor and no projections at all on the third floor – with an offset belvedere to the western side of the façade. Furthermore, at the corners Wright proposed glass inserts to emphasise the vertical aspect of the scheme. It would have made a theatrical addition to the Grand Canal, Wright claimed: 'Alongside the corner-feature a glass lighting-feature rises – lighting outside and inside by way of neon tubes (low candlepower) when appropriate.'[27] Wright described a reinforced-concrete construction founded on piles, its façade dressed with marble emerging from the canalside: 'The intermediate piers of construction rise like reeds from the water and should be seen below the surface.'[28] The façade was in fact a tribute to the academic architecture that Wright had always severely dismissed in the past as irrelevant, and a reversal of his earlier 'organic' architecture. Curiously, the original scheme had a belvedere on the west side of the elevation with a roof garden that Wright had designed as his own pied-à-terre for whenever he visited Venice.[29] Was this belvedere perhaps a tribute to the Villino Belvedere that Wright had rented in Fiesole with Mamah back in 1910? That had been a small house with an intimate private terrace and had captured the image of a past Italian idyll in Tuscany. Wright's design for the Masieri Memorial was developed over the subsequent years, and at one stage the belvedere was moved to the east side against the Palazzo Balbi, a desperate move to show that the new memorial was subservient to the adjacent Mannerist palace.

By releasing his proposed designs in New York before they were presented in Venice, Wright provoked a harsh reaction from Italian conservationists, who objected both to Wright as an American architect and to the idea of a modern building on the Grand Canal.[30] The debates regarding the scheme were often personal and did not really consider the architecture on its merits. Furthermore, there was a long delay before any of the information was released, and this allowed the Italian press to escalate the personal attacks on Wright and spread misinformation about the scheme.[31] Even a special edition of the *Metron* (1954) under the guidance of Zevi was another 'wasted' opportunity to appease an architectural debate that was caught in a perfect storm of controversy.[32] The article sought to make a connection between the organic character of the city and Wright, the self-anointed master of 'organic' architecture. Furthermore, the theatrical aspect of the façade that Wright had developed and removed from the internal plan was entirely in keeping with Venitian architecture. Wright responded to the controversy with a well-mannered letter in 1954, in which he sought to reassure Venetians that, '[the Masieri Memorial] is no ruthless sacrifice of an ancient culture to a modern ambition, but is, I am sure, a worthy tribute to you all and harmonious with your great tradition.'[33] As another former resident of Oak Park, in Chicago, Ernest Hemingway said that he would personally allow the memorial to be built, but only if it was burnt down afterwards[34] – to which Wright replied: 'a mere voice from the jungle!'[35] The controversy lasted for nearly three years and gathered worldwide press coverage before the scheme was finally rejected in 1955.

For me, the Masieri Memorial proposal can also be framed as a reflection on Ruskin's *The Seven Lamps of Architecture* (1849). In his essay on the 'Lamp of Memory,' Ruskin noted: 'Architecture [we] may live without her, and worship without her, but we cannot remember without her. How cold is all history, how

Drawing of the Masieri Memorial Student Library and Dwelling, Venice, Italy (1953) by Frank Lloyd Wright

Internal view of the Masieri Memorial, Venice, Italy (1970–83) by Carlo Scarpa

lifeless all imagery, compared to that which the living nation writes, and the uncorrupted marble bears.'[36] The memorial was thus part of Wright's troubled legacy, it was a site where Masieri memory was to be made material, and was a place for Wright to secure his legacy. So desperate was Wright to realise his dream that he departed from the structural 'truth' of the Gothic that he and Ruskin had professed. His 'organic' mantra was no longer a unified architectural philosophy and he was content to remove his mannerist façade from its functional plan to ensure his legacy. It is ironic that Wright's most contextually nuanced scheme was eventually defeated by a conservation lobby.

I returned in the afternoon to visit the Masieri Memorial as eventually designed by Carlo Scarpa (1970–83), and the administrator began our tour in the dark and congested entry hall. From this vantage point, I experienced the space opening out to face the light glistening off the Grand Canal, which was framed by the central door opening. In keeping with tradition, a metal grille protected the opening and, inside, Scarpa had introduced a glazed lobby that allowed the water to penetrate the façade during high tides. This indeed was the language for the whole project, with the façade acting as a permeable screen in front of a new dual-columned steel structure that held the concrete floors and exposed services. Scarpa also indulged in judicious cutting back of the new floors to create a dialogue between them, expressing the qualities of the concrete, steelwork and servicing pipework – and thereby adding spatial play to the layers of materiality. The upper storeys possessed circular bathroom pods that were finished in blue-and-white polished plasterwork, and the open-plan offices sought to make the best out of the remaining spaces in a number of different desk configurations. For the problematic Grand Canal façade, Scarpa had found an old sketch by Giovanni Canaletto and used it as a basis to placate the conservationists with their neo-Ruskinian desires, resulting in what can be called a neo-Venetian solution.

Carlo Scarpa was the natural choice to complete the Masieri Memorial. Angelo Masieri had been a pupil and collaborator of his, and their admiration of Wright was a common influence. Scarpa was born in Venice in 1906 and studied art at the Royal Academy of Fine Arts in the city, before working briefly as an architectural assistant and also as a designer for the glassmakers of Murano. He returned to the Academy to become Professor of Design in 1926 aged only 20 years old. His first exhibition design was for the Venice Biennale in 1928, and his first architectural commission, in 1935–7, was for the headquarters of the University of Venice, the Ca'

Upper detail of main hall (*magna aula*), Venice, Italy (1935–7) by Carlo Scarpa

Foscari, which involved restoring and remodelling the main hall (*magna aula*). Ca' Foscari (*c.*1450) was an impressive Gothic mansion built by Doge Francesco Foscari and which Ruskin called 'the noblest example in Venice of fifteenth-century Gothic.'[37] The palace sat on the corner of the Grand Canal and the Rio de Ca' Foscari, north of the Accademia bridge and beside the site of the Masieri Memorial. It possessed an impressive four-storey façade with a finely detailed central arcade on the first and second storeys with marble tracery and Gothic detailing. It was a typical example of Venetian domestic architecture, albeit at a large scale: 'with their great central window arcades lighting the huge halls behind, flanked by side wings of smaller rooms lit by single windows.'[38]

Ever since 1867, the Palace has been the home of Ca' Foscari University, and I entered the campus from the rear – its land side – into an enclosed internal courtyard with high walls, where I met the administrator on the ground floor. I was escorted up a wide medieval stair to the first-floor piano nobile, where the vast main hall was revealed behind a large landing space. The screening designed by Scarpa divided the room in two, allowing the senate to meet in privacy and others to pass beside the hall to get to the rooms beyond. A number of abstracted 'tree' forms made from standard wood sections supported two layers of screens, with a permanent glass barrier and a secondary hinged cloth screen for added privacy. The abstracted trees were reminiscent of those in the Taliesin North and Taliesin West drafting studios, and were detailed carefully using simple square sections to generate an abstract geometry similar to Wright's own tectonic meditations. It was a wonderfully modern, abstracted, yet poetically articulated, solution. In the early morning, the light again reflected off the Grand Canal, illuminating and animating the tri-lobed ogee arcade to the main hall and casting shadows against the oscillating sheer blinds thus making the external façade dematerialise. This was my magical Venetian memory.

VENETO

I followed Inigo Jones to the Veneto in search of one of Palladio's famous villas. Venice saw dramatic changes in its economic and political climate in the 16th-century. With international commerce declining, the republic had sought to increase agricultural production in its adjacent colonies by draining the land and farming it.[39] A new class of Renaissance landowner-farmer emerged, and in his work Palladio articulated a new kind of country dwelling that embraced their aspirations. From his detailed study of ancient precedents, Palladio developed a rigorous proportional system that was 'more rationalist than the Romans.'[40] As a consequence, Palladio's villas seem to be static compositions, which enhance the importance of the owner, and are supported by strict proportions that also tie them back to their ancient lineage. The Villa Emo (1556–65) by Palladio, was typical of the 'colonialist' endeavours of the Venetians on the Italian mainland. It featured an imposing symmetrical façade with a central temple façade flanked by two long side pavilions that embraced the landscape. The elevation and plans were organised according to the Venetian module.

The Villa Emo was busy with coach trips on the day I visited. I was surprised at how simple and well balanced the composition was. I ascended a very shallow ramp: it was claimed that the entry steps had a proportion of 1:2, which was ideal for threshing wheat. In addition, the side pavilions were specifically constructed for agricultural use. At the end of the ramp stood a dominant portico with a central door leading to nine formal rooms that were arranged according to a strict geometry and beautifully adorned with frescoes. It was a ritualised procession from one formal space to another around a central space, a kind of early Renaissance dance. Nowadays, the side wings are given over to the supporting roles required at any heritage site these days – in other words a tourist shop, conference suites and meeting rooms. In the gift shop, I purchased a pencil and ruler set as a souvenir of Palladio's stately measured villa.

Wright's homes had progressed beyond Palladian villas to form a very different concept of the home. The American historian Vincent Scully summed up the progression brilliantly: 'The Palladian plan is an excellent expression of a pre-industrial, humanistic world where the human being occupied a fixed, central position. The Wright plan is an image of modern man, caught up in constant change and flow, holding on, if he feels he must, to whatever seems solid, but no longer regarding himself as the center of the world.'[41] In summary, Palladio adopted the classical tradition of establishing a rigid proportional system for both the plan and elevation, whereas Wright generated a more flexible method of planning using geometric modules. And the two architects articulated their homes very differently, with Palladio's villas possessing imposing, pristine geometrical forms, where Wright's homes are intimate, informal, irregular and rich in natural textures and colour.[42]

I travelled beyond Veneto to the adjacent region of Fruili and to the town of Udine. It had been part of the western Roman Empire before being conquered by the Venetian Republic in 1420 and becoming the second city of this expanding regional power. To consolidate the Venetian influence, the new town hall of the Loggia del Lionello (1448–57) was built in the Venetian-Gothic style, essentially as a miniature version of the Doge's Palace. This was colonial architecture at its most literal. Udine today retains its own medieval identity with an enclosing perimeter wall, narrow winding streets, small piazzas and an abundance of street life. At the tourist centre, the work of Gino Valle is promoted as that of a famous local architect. The work of Angelo Masieri is also acknowledged on a local listing plate, but he is less well known here. Masieri's Giacomuzzi House (1947–50) is a low-level insertion into a city block, with a low boundary wall, and is hidden from the street by two mature trees and an area for car parking. The house has an abstract cubic form and exhibits a definite horizontal quality through a sequence of terraces that recede towards the rear of the site. Externally, it is finished with a natural coloured render with horizontal banding and patinated copper features. All in all, it is an interpretation of Wright mixed with cubism, and thus similar to the work of the Dutch architects, W. M. Dudok and J. J. P. Oud.

A short drive beyond Udine's old town wall is the Romanelli Villa (1950–55) by Masieri and Scarpa, which is now set within a modern suburb. I had managed to make an arrangement with its owner to view the house and I instantly recognised the villa from the street, noting also that there were a number of other similar properties beside it, as if sharing its reflected glory. The Romanelli Villa sits to the north of the site, with a large garden to the south. The owner welcomed me in and was evidently keen to show me around his house. We started in the garden, where the concept of the property was explained to me:

> It is a long wing that spans from one side of the property to the other. You have just entered via one part of the wing and at the other end is the garden. The house is in the middle . . . The original design was by Angelo Masieri, but when he died in a car crash, the house was finished by Carlo Scarpa. The horizontal roof on the right of the house was introduced by Scarpa, as it was originally pitched.

The Villa faced the garden obliquely, the wing feature that the owner had identified began at the entry, passed through the house and formed an abstracted pergola and the roof followed the same orientation. But the central part of the house was rotated so that its leading corner addressed the garden. In addition, the elevation was articulated by wide vertical render bands, forming an abstracted set of columns.

Looking at the house from the garden, I could recognise that it had been inspired by Wright's Taliesin West, with its geometrical spatial planning, while it also possessed certain details from the Prairie House period – that is, the projecting roof forms, compression of the entrance space, and the corner window details. The embracing wing seemed to ground the design in its site, making me think of Palladio's own work within the same landscape. Thus, whilst the 'organic' architecture of Wright might be considered as the opposite to Palladian architecture, the Romanelli Villa seeks to reconcile this conflict.

The owner then led me inside the house and opened up the shutters to show off the internal space to its best advantage. Here, the space flows seamlessly around the central hearth in the approved Wrightian manner. Part of the living room was a double-height space divided by the external wing, forming

Garden View, Romanelli Villa, Udine, Italy (1950–55) by Carlo Scarpa and Angelo Masieri

a close dialogue with the garden beyond. This space also extended into the dining area and linked it back to the kitchen and utility area located towards the rear. The kitchen had since been adapted to cope with family demands, and the owner was proud to show me the five-sided table that he had designed to fit the geometry of the site. I had to agree that it was a great addition to the 'organic' design. We returned to the entrance lobby to go upstairs to the bedrooms, which were all serviced off the upper part of the wing form. The master bedroom was positioned at the back and faced the rear garden. The other bedrooms faced out onto the street, but were set back from the road and its noise. This family house was evidently still very much in use, although I noticed that the children had now grown up and left.

LIGNANO PINETA AND TRIESTE

During my research, I came across several Wright-inspired sites located around northern Italy and I explored these schemes using Venice as my base. About 140 kilometres (87 miles) west of Venice, the settlement of Lignano

Pineta on the Adriatic Sea had been planned as a holiday resort by Marcello D'Olivo. It was conceived around a spiral plan that sought to integrate the buildings into the landscape and, as such, was a reaction against the neo-classical or grid-iron method of planning. The intention was that the spiral form would replace the traditional orthogonal beach esplanade, with its commercial hierarchy related in its proximity to the sea, and with a new form that could be more democratic and equitable. I arrived at the town in mid-October and found it deserted, with very little traffic and hardly anyone walking on the streets despite the warm weather. I gravitated towards the town centre, which was next to a roundabout. There, I found a map posted on an information board with a church and a small post office behind it, and a petrol service station and some small shops opposite. The traffic island effectively formed the civic centre – this was at once unsettling and revealing, being a core without any imposing architecture or piazza, yet one that responded to the primacy of car ownership and its appetite for fuel and parking. The town possessed the stilted atmosphere of the *Truman Show* or *Stepford Wives*.[43] I inspected the well-crafted church, which had elements of 'organic' design in its dynamic roof form and exposed concrete trusses and brickwork. The remaining town was also planned around the car. The main curved street linked the church to the sea, and on this stood a low-level pavilion containing shops, cafés and offices that again exhibited a number of 'organic' features from Wright's late period, albeit used in a very playful manner. The street ended at the seafront in the Piazza D'Olivo, complete with a small fountain, another roundabout and car park, making for a somewhat ironic urban setting whereby only the car user could inhabit the space.

I knew there were a number of villas designed by D'Olivo in Lignano Pineta, and so I drove around the spiral plan, literally going around in circles looking for them. Next to the Ernest Hemingway Park (he visited the town once), I found a real estate office that was open. When I asked about D'Olivo, the agent swivelled in his chair, reached for a book and, laughing loudly, showed me an image of D'Olivo with Saddam Hussein. After a good humoured encounter, the estate agent pointed me towards the Villa Spezzotti (1958) and the other homes completed by D'Olivo. The Villa Spezzotti adopted the urban form of the town, with a spiral ramp climbing up around the large, circular building. The house features blue-and-white rendered elements decorated with abstract patterns based on a sunflower motif. It was difficult to make out any other features of the property, as the creeping vegetation obscured my view. The adjacent Villa Mainardis (1958) was another circular house, but with an inverted form to the Villa Spezzotti: this time, the central entry ramp circled around a void. This use of circular planned homes made the town seem even more surreal and futuristic, similar perhaps to some of Wright's rendered images and his circle-inspired projects such as Pleasantville in New York state. An article of the time noted: 'D'Olivo clearly draws inspiration from F. L. Wright, of whom he is an enthusiastic, if indirect follower.'[44] Whilst D'Olivo developed the 'curved line and the spatial continuity that Wright developed for his second Jacob's House,' he also worked in a more abstracted and formal way, generating spaces that in the end were subservient to the over-riding geometry.[45] Nevertheless, D'Olivo had managed to create a distinctive form of architecture that questioned the underlying orthodoxy of modernism.

Later that afternoon, I travelled further east to Trieste, driving up small hills and passing through tunnels, being mindful to turn off the motorway before I reached Slovenia. It was within the small suburb of Opicina that I gained directions for the Villaggio del Fanciullo (Children's Village; 1949–57) by D'Olivo. The project was built to house juvenile delinquents and neglected children, and D'Olivo tried to deliberately remove 'all reminders of the old-fashioned prison-like edifice, and generally speaking of all vertical structures' and to preserve the exiting site to encourage an 'open-air life.'[46] It was another example of D'Olivo's all-embracing vision of architecture, with the triangular plan of the Villagio also informing the site planning of individual pavilions and buildings as if it was an integrated design solution. The site is still used extensively today, with many cars dropping off children at the adjacent gymnasium, and within the complex there are dormitories, a refectory, a school, a workshop space and a printing shop. I recognised the main administration building with its dynamic geometrical form and another variation on a triangular theme, with a broad base to the ground that seemed to taper towards the middle, and a roof with an upturned triangular geometry. The building was being repaired and was hidden behind a protective fence. Nonetheless, I could see that the original staircase with its triangular cantilever treads was being restored. In many respects the architecture had achieved its aim of breaking away from a dominant rectilinear geometry, yet I feel that D'Olivo struggled to master both the circular and triangular geometries. In fact some of Wright's work using these geometries was not always successful either, making the architecture seem ponderous and unbalanced.

IVREA

North of Milan, in the Piedmont region of Italy lies the city of Ivrea. This is home to the Olivetti Factory, a complex that was initiated by Adriano Olivetti as a paternalistic industrial settlement, based around the manufacture of typewriters. The company had been founded in 1908 by Camillo Olivetti, and was then extensively developed by his son, Adriano, who inherited a business with 30 employees working within a single workshop. He went on to build a large modern factory designed around the Taylorist management philosophy, with the help of the architects, Luigi Figini and Gino Pollini, who were responsible for designing many of the new rationalist buildings that represented modern manufacturing techniques. Their extension to the Olivetti Factory (1939–40) was based on the works of the famous American industrial architect Albert Kahn, who had designed the main Ford factories. However, after the Second World War, there was a reaction against the modernism of Mussolini that was propagated by Bruno Zevi and many other critics. Adriano Olivetti responded to this change in architectural thought and sought also to project a 'social' and progressive image of the firm and so he commissioned the Social Services Building (1954–7) once more with Figini and Pollini.

As I approached the complex by foot, I found the 'organically' inspired Social Services Building from the 1950s facing the rationalist factory extension from the 1930s, both by Figini and Pollini – it was a dialectic for the image of the Olivetti company. Whereas the factory extension was dominant, with three broad bands of linear glazing framed by a grey render façade, the Social Services Building was a subservient, two-storey abstracted form, with a projecting first floor canopy that enclosed a row of trees and had exposed textured concrete. The Wright-inspired Social Services Building is based on a hexagonal planning module and is divided into two masses at a slight angle to each other, responding to a turn in the road. One wing was for cultural functions and social welfare, whilst the other wing acted as a health centre. Wright had used the hexagon module for the Hanna House (1936–7), and claimed that it was more flexible than the square or triangular module, which Figini and Pollini obviously also believed.[47] There was no formal elevation to the Social Services Building, because the dominant canopy to the front projected so far into the street. This overhang offered shelter, while its dynamic hexagonal openings allowed the tall trees to penetrate it. There were tall, carefully composed glass openings to the building, and the whole edifice was wrapped in exposed concrete.

Arriving late and flustered, my escort from the Olivetti Foundation proceeded to show me around the cultural wing. I could see that it still possessed many of the original features, such as a hexagonal central staircase with exposed treads and hexagonal skylights above. We met the local administrator who was slightly bemused by my interest in the building. However, she allowed me to walk along the generous first-floor terrace on the canopy roof, where the trees growing through the large openings made an interesting interplay between the real organic form and its hexagonal abstraction. In the fading light on the terrace, the human scale of the Social Services Building was juxtaposed against the more impersonal expanse of the factory; despite its brutal materiality, the building reflected an architecture that wanted to start a new kind of social order. It was also a building that sought to advance the ideas of 'organic' architecture: it was inventive on many levels, with its dynamic form, its lack of a formal elevation, its embrace of nature and its expressive materiality.

FLORENCE

Returning to my Grand Tour, I left Venice in the late afternoon and travelled south-west towards Florence. The horizontal and fertile landscape was at its most resplendent in the evening. I turned off the motorway south of Padua to look for the Villa Molin (1597) by Vincenzo Scamozzi, which Inigo Jones had visited and studied extensively, deriving elements of its design for the Queen's House (1616) in Greenwich, London. I found the Villa Molin within the encroaching modern sprawl of Padua. It lies behind a high-level canal embankment and I easily recognised its imposing pedimented temple façade. The Villa retains a sense of gentle country life, out of step with the harsh realities of the encroaching 21st century, with a busy road and a service station nearby and Italian teenagers zipping up and down the road on their mopeds. The Villa seemed to be in private ownership, with little to identify the site or any information concerning visiting times. Nonetheless, I felt an emotional connection with the original Grand Tour, being there 365 years later with the same excitement of a new episode beginning at the next new destination. I returned to the motorway, crossing the wide River Po delta in the twilight. The night closed in as I crossed the Appian Mountains and arrived late in Florence. I followed a coach tour towards the city centre and as it pulled up close to the railway station, I decided to join the horde and booked myself into the Leonardo da Vinci Hotel. It was dark as I went to bed, and I had to wait until morning to see if my room had a view.

When, in the morning, I drew back the curtains, I found myself looking onto an apartment block and a railway viaduct. This would have caused much anguish for the early 20th-century travellers depicted in E. M. Forster's book *A Room with a View* (1908).[48] Wright's first visit to Italy in 1910 was almost concurrent with that of Lucy Honeychurch, the lead character in *A Room with a View*, and he was on a parallel romantic adventure with his mistress. Yet, why did Wright choose to work in Italy, and especially Florence, during his first visit to Europe? His distaste for the Renaissance was already well known, and so, to visit the home of its origin was a curious choice. One source of inspiration for Wright may have been Louis Sullivan, who devoted a whole chapter in *The Autobiography of an Idea* (1949) to his European adventure – mostly describing his time at the École des Beaux-Arts in Paris, but with a short passage on Florence and Rome. Sullivan had visited Florence in 1874 and stayed there for six weeks, noting (in the third person): 'Louis saw Florence and does not know how he came to break the golden chains that bound him there, a too willing captive.'[49] The robustness and scale of the Renaissance palazzos built by the powerful families of the Medici, Pazzi-Quaratesi and Strozzi in the later half of the 15th century were to influence Sullivan's Auditorium Building (1887–9) in Chicago, which possessed a heavy rusticated base with a severe Romanesque elevation and was topped with a tower. It is very plausible that Sullivan might have suggested the pleasures of Florence to Wright during the time they worked together on the Auditorium Building and other commissions.

I caught a local bus from Florence to Fiesole and met an American woman who was undertaking an intensive Italian language course. She was familiar with Fiesole and described a number of local attractions within the small town, including the archaeological site, museum and monastery. I told her that I was looking for a house where Frank Lloyd Wright had resided when he ran away with his mistress – she shook her head with distain and called him a 'philanderer.' The bus meandered for half an hour up a steep hill; in Wright's time there would have been an electric tram, apparently the first to be used in mainland Europe.[50] Fiesole was infused with an air of antiquity: the site was first settled during the Bronze Age and the Etruscan's presence can be traced back to the seventh century BC. The archaeological museum had a number of well-preserved relics that included a Roman theatre and thermal baths from the first century BC and temples dating from the third century BC.

The local bus terminated in the lower section of the main Piazza Mino, next to the Duomo. The recently paved upper part featured an allegorical statue, behind which stood the 14th-century Palazzo Pretorio (town hall). I had made an appointment to see an official at the Commune who wanted to talk about a new exhibition of Wright's work in 2010, held to celebrate the centenary of his visit to Florence and Fiesole.[51] We discussed my research and then set off to visit the Villino Belvedere where Wright had resided in 1910, during the spring and summer months. Via Verde rose steeply from the main piazza, with room for only one small car to pass at a time. After about 400 metres (1312 feet), there was a small plateau, with an open vista over the olive groves below and Florence in the distance, sheltering beneath dramatically dark, autumn clouds. The road divided into two at the small piazza, the southern Via Della Doccia descended back down the hill, whilst the northern Via Motececeri climbed upwards. I found the Villino Belvedere with its entrance at the first floor level and the main floor and garden below, enjoying this same, uninterrupted southern view towards the city. The Villino has been much altered, with the projecting south-facing balcony now fully enclosed. Yet the north entrance and the garden were just as Wright would have seen them. Unfortunately, the current owners did not allow me to visit, and the officer told me that even Wright's cousin had previously been turned away. We returned to the main piazza, stopping to smile wryly at a commemoration plaque to Wright that had been placed on the wrong house – something that should be corrected by the centennial celebration.

Wright described his idyllic hideaway in a chapter in *An Autobiography* entitled 'In Exile.' He recalled the Romantic poet Percy Bysshe Shelley, and expanded upon his own particular situation: 'In ancient Fiesole, far above the romantic city of cities, Firenze, in a little cream-white villa on the Via Verdi, the rebel. How many souls seeking release from real or fancied domestic woes have sheltered on the slopes below?'[52] Wright's romance with Mamah Cheney was thus played out within this modest town and small Villino: 'Walking hand in hand together up the hill road from Firenze to the older town, along the way in the sight and scent of roses, by day.'[53] In addition, the passage expands upon Wright's time in Florence and his wider Grand Tour through Europe: 'Together again tired out, sitting on benches in the galleries of Europe, saturated with plastic beauty, beauty in buildings, beauty in sculpture, beauty in paintings, until no Chiesa however rare and no further beckoning work of human hands could waylay us any more.'[54] It was within this blissful existence that Wright composed his 'Introduction' to the two-volume monograph.

Wright situated his introduction in Florence in order to acknowledge the importance of the city in art and architectural history: 'What these men of Florence absorbed from their Greek, Byzantine and Roman forbears, they bequeathed to Europe as the kernel of the Renaissance; and this, if we deduct the Gothic influence of the Middle Ages, has constituted the soul of Academic fine arts on the Continent.'[55] Furthermore, Wright noted the proliferation of the Italian 'flames' spread across Europe which lit 'myriads of French, German and English lights.'[56] However, for Wright, the academic proliferation of the Renaissance had questionable results beyond Italy. They were essentially copies using a set of coding devices to generate originality: 'those buildings were more or less "professional" embodiments of a striving for the beautiful, those buildings were "good school" performances, which sought consciously to be beautiful.'[57] Wright constructed a counter-position, taking his inspiration from wider surroundings, that excluded the academic approach. He proposed that 'The true basis for any serious study of the art of architecture is in those indigenous structures, which are to architecture what folklore is to literature or folksongs to music.'[58] Wright therefore reflected on the indigenous, vernacular architecture that he had experienced: 'No really Italian building seems ill at ease in Italy. All are happily content with what ornament and colour they carry, as naturally as the rocks and trees and garden slopes which are one with them.'[59] They were all basically 'organic.' It was also a symbolic end of the 'Prairie Style' period for Wright. His reflections in Italy contextualised the 'Prairie' idiom in a wider 'organic' framing that embraced vernacular architecture.

Wright returned once more to Florence in June 1951 to open an exhibition of his work entitled *Sixty Years of Living Architecture*. The exhibition had been conceived in the corridors of power in America as a response to an upsurge in communism in Italy.[60] Arthur C. Kaufmann, head of Gimbel's Department Store, and Congresswoman Clare Luce made plans for a cultural project, which sought to propagate American creative power and to show how it was derived from American values and freedom.[61] Wright was the perfect candidate. Conceived as a retrospective of Wright's career, but whilst he was still alive, the exhibition included 800 drawings and 28 models and occupied 15 halls within the Renaissance-style Palazzo Strozzi.[62] It covered Wright's development as an architect, beginning with his first houses in Chicago and concluding with a model of the Guggenheim Museum in New York. Dominating the main space was the large refurbished model of Broadacre City. Wright promoted his dis-urbanist theories in a talk to accompany the exhibition. It was a de-territorialised, global agenda, whereby the ideas underlying Broadacre City were applied to Italy, just as they could be to any other nation, and, as such, should have been an inspiration to Italian architects and planners.[63] Despite all the publicity, the exhibition was viewed critically at the time, not least by the left-wing, with the Florentine critic Nicco Fasola questioning Wright's whole approach.[64] Perceptively, Fasola branded Wright as a kind of cult figure who worshipped nature – considering how the Taliesin Fellowship operated, I think this was quite an accurate portrayal. Fasola believed that Wright's best work was during his early career, whereas the later works were just 'comfortable formalism stuffed with pleasing aesthetics.'[65] Furthermore, there were other cultural issues that the retrospective highlighted, and it was argued that the individual values propagated by Wright were not compatible with the traditional collective principles of Italian society.

Wright's two visits to Florence thus highlighted a number of contradictions that are endemic in any analysis of his work and writings. In Fiesole in 1910, Wright concluded his 'Prairie Style' period, and embarked upon his reinvention as a global architect – not wishing to be dismissed and discarded as a regional architect (as Sullivan had been). Wright thus began to advocate an 'organic' architecture that was based on a universal 'folk' theme, which embraced the individual practice of the architect. His first Grand Tour in 1910 was an example of Wright using a European journey to galvanise his reputation back in America and to broaden his architectural knowledge yet, ironically, his tour was to lead to professional isolation and less prestigious work. On his return to Florence in 1951, Wright had essentially become a global brand, promoting his own individualist American view of architecture without any regard for local culture or place. And Wright's de-territorialised suburban Broadacre, stuffed with suburban homes, was never going to placate the communists.

ROME

A number of authors have, over the years, sought to define Italy's relationship with Wright's work, which began at the turn of the 20th century with a number of journal articles. By the 1930s, there was a far wider appreciation of Frank

Lloyd Wright in Italy, beginning with the Milan Triennale V, in which Wright's work was included among the forerunners of contemporary architecture, albeit basically suggesting that Wright's work was somewhat isolated and that his architectural career was already over.[66] However, in 1935 in a lecture titled 'Architectural Prophesy', the critic Edoardo Perisco brought Wright to the very forefront of architectural, cultural and political discussions within Italy. His talk reviewed the innovative nature of Wright's work and, as such, concentrated 'on the spirit of stimulating Wright's architecture: his appeal for liberty and his rejection of the authority principle.'[67] In addition, Perisco made a compelling analogy of Wright with impressionism. He suggested that 'Wright's work had, in the history of modern architecture, the same breaching function that impressionism had had for academicism in painting,' thereby linking Wright to Cezanne.[68] Despite this eulogy to freedom during the tyranny of Mussolini's Fascists, Wright was also regrettably involved with the Fascist movement in Italy. He sent a message to the Congress of International Architecture in 1935 in Rome advocating his Broadacre City scheme and offering support to the ruling regime: 'Mussolini and his architects will lead their country to a new lease of life by abandoning the old academic order and working to establish the more natural and humane order.'[69]

Zevi actively advanced the concept of 'organic' architecture after the Second World War and even tried to manipulate Italian Renaissance historiography to include Wright. As such, he sought to establish a new language of modern architecture, leading him to equate Frank Lloyd Wright with Francesco Borromini and the baroque tradition. In 1950, Zevi published *Towards an Organic Architecture* as a direct attempt to reclaim the spirit of modernism away from Le Corbusier's functionalist manifesto, and conceived a new history of 'organic' architecture. Zevi devoted a short chapter to the 'Meaning and Scope of the Term Organic,'[70] and included a number of commentators, such as Louis Sullivan claiming that 'organic' was a 'searching for realities – the ten-fingered grasp of reality.'[71] He then cited Sigfried Giedeon's dialectic definition: 'Throughout history there persists two distinctive trends – the one toward the rational and the geometrical, the other toward the irrational and the organic.'[72] To amplify his case, Zevi listed 15 items, beginning with a reference borrowed from Johann Wolfgang Goethe, to show why organic may be considered a 'formative art' and inorganic a 'fine art.'[73] Zevi also quoted Giorgio Vasari, who, when he saw the Farnesina Palace in Rome 'praised it in these terms: 'NON MURATO, MA VERAMENTE NATO' (not built, but born).'[74] [Capitalisation by Zevi] It is not actually a helpful definition of 'organic' architecture, but it does illuminate the commonly held belief (and one that Wright himself promoted) that 'organic' architecture had to be conceived and delivered as a complete work of art, and thus as an act of genius – a typically Wrightian idea, of course! Perceptively, Zevi warns against two fallacies that do not adequately explain organic architecture; the use of the terms 'naturalistic' and 'biological'[75] and this brings to mind the contemporary use of 'organic' which has become too loosely defined.

In *The Modern Language of Architecture* (1978), Zevi explicitly confronted *The Classical Language of Architecture* (1964) by John Summerson, itemising seven 'invariables' to modern architecture that describe and communicate an 'anti-classical language.'[76] Again, Zevi did an expert job in condensing the idea of 'organic' architecture into a realistic proposition, something that Wright himself often made obtuse. The seven variables cited by Zevi were: listing content and function; asymmetry and dissonance; anti-perspective; fourth-dimension decomposition (after De Stijl); cantilever, shell and membrane structures; living, dynamic, fluid space; and continuity with the landscape. Using this new language, Zevi sought to make a definite break from neoclassical history by embracing 'the heresies and dissonances of history, those countless "exceptions to the rule" which have finally been emancipated and which can provide the back bone of an alternative language.'[77] Furthermore, Zevi wanted to realign Italian historiography with modernist architecture and to 'interpret history in a modern [way] . . . so as to make it act effectively as an incentive to creativity.'[78] Zevi illustrated his new approach to historical interpretation by juxtaposing 'the Middle Ages and the Arts and Crafts movement, Gothic and art nouveau, Renaissance and modern rationalism, baroque and organic architecture.'[79] For Zevi, the Baroque and 'organic' architecture shared the same 'linguistic phenomenon' because they were derived from similar sources: the baroque represented the dissolution of Renaissance rigour, and similarly Wright's 'organic' architecture offered a break from the rationalism of Chicago's industrial architecture.[80]

Zevi identified Francesco Borromini as the exponent of baroque architecture most closely related to Wright. In his essay 'A Recollection' (1999), Zevi described his last day with Wright during the 1951 visit; 'wandering much of the afternoon around Rome, where he met the architect I love most after Wright, the baroque master Francesco Borromini.'[81] Provokingly, Zevi compared the internal and the external manifestations of Sant'Ivo alla Sapienza (1642–60) with the Guggenheim Museum (1946–59). This analogy establishes a number of themes: the spatial qualities of baroque and 'organic' architecture, and the evocation of nature within Borromini and Wright's work. During my visit to Rome, I was fortunate to view the Sant'Ivo. It is encircled by an austere defensive wall, and is set within an imposing two-storey cloistered courtyard that houses a library and other academic functions of Sapienza University. At the far end of the cloister, the Church mutates from a dynamic concave form in its lower two storeys to a convex drum form above, and to complete this dramatic geometric transformation, it is topped off with a dome and a lantern in the form of a ziggurat. Internally, the space was intimate and drawn upwards, with a simple hexagonal plan that was based on the intersection of two triangles 'to form a hexagonal six-pointed star – the symbol of wisdom – and a hexagonal central space.'[82] The hexagonal plan was articulated with semi-circular chapels that alternated between concave and convex form which surrounded the consecrated space. Above, a deep cornice reconciled and simplified the geometry, so that the dome had six identical panels, each with a window and ornate decoration, culminating in a lantern.

The art historian Anthony Blunt claimed that Borromini 'believed that architecture was based on nature'[83] – a concept that was traceable to Galileo, who had written that 'the great book of nature is written in the language of mathematics, and its characters are triangles, circles, and other geometrical figures.'[84] Borromini therefore looked beyond the more static Renaissance method of interpreting nature via classically proportioned columns and regulated space. Instead, his ideas were 'consistently geometric' and his plans were 'generated by shapes that are divided into geometric sub-units, irrespective of modular proportions.'[85] In this way, Borromini developed a more flexible means of exploring different geometries that he used to generate new spatial relationships. These sentiments could be equally applied to Wright, and his abstraction of nature and the consistent use of a geometric planning module was thus another common point for both architects. Wright had used a similar abstraction of nature, using a hexagonal planning module to develop spatial continuity at the Hanna House, as had Figini and Pollini at the Olivetti Social Services Building. Similarly, for the Guggenheim, Wright adopted a circular planning module and generated an inverted ziggurat form. Its concentrated internal space with simple geometry seems a convincing manifestation of the baroque tradition. I would certainly concur with Zevi's provocative comparison and agree that it provides an innovative and playful interpretation of 'organic' architecture.

Looking more closely, there were certainly examples of baroque tendencies in Wright's early work. In the Unity Temple, the centrality and massiveness are emphasised, whilst for the Robie House, its elevation seems to be in a state of perpetual movement and distortion. Let us not forget his love of baroque music as well, a touchstone maintained for a lifetime. However, towards the end of his career, Wright displayed a bombastic tendency towards baroque-rococo designs such as the Baghdad Cultural Quarter scheme. Thus, by adopting a more baroque style at the end of his career, Wright contradicted his own principle of 'organic' architecture, by applying curious cultural motifs to ponderous circular masses.

Zevi's juxtaposition of Sant'Ivo and the Guggenheim provided another innovative narrative, namely the displacement of religion by the new 'cathedral' of culture, the art gallery. The baroque rhetoric of the Counter-Reformation had indeed found a natural successor in the iconic Guggenheim Museum. Cultural production, dissemination, display and commodification have become the new global tendency dominated by global institutions like the Guggenheim. More recently still, the MAXXI Museum in Rome (2010) marks the latest incarnation of Roman baroque combined with the iconic form, generated by one of the most fashionable star-architects, Zaha Hadid. The principles of spatial dynamics, manipulation, play of light, massiveness and grand scale are all represented here; Hadid certainly paid an inadvertent tribute to the baroque, Borromini and Wright. Furthermore, the curving and tilting walls within the MAXXI museum make exhibiting art as problematic as it was for the Guggenheim in New York. They share a similar iconic presence, except that one is set within a dynamic urban city, while the other is in a residential suburb. The sense of disruption is, however, possibly greater within suburban Rome than in central Manhattan. The global baroque rhetoric continues with the MAXXI; it demands to be heard, to be a global presence with or without art. The museum is the art, a global art form. It even led Pope Benedict XVI to complain to an audience of 500 design practitioners, including Daniel Libeskind and Zaha Hadid, 'that modern ideas of beauty were often 'illusory and deceitful, superficial and blinding, leaving the onlooker dazed.'[86] In other words, the museum was similar to the colonial baroque of the Catholic Church. The baroque is dead, long live the baroque!

6

A SHORT TAXI RIDE AROUND THE PERSIAN GULF

Frank Lloyd Wright's imagined and fantasy projects in the Middle East were prophetic of a search for architectural identity within the region around the Persian Gulf. Wright was a star-architect who claimed that he respected the architecture of the region, yet viewed the Orient as one entity and often muddled his way between Arabian and Persian precedents. For instance, he mused in his 1937 book, *Architecture and Modern Life: Some Aspects of the Past and Present of Architecture*: 'the opulent Arab wandered, striking his splendid, gorgeous tents to roam elsewhere. He learned much from the Persian; the Hindu, learning from the same origins.'[1] In addition, Wright often quoted his admiration for the tales of *The Arabian Nights* and, indeed, at Wright's home in Oak Park, there was an illustration from 'The Fisherman and the Genie' in the children's playroom.[2] Wright was so captivated by the stories that he identified himself as 'the young Aladdin' of the *Thousand and One Nights* in *An Autobiography* and recalled that a childhood 'party grew so real in his imagination, as he rubbed his lamp.'[3] Wright equated his own powers of creativity with Aladdin's, and the lamp became a symbol of his imagination.[4] So when Wright was invited to Baghdad in Iraq to design an opera house in January 1957, it was a chance to prove unequivocally his creative genius. Typically, he developed the project into a grander Cultural Quarter – an unrealisable personal fantasy, but prophetic of the fantastical schemes and the search for identity currently being undertaken on a lavish scale within the Persian Gulf.

THE ARABIAN PENINSULA

Wright reflected that Owen Jones was a founding influence on his architecture, alongside Viollet-le-Duc and Victor Hugo.[5] Jones's book *The Grammar of Ornament* (1856) represented an early imperialist and orientalist transcultural global encounter. While the images contained displayed the richness and variety of ornament beyond the known European precedents, I am always surprised that there was not a deeper analysis of the architecture that situated the ornament. Nevertheless, the book disseminated 'other' cultures to a wider audience of aesthetic thinkers and producers. Two such artists were Sullivan and Wright. They saw themselves as Celtic 'outsiders' who 'searched for an "other" culture with which to overcome the spiritual bankruptcy of the West' – and, indeed, it was believed that Celtic art had originated in the East.[6] The book also alerted the two architects to the richness and inventiveness of other cultures. Jones's book influenced these Chicago architects in such a way that they were inspired to use these new abstractions of nature to generate an architecture that reflected their own American culture and would, in time, become part of a great modern civilisation.

When reflecting on past architectures in *Architecture and the Modern Life* Wright attempted to remap ancient history to accord with his 'organic' manifesto.[7] He plotted a persuasive history of masonry construction, noting an admiration for the Byzantine arch that informed a 'sophisticated building act resulting in more sophisticated forms.'[8] He admired the method of restraining the arch with heavy walls, so that it could support a 'low, heavy, stone dome,'[9] of which 'St Sophia is the greatest remaining, but a late example.'[10] It is not known whether Wright ever visited Turkey to see Hagia Sophia but he did see the Byzantine cathedral at Monreale, Palermo, during his first journey to Europe in 1910.[11] His admiration for Hagia Sophia must have derived from secondary sources, such as Lethaby's book on *The Church of Sancta Sophia* (1894),[12] Wright waxed lyrically that in the 'domed buildings of Persia we see the Byzantine arch still at work.'[13] The Persians, according to Wright, were from the 'valley of the Euphrates and the Tigris.'[14] He thus confused the ancient civilisations of Mesopotamia with its later Persian conquest and subsequent Arab occupation. The blue colour of the dome captivated Wright too, and he claimed that it possessed a mystical power.[15] It is also tempting to speculate if Wright's evocation of the dome was derived from *Kubla Kahn* (1816) by Romantic poet Samuel Coleridge Taylor, in which 'the pleasure dome' becomes the symbol of harmony that 'combines ecclesiastical and secular architecture, palace and religious dome structures.'[16]

Wright muddled references when he returned to talk about his favourite hero: 'What mystic romance this Persia! Aladdin with the wonderful lamp? The wonderful lamp was Persian imagination.'[17] The tale of Aladdin had in fact been added to *The Arabian Nights* by the French translator, Galland. Within the first version of the story, Aladdin was actually Chinese and the setting for the story embraces an early global perspective that extended from China (perhaps Turkestan) in the East, to the Maghreb (North Africa) in the west.[18] For Wright, the Arab was the nomadic tent dweller who had learnt his architecture from the Persian, with 'terraces and domes of masonry or copper or gold . . . but [they] seemed to lack the pure and simple synthesis of form and clear pattern and colour achieved by the Persian.'[19] Wright's historical narrative then concludes with Persian architecture passing to 'China, Java, Bhutan, and Thibet by way of the Buddha.'[20] There are regional connections, and early global trading empires certainly overlapped in many of these regions. Wright believed that the work of the 'Chinese, Japanese, Persians and the Moors, Orientals all, developed a somewhat different sense of building.'[21] And whilst he respected these buildings, he also saw them all as essentially one 'Oriental' identity. To this Oriental sense of building, Wright ascribed 'plastic' qualities derived from the 'spirit,' meaning that consequently 'the building was treated more consistently as a unit or consistent whole.'[22] Thus, he believed that Oriental buildings were 'organic', and he used their alterity to dismiss the formal and 'classic' buildings of Greece and Rome.[23] More importantly, Wright was beginning to assemble a globalised 'organic' narrative that would, of course, situate him at its centre.

KUWAIT DETOUR

Following the Third Gulf War (2003), centred around Iraq, the country and wider region has remained notoriously unstable. Consequently, my field trip to Baghdad was never realised. In addition, the election in Iran in

June 2009 de-stabilised that country and a visit there was not considered advisable either. I was, however, able to visit Kuwait, Dubai and Abu Dhabi, and although not following directly in the footprints of Wright, I was still able to experience the region and to reflect on Wright's impact within these emerging cities. This, therefore, is a summary of my short and focused visit to the Arabian Peninsula in September 2009, in which I took taxi journeys to specific sites to provide a narrative about Wright's influence in Kuwait, Dubai, Abu Dhabi, and the wider Middle East region. The taxi was to be my sole means of transport and, as a friend had warned, it would also become a solace from the pervasive heat. At a peak of 41 degrees celsius, I was constantly looking for some shade and a cool interior.

The region of Mesopotamia was part of the 'fertile crescent' that linked the Persian Gulf to the Mediterranean Sea, and there was evidence of an advanced Mesopotamian civilisation on Failaka Island, near Kuwait, in 3000 BC.[24] Alexander the Great famously expanded his Greek empire eastwards during the third century BC, establishing a fortress on Failaka. Yet, Kuwait City on the mainland developed separately. Under the Islamic Caliphate, the town of Kathima was established at the end of Kuwait Bay, and it was invoked in a number of Arab histories, poems and songs.[25] Kuwait was probably in existence at this time, but it was really to gain prominence when the sheikhs of the Bani Khalid chose Kuwait as a summer resort in *c.*1670.[26] In 1756, a Danish explorer reported that the town had 10,000 inhabitants who lived on the produce of pearls and fishing, with a fleet of 800 sailing boats.[27] The name 'Kuwait' was derived from the Arabic for 'a small fort'[28] and its existence relied on connections back to the desert, together with sea commerce. Yet, as the town prospered, it became embroiled in more regional conflicts. The conquest of Basra by the Persians in 1776 led to Kuwait becoming the main Arab port at the head of the Persian Gulf.[29] In 1859, Kuwait signed a pact with the Ottoman Empire, but was somewhat wary of the latter's power, so in 1899 it signed a new treaty with Britain which gave greater protection to Kuwait's sea trade.[30]

In wake of the First World War, the defeat of Germany and its fellow Axis powers led to the break up of the already declining Ottoman Empire. Whilst Kuwait's borders were already fairly defined and strongly supported by Britain by this point, its newer neighbours tended to consist of amalgamations of different tribes and alliances within national borders, which had simply never existed previously. These new nations – Iraq, Iran and Saudi

Arabia – were engineered largely by the British Empire as an attempt to dilute Arab influence, a solution, which, unsurprisingly, has led to long-term instability in the region. This meant that Kuwait came under attack from neighbouring tribes in 1920, requiring the building of a new city wall to control the access to its capital city from the interior.

Kuwait City had hitherto been an excellent example of an integrated desert settlement with a protective outer wall, an organically ordered town plan formed by layers of accretion, close-knit low-rise buildings with narrow lanes, and a visibly democratic city in form, and structures generally no higher than two-storey. Even the mosques of Kuwait City were low-lying; in 1912 it was noted that 'they hardly show above the houses.'[31] The organic pattern within a Muslim urban settlement was never structured according to an overriding design ethos, but rather exhibited the well-formulated social structure whereby 'tradition' was the dominant principle.[32] It was a communal settlement, yet it lay within an established hierarchy that fitted into its coastal setting with an open seafront and a protective outer wall to the desert. The most prominent homes were the merchant homes on the seafront, with smaller homes behind, and the area beyond the city wall was inhabited by migrant workers and Bedouin.[33] The form of the settlement developed incrementally in response to traditional concerns for 'custom, ownership, and the Muslim's right to visual privacy.'[34] In addition, Kuwait City was a settlement that was 'vernacular, anonymous, spontaneous, rural,' that had an imbedded 'organic' character.[35] Within the city most of the homes retained a simple blank façade, with only the decorated timber doorway indicating the status of the homeowner, some of these doors being particularly intricate. With its mud-wall construction, Kuwait remained a peripheral settlement, lacking an informed urban society and any traces of sophisticated architecture culture. Despite this lack of material culture, Kuwaiti identity was derived from verbal and traditional cultural sources that were recorded in poetry, religion, and tribal hierarchy.[36] Such non-material aspects were at odds with the 20th century.

By 1950, Kuwait's population had grown to 150,000, of which almost half were immigrant workers, and traffic congestion was becoming acute. This led the Kuwaiti government in 1951 to address the material construction of the organic city and commissioned British architects; Minoprio, Spencely and Macfarlane (MSP) to prepare a masterplan. This modernist vision for Kuwait City was based on the British New Town precedent, with a new road network, clear zoning for different uses, and a protective 'green belt.' MSP had recently completed the plan for Crawley in West Sussex, with Minoprio admitting: 'We didn't know anything much about the Muslim world and the Kuwaitis wanted a new city . . .'[37] And what they got from the masterplan was: 'primarily a road plan.'[38] Another aspect of Kuwait's new city plan that tied it to the New Town movement in Britain was the role of a new kind of welfare state: Kuwait's oil revenue provided a new paternal educational, health and housing provision for its residents as a birth right. Kuwait City gained independence in 1961 and its urban growth continued. By 1970 its population was 733,000, of which only 47 per cent were Kuwaiti. Hence, a second masterplan was commissioned, but this time around, neither the design process nor the resulting masterplan proved at all successful. Indigenous Kuwaiti architects and planners were now beginning to question the wisdom of Westernisation. Jamal, a local architect lamented in 1973: 'Traditional Kuwaiti character will not be reflected in the new urban and physical environment, while the traditional environment will deteriorate further . . . Generally speaking, Kuwait should not assume that economic growth equals, or automatically brings, personal social happiness. The Kuwaitis' way of life should not be geared to consumption or wasteful living as seen in the West.'[39] Yet urbanisation and Westernisation continued, with additional masterplans that contributed to the destruction of the old democratic building fabric of Kuwait City, so that all that now remains are old isolated relics and ephemeral poetry of a lost city.

I had booked a room at the Ghani Palace Hotel (2002) by Saleh Al Mutawa. It was modelled on a conventional Yemeni townhouse, with white-washed walls, inset coloured glass, intricately detailed timber screens and balconies, projecting timber joists and water spouts. Inside, its thin atrium alluded to a traditional alleyway, with an open arcade of shops and projecting screened balconies giving it a nostalgic cultural representation. Al Mutawa's work is said to embody a Kuwaiti traditional architecture that is part of a wider Arabic consciousness.[40] I couldn't help feeling that the hotel was like staying at Wright's Imperial Hotel in Tokyo because of the heightened sense of cultural intensity. From my bright two-storey studio room on the sixth floor, I viewed Kuwait City confronting the Persian Gulf, but a six-lane motorway mediated the connection – a legacy of the city designed for the highway.

Detail of elevation and upper tower to Ghani Palace Hotel (2002) by Saleh Al Mutawa

The next morning, I met with Dr Yasser Mahgoub of Kuwait University at the classically inspired Central Mall, which sits next to the Ghani Palace Hotel. He kindly offered to drive me to a museum of my choice, and so we agreed to visit the Tareq Rajab Museum. We passed a cluster of water towers en route, designed as giant representations of palm trees, and often grouped together as if to form an oasis. It is a brilliant idea for retaining water, with genuine architectural presence in their conception and scale, and I was thrilled to see them by the roadside. These water towers even had a passing reference to Wright's dendriform columns in the Johnson Wax Administration Building.[41] In addition, they both carried out similar functions, the water towers stored water, whilst in the Johnson building the columns acted as downpipes for rain water. But Wright's columns have a pin-joint at their base, so that they would have toppled over in Kuwait!

The Rajab Museum was located along the fifth circular highway in the Jabriya district – House 22 in Block 12 on Street 5, to be precise – and we got lost for a short time whilst negotiating the suburb. The museum sits beside an imposing villa that exhibits the most Islamic character on the street with projecting screened rooms displaying an Islamic pattern and heavily decorated timber doors. In stark contrast the museum was hidden within a basement, and at street level it had a well-decorated ornamental door with two guards outside. They opened the door for us and we proceeded down the stairs to the basement where the artefacts were displayed. It was the basement setting that had saved the museum during the Iraqi occupation of 1990–91: apparently, they could not find it in all the chaos. These were perhaps the hidden remnants of Kuwaiti culture. There was an eclectic mix of high quality artefacts from across the Islamic world, in terms of garments, jewellery, pottery, guitars, old doors, firearms and antique copies of the Koran. We discussed Wright's legacy in the region and questioned whether there were any 'organic' inspired designs within Kuwait City. Dr Mahgoub did not believe there were any Wright-inspired buildings in Kuwait. I then asked him about the planning of the city and its dispersed motorised suburbs, did they bear any relation to Wright's Broadacre City? He replied:

> No, not at all; here the city planning was based on the Garden City typology, not Broadacre. But I think that the Mile High Tower by Wright was a concept that has caught on in the Gulf with the Burj Dubai, and now there is a 1001-metre tower proposed for the new Silk City scheme in Kuwait. The size of that tower is inspired by the 1001 tales from the *Arabian Nights*.[42]

It was very interesting to hear about the 1001-metre (3284-foot) tower proposal in Kuwait as Wright was such a fan of *The Arabian Nights* and he would have loved to make such a tower himself in the Middle East. Yet, despite the fondness for citing the Garden City[43] as the inspiration for Kuwait, the city developed as a typical 'City on the Highway,' possessing all of the 'four main foundations' for a motorised suburb: new roads to open up more land, zoned land uses, government-provided mortgages, and a population boom.[44] Wright often eulogised about the virtues of America's road network, declaring that 'along these grand roads as through veins and arteries comes and goes the throng of building and living in the Broadacre City of the Twentieth Century.'[45] As such, it represented a particularly American viewpoint about travel, democracy, freedom, and architecture's role within them. As Wright proclaimed, the city of the future could be 'everywhere and nowhere.'[46] I would contend that Kuwait is now similarly affected by possessing a suburban condition which lacks any identity specific to its geographical location or environmental conditions.

Some authors argued convincingly that Broadacre City attempted to attain an 'oriental paradise garden'[47] whilst Wright claimed that it was a 'democratic' expression of the future – but neither of these ideals were visible in Kuwait. Its suburbs had no engagement with the landscape; they were just Westernised villas dominating the whole plot with congested roads full of parked cars. They were drab and colourless without any metaphorical garden or greenery. In addition, only affluent Kuwaitis are allowed to own property, so there is no underlying egalitarian ethos. Kuwait City is thus divided between the affluent suburbs for the Kuwaitis and an abandoned city centre for the migrant poor, and the neglected desert for the Bedouin and the other nomads. The city neatly summarises the inequality of globalisation within the region, whereby the indigenous Arabs enjoy the benefits of oil wealth, whilst the migrant and the nomad are all but excluded. It also underlines the narrowness of Wright's vision for Broadacre City, which required a broad based property-owning democracy to support its agrarian vision. However, it may also be claimed that Broadacre was the ultimate subversive architecture of change, which challenges the inequities of contemporary Kuwait to achieve a lasting inclusive democratic solution.

On Friday morning I decided to visit the largest market in Kuwait, which inevitably was a taxi ride away, beside the fourth arterial roadway. Turning off the motorway, the taxi negotiated a vast car park and I was dropped off beside a row of unassuming beige metal sheds. Beneath the high canopy, the market was divided into several areas, each specialising in certain goods. The haberdashery sector had a vivid collection of drapery and curtains of the most intense colours, reminiscent of a scene from the *Arabian Nights*: I imagined that behind each curtain, a new Arabian adventure could unfold. Other parts of the market were far more mundane, a wall of washing powders that Andy Warhol would have enjoyed, a vast collection of brass kettles and perfume bottles. Yet, there was a real excitement around the crowded market: it was noisy and animated with lots of shouting and pushing. Wright believed that the roadside market was an emergent urban condition for the city on the highway and, in Kuwait, the vast Friday market was certainly a great spectacle that possessed a real sense of community. The transience and mobility of the Friday market was reminiscent of the caravanserai of the past, but it also reflected the present city on the highway, as well as pointing to dispersed city of the future.

Following on from the first urban masterplans, there was also a concerted effort within Kuwait to design individual 'architectural' buildings that would enhance the urban vision. These architectural insertions were directed jointly by two architects, the Englishman, Leslie Martin, and the Italian, Franco Albini.[48] One of the projects that they orchestrated was the National Assembly Building (1985) by Jorn Utzon. The architect had come to prominence by winning the design competition for the Sydney Opera House, but Wright had been scathing in his review of the edifice, calling it a 'reckless design . . . [with] neither rhyme [nor] reason,'[49] seeing it as an 'inorganic fantasy.'[50] Wright's criticism, though, must be balanced against his towering ego and sense of entitlement. Naturally, he believed that such a prominent design should have been given to him by right. I have always felt that Utzon followed a Scandinavian or 'Nordic' tradition of 'organic' architecture, and I was keen to see his icon of European democracy in Kuwait. The next day, I took a taxi to Arabian Gulf Street, with the heat gradually waning in the evening and a breeze coming off the Gulf. The Kuwait Assembly Building was now closed to tourists, and fortified with high railings and security guards within pillboxes. From the opposite side of the four-lane highway that makes up the Arabian Gulf Street, I took some photographs of the sweeping canopy and noted a future extension being made to the Assembly.

The Kuwait Assembly Building was funded by the increased revenue from oil during the 1970s. Utzon's winning design sought to reflect aspects of 'traditional Arabic' architecture such as the nomad's tent, the internal souk and the covered square.[51] Yet there were a few contradictions. For example, was the bold, sweeping entry canopy merely a simplistic Western reference to an Arabic tent[52] or was it a tacit acknowledgement of the Emir's Bedouin past? Moreover, the tent is traditionally a transitory element, usually black or brown, and not a ponderous white reinforced-concrete construction, as it is here.[53] Wright was also guilty of propagating this rather narrow view of Arabia: as noted, he often marvelled at the 'Arab and their wonderful tents.'[54] The National Assembly was planned about a central street that was based on a traditional bazaar that linked the parliament to the covered square and the Gulf beyond. To support democratic participation, Utzon designed a covered plaza, a typically Western symbol of democracy.

Interestingly, the original scheme had a mosque placed beside the democratic square, and beneath the sweeping canopy, giving it some relevance as a place of congregation.[55] But for some, the remade Bedouin tent and the covered square has become a 'monumental carport . . . [where] leaders meet their chauffeurs.'[56] The National Assembly is nonetheless seen as a progressive statement within the Persian Gulf and, despite the various contradictions, great care was taken after the hostile invasion by Iraq to restore its image.

I considered the National Assembly to be a successful integration of 'organic' architecture into the Persian Gulf, with its democratic open plan and abstracted low-level elevation. Furthermore, it attempts to foster wider democratic participation and its prominent location means that it acts as a focus for any discontent. Within the National Assembly, gradual change has been achieved: in 2005, women were allowed to vote; in 2006, the roles of Crown Prince and Prime Minister were separated; and in 2009, three women Members of Parliament were elected. The voting base has been expanded, but even so, only about 10 per cent of the Kuwaiti population of 3 million are currently allowed to vote. The recent 'Arab Spring' has resulted in a number of demonstrations with some calling for a new prime minister, but not a change of regime, and likewise Bedouins have called for improved rights.[57] These protests were appeased by legislators promising to look at civil rights, and so seemingly a reduced form of democracy does function within Kuwait.

DUBAI

I arrived in the evening at the cavernous and glitzy Terminal 3 at Dubai International Airport (2008). Its scale and ambition certainly made Kuwait seem totally provincial by comparison. There was a short queue at the tourist visa booth, and I had one of my few encounters with an indigenous resident. I searched the airport for a station on the newly inaugurated Dubai Metro system. But not everything was going to plan. At the metro station, despite displaying the presence of two new metro lines, only ten stops on one of the lines were actually in operation. I joined the other confused tourists and migrant workers around the ticket booths trying to buy economy-class tickets. Curiously, there were two tickets types that divided the passengers between Gold (residents) at the front carriages with leather seats, and Economy (migrants) to be seated on the plastic seats behind. Once we were on board, the excited passengers began to take photographs of each other using their mobile phones: it was a very touching shared experience. While this particular journey went smoothly, significant problems have plagued the metro system, and in a good-humoured article, the local English-language paper, *The National*, challenged four reporters to cross the city using various transport options. The winner, unsurprisingly, was the reporter who used their car, followed by the taxi, then the metro (which had broken down), and finally the bus.[58]

The following morning, I explored the old settlement around Dubai Creek. What was once the old fort now had a basement extension, which contained Dubai Museum. It was sun-baked upstairs and blissfully cool downstairs. In the museum, I followed a path around several Arabian experiences, including a Bedouin tent, small workshops, a fishing dhow, a pearl diver and a gift shop. As the most urbanised Emirate, Dubai has a population of 1.5 million and its second largest income is from oil. The city has expanded beyond all recognition from the once modest settlement to embrace international shipping, property development and tourism. Ideally situated between London and Hong Kong (it is a seven-hour flight to both cities), Dubai can justly claim to be at the crossroads between east and west.

The Bastakai quarter was nearby, with a collection of traditional homes turned into cafés, restaurants, galleries and administration centres. Wandering around its narrow, empty alley was a slightly unnerving experience. These 'traditional' Dubai houses have plain façades, only the occasional simple door or projecting screened balcony, no windows, and a profusion of wind towers with projecting timbers at each corner. They were finished in a uniform light brown, earthen hue. Inside these renovated homes were common courtyards with either a tree and or a cloth cover to offer shade from the sun. Despite this being a manipulated tourist experience, these courtyard spaces were evocative of an obsolete lifestyle. Until, that is, I came to one house which had a bank of metal louvres that hid a mechanical chilling plant, and the illusion of a return to courtyard housing and 'organic' planning was instantly dispelled.

The recreated district in Bastakai exemplifies two general concepts that epitomise Islamic architecture: the absence of any specific building form and a focus on the interior space.[59] Consequently, Islamic architecture is hidden behind a static frontage that does not reveal any specific function or status. Internally, there are often oblique turns upon entry, and the plan is the result of accretion, thus displaying the 'principle of organic growth.'[60] Similarly, Frank

Lloyd Wright was to develop these basic elements of Islamic architecture in his own work, particularly the internalised inner space and free planning. Several scholars have identified the internally concentrated spaces within Wright's architecture, especially his non-residential designs which, in his case, were largely derived from Japanese architecture.[61] Wright used thick enveloping masonry walls to separate occupants from the city and to define his internal spaces. In this, there are clear spatial similarities with traditional Islamic space, but Wright never acknowledged any such link. Although his informal planning seems similar to the Islamic tradition of adding spaces, Wright underpinned his spatial plans with a carefully controlled planning module that was again taken from Japan and the tatami mat method of planning.

The importance of the interior space in Islamic architecture is articulated by its all-enveloping decoration, which creates a 'non-tectonic' surface, so that the walls and roof that support the room are negated visually.[62] Tiles and mosaics with abstracted geometry, floral patterns and calligraphy[63] contribute to achieving this concept of space that is very different from Western spatial concepts. Wright's work sought such an integrated ideal, and he developed the Textile Block construction as a means to unite a number of long standing concerns. Firstly, the blocks could be mass-produced by the machine – thus attaining his early aspirations for 'The Art and Craft of the Machine' (1901). It was cheap to build and thus egalitarian; and the inscribed abstract pattern was a fusion of nature and culture.[64] Essentially, the construction involved the on-site assembly of textile blocks with steel wires acting as reinforcement to support the blocks and the wall. Their first proposed use was in the desert setting of Death Valley for Albert M. Johnson (1921), but it was not used in construction until the Millard House (1923), also in California. Yet the textile tile had two distinctive identities: 'the otherworldly, Xanadu-like grandeur' of Wright's grand schemes in the desert of America, and 'the down-to-earth, democratic economy' of his single residential schemes.[65] The textile block was a brilliant abstraction of Owen Jones's *Grammar of Ornament*, to form a wonderfully animated surface to support a new spatial experience. Furthermore, it could be argued that Wright's 'Text-tile tectonic' was to reach its pinnacle in Broadacre City: 'an infinite "oriental rug" as a cross-cultural, ecological tapestry writ large, as an oriental paradise garden combined with the Cartesian grid of the occident.'[66]

In nearby Tehran, Wright designed the Amery House (1957) for his former student, Nezam Amery. The Amery family was part of the ruling elite in Iran before Shah Reza Pahlavi came to power: thereafter, Nezam Amery sought his education in America and came to know Wright's work and even joined the Taliesin community. Amery assisted Wright's design for the Greater Baghdad scheme (1957–8) and also contributed to the design of his new family house. The Amery House was based on the Millard House (1923–4), but it was rescaled to metric dimensions.[67] The plan attempted to update the traditional Islamic dwelling with an open ground floor, a formal living space with a balcony on the first floor, and the private bedrooms on the second floor. Furthermore, it was claimed that the home was made intentionally narrow to allow for cross ventilation, although I would question whether that was ever used following the advent of affordable air-conditioning. The internal planning articulated the emergent progressive, Westernised middle-class sensibilities and the use of Wright's textile block reflected his admiration of 'Persian' masonry, endorsing the Textile-Block system as a combination of Islamic text and texture.[68] Indeed it was the ideal choice of material. However, it was also yet another imported cultural aesthetic and technology from America, and another example of Wright's global ambitions for his architecture. Furthermore, the use of such a highly decorated façade also represented a denial of a traditional Islamic dwelling with its plain façade.

Back in Dubai, I caught a taxi to the landmark Burj Khalifa. We pulled off the highway into an underground car park and entered the luxurious world of the Dubai Mall, complete with its ice rink, cinema, aquarium, restaurants (then all closed for Ramadan), clothing shops and department stores. It was a fully integrated leisure destination, carefully controlled, both climatically and socially – an escapist dream from the scorching sun and desert. At the information desk, I was told that the best view of Burj Khalifa – still unfinished when I was there – was from the Star Atrium, but even from this viewpoint, it was impossible to contain the soaring tower within my camera viewfinder. Having the world's tallest building carries a certain status that Dubai obviously craves. The Burj Khalifa Tower is 829 metres (2720 feet) tall, the ultimate expression of global identity, branding and boasting. It was designed by the global American architectural practice, Skidmore, Owings & Merrill (SOM), built by migrant labourers from poor emerging nations, and constructed in the Middle East for offices and apartments that may well be occupied by a multitude of nationalities. It is a contemporary Tower of Babel built on sand! It is the first time the world's tallest building has been

Burj Khalifa Tower, Dubai, United Arab Emirates (2010) by Skidmore, Owings and Merrill

Mile High Office Tower, 'The Illinois', Chicago, Illinois (1957) by Frank Lloyd Wright

located in Arabia since 1311, when the spire of Lincoln Cathedral overtook the Great Pyramid of Giza. There was a similar ambivalence towards the cheap labour used to build these ancient and modern symbols of power and, even in the 21st century, some Arabians have claimed that 'we need slaves to build monuments.'[69] There are several hundreds of thousands of migrant workers living on low wages in congested work camps within the UAE, which certainly questions the integrity of these architectural monuments. In addition, the environmental cost is great, as Dubai possesses the highest per-capita carbon footprint in the world. Before it opened in 2010, there was dramatic change of name from the Burj Dubai to Burj Khalifa Tower – an acknowledgement that the nearby Emirate of Abu Dhabi (under the rule of Sheikh Khalifa bin Zayed al-Nahyan) had effectively bailed out Dubai when the latter was unable to pay back its short-term loans and was becoming crippled by its own debt during the global recession. It is a dubious monument to anything other than debt-fuelled avarice and ego.

Wright's Mile High Tower (1957) was undoubtedly prophetic of the present need to build ever taller towers, as Dr Mahgoub had mentioned to me in Kuwait.[70] The Burj Khalifa is certainly similar to the Mile High Tower with its triangulated plan, diminishing mass and a stepped profile. It was said that Wright's initial brief had been to design a television antennae, but that he had developed it into a tower that would contain 'all Illinois state government offices and consolidate commercial, governmental, and civic functions.'[71] Furthermore, Wright claimed it 'would mop up what now remains of urbanism to leave us free to do Broadacre.'[72] It was a curious building for Wright to design, as he often denigrated the city and the skyscraper. However, it makes more sense when one relates it to the parable of the Tower of Babel.

The idea of the tower has long captivated the human condition and has long been part of a fantasy architecture, with the ancient Babylonians creating tall structures that were in 'harmony with the universe and reminder of human limits.'[73] In the medieval period the tower became an 'architectural vision' which symbolised power and security, particularly in the hill towns of northern Italy.[74] But it was during the Renaissance that the Tower of Babel was to become 'a model of for architects . . . as a self-contained miniature city, a vertical city within the city.'[75] Following the Industrial Revolution, the Renaissance ideal became reality in America, with Louis Sullivan, Wright and others struggling to give the behemoth an architectural identity. Thus, Wright's

Mile High Tower can be seen as a reaction to commercial, government and civic institutions and to a universal modern architecture. For Wright, the Mile High Tower was to be an asylum for bankers, civil servants and academics. And it was also a critique of the universal language of the 'International Style' architecture that sought to impose a single architectural language. Wright's tower was a rich brocade of glass and copper, and not the severe language of international modernism. More importantly, his tower was pushed to the ultimate dimension of one mile – a symbolic height that implied infinity and immortality, and hence it was a prototypical legacy project.

ABU DHABI

At Dubai bus station, there was a queue of migrant workers waiting for a bus to Abu Dhabi. They were the marginalised occupants of the city without the essential symbol of freedom – the car. Following a crush at the coach door, I was lucky to get onto the bus and find a seat. Beside me was a Filipino worker who was visiting his sister in Abu Dhabi. He slept for most of the journey, but was very cheerful and chatty when he awoke. In fact, most of the passengers immediately drew their curtains and fell asleep. Being a tourist, I kept mine open to view the desert beyond. But there was hardly any break in the linear urban sprawl, as we duly passed through the Internet City, power stations, docks, billboards advertising new developments, and fenced-off areas that were perhaps the infamous labour camps for migrant workers. As we approached the city of Abu Dhabi, I glimpsed a mixture of new architectural icons, the new Grand Prix racing track (2009), the circular high-rise Aldar Headquarters (2010), and the Grand Mosque (2007). But Abu Dhabi bus station was somewhat dated, with a number of repeated arches supporting a roof canopy. Indeed, it reminded me of Wright's Marin County Civic Center (1957–70) building with its repeated arch motif. I waited patiently in the searing heat for a taxi, while reading the many advertisements for shared apartments and bedrooms for migrants.

As the richest Emirate, Abu Dhabi has a population of 1.6 million with the largest land mass and the greatest oil reserves. Its citizens are amongst the very wealthiest on the globe. The city consists of number of islands that are connected by road bridges and a rationalist grid divides these islands into real estate parcels. Under the rule of Sheikh Khalifa bin Zayed al-Nahyan, the city attempts to be everything that Dubai is not. Yet, property development remains a cornerstone of the overall economic vision for Abu Dhabi, which includes other 'niches,' such as the financial sector, business conferences, international media, sports and tourism.[76]

My first destination was the old fort, but it was closed for restoration: the National Library and Cultural Centre (1978–81) designed by The Architects' Collaborative, however, was open. It was a successful modern interpretation of an Arabic building and was modelled on the fort typology and built with massive perimeter walls, which enclosed an open courtyard with a perimeter arcade. The walls had discrete openings and were finished with exposed concrete, and their arches were lined with magnificent blue tiles. The main entry gate was closed, so I entered from the car park into a covered arcade lined with boutique shops which led to the main open courtyard with its fountain and the formal entrance to the Cultural Centre. Inside the centre there was a similar play of materials with finished concrete, expanses of decorative tiles and dark-stained timber detailing. I was hoping to view the exhibition on Saadiyat Island, but the ground floor was deserted, so I ventured upstairs to look around. At the landing I was confronted by a black Bedouin tent with a number of women weaving gifts. It was an unsettling scene, a tent within an air-conditioned space and the women themselves seemed ill at ease with the spectacle. They were there as living artefacts within the Cultural Centre, a defeated nomadic culture on display. Beyond was an open gallery that displayed more cultural artefacts, which included model boats, doors and keys. There was an air of lethargy, with no exhibitions running during Ramadan. I enquired about the Saadiyat Island exhibition and the guard suddenly became animated. He told me to visit the Emirates Palace Hotel – a 'beautiful building,' he enthused, where apparently 'I would wear out my camera taking photographs!' It did not seem appropriate to say that I rather liked the Cultural Centre too.

At the bus stop, I had another long wait, which I passed by reading the personal advertisements posted there. Giving up on the bus I eventually secured a taxi and we navigated the gridded city towards the dramatic 'corniche,' with its glimpses of the sandy bay and the Persian Gulf beyond. The city was intimate and the buildings appeared dated: it felt like a regional centre with an air of neglect. As I approached the Emirates Palace Hotel, I recognised a triumphal arch with a large image of the ruling family. The hotel itself had a strangely civic character and the scale and architecture was reminiscent of Mughal architecture of Pakistan or India. Inside, it was very polished and I attempted to tidy myself up to look more presentable (I didn't want to get thrown out for looking poor). Despite its claim to be a people's palace, the hotel seemed more exclusive than inclusive to me. At the reception, I was ushered towards the exhibition spaces and, at another long desk, four receptionists greeted me, and an overly eager Australian woman offered to show me around. She proceeded to recap the official view of the scheme and I listened attentively whilst she proudly explained the five sections of the exhibition: introduction, inspiration, context, masterplan, and cultural vision – with detailed models and drawings of the four new cultural icons. She introduced the concept of the Cultural Quarter on the island, the careful analysis contained within the masterplan, and the 'four pearls' by the latest star-architects: the Guggenheim Abu Dhabi by Frank Gehry; the Louvre Abu Dhabi by Jean Nouvel; the Performing Arts Centre by Zaha Hadid; and the Maritime Museum by Tadao Ando.[77]

According to the marketing information, the 27 square kilometres (16¾ square miles) Saadiyat Island development comprise seven themed experiences, which include the Cultural Quarter, Al Marina, Saadiyat Beach, Saadiyat Promenade, Saadiyat Reserve, Saadiyat Lagoon and South Beach.[78] The expected total population of 150,000 on the island would be similar to those living in Hollywood or Oxford. The description of the concept recalls a set of random global spatial experiences and each district will be marketed as an already existing identity – South Beach in Saadiyat would be like Daytona Beach in Florida, for example.[79] Within the Cultural Quarter, the 'four pearls' are to be located on their own man-made island which projects into the Gulf and looks back towards Abu Dhabi. The masterplan also intends to support a biennale modelled on the Venice model, and a new university is planned with an academy of fine arts focussed on teaching Arab students.[80] Whilst the expansionist Guggenheim Museum has no difficulty in subscribing to another global franchise, there were 5000 French petitioners objecting to sale of the Louvre overseas rights – it was claimed that the Louvre was paid $548m just for the privilege of using its name.[81] Underlying the whole concept was the premise that Abu Dhabi was a global brand, that culture was a commodity that could be freely traded, and that tourists would willingly fly to Abu Dhabi to experience an Arabian setting for Western art.

In nearby Iraq back in 1957, there was a similar attempt to remake the city of Baghdad as a Western cultural enclave. Iraq had nationalised oil after the Second World War and a development board was inaugurated in 1950 to distribute its newly acquired wealth. Whilst the first six-year plan (1951–6) focused on providing infrastructure and institution buildings, the second six-year plan (1955–60) included cultural representations such as the royal palace, the house of parliament and the Iraqi Museum.[82] In particular, the Hashemite rulers sought to maintain their power and to dispel any insurrection, so that 'visible' development became a priority to show that the vast oil income was being fairly distributed.[83] A Development Board pamphlet in 1957 described the aspirations of the state, which included plans for Walter Gropius to design the university, Le Corbusier to design the stadium, Alvar Aalto to design the museum and Gio Ponti to design the office building headquarters of the Development Board.[84] Wright was not initially included in the list, but a musical expert, Abdul Jabbar Chalabi, recommended Wright for a new Opera House[85] and another supporter, Muhammed Fadhel al-Jamali, impressed upon the Americans the need to engage with a wider cultural exchange with Iraq. Consequently, a performance from the Minneapolis Symphony Orchestra in a garden beside the river in 1957 began to consolidate the emergent relationship.[86] Thus, the Iraqi monarch was engaged in a careful balancing act to prove their commitment to nation building whilst also being embroiled in political machinations.

The designs by Gropius, Le Corbusier, Aalto and Ponti were all in the dominant 'International Style' architecture of the period, and were derived from previous schemes with the addition of superficial solar shading to guard against the omnipresent sun. This multinational approach was common amongst architects in the 1950.[87] However, Wright claimed a different inspiration from the *Arabian Nights* and, when addressing architects and engineers in Baghdad, he stated he was 'one of the 'subjects' of Harun Al-Rashid (the 5th Caliph).[88] Wright called on Iraqis to 'preserve your own spiritual integrity according to great oriental philosophies.' He also claimed that the greatest inspiration of his life was Lao-Tze.[89] Furthermore, he said that the designs for Baghdad 'demonstrate that if we are able to understand and interpret our ancestors, there is no need to copy them' – and he also warned against adopting 'the materialistic structures called "modern" now barging in from the West upon the East.'[90] Thus, Wright viewed Iraq in the 1950s in the same light as he did Japan in 1913, equating the 'Orient' with one vast related identity, possessing an indigenous culture that he alone could expose and recover. The proposed opera house was to be an updated

Imperial Hotel, an intense Wrightian manifestation of universal culture. Wright saw himself as the visionary 'white agent' once more in the Orient. When introducing his scheme in a 1957 issue of *Architectural Forum*, the editor proclaimed: 'For Frank Lloyd Wright, here was a chance to demonstrate what he had tried to teach in Japan and to preach in the US – that a great culture deserves not only an architecture of its time, but of its own.'[91]

During Wright's visit to Baghdad in May 1957, he saw the site for the opera house in the old city, but then contrived to nominate an island on the Tigris River as an alternative location. He made no reference to experiencing the old city, the sights, smells or heat. Instead, as part of a typical modernist narrative, Wright identified his new site on Pig Island whilst flying over the city on his approach (a metaphorical flying-carpet view of the city).[92] Pig Island was a low-lying island to the south of the city that was prone to the Tigris's seasonal flooding, and was so called because only the marginalised swine were allowed to inhabit it. Having secured the use of Pig Island during an audience with King Faisal II, Wright typically then expanded the commission into a much larger plan for Greater Baghdad. It was a full-scale cultural assault on the capital that consisted of:

> the opera house doubling as a civic auditorium, a landscaped park with fountains and cascading waterfalls, a three-tiered parking ziggurat, museums for both monumental ancient sculpture and contemporary art, a grand bazaar, the King Faisal Esplanade, various bridges, big and small, lined with shops, a monument to Harun al-Rashid, a botanical garden and zoological park, a casino and amphitheatre, a university complex, and several radio and television towers.[93]

In addition, Wright secured the design commission for the new Post and Telegraph Building in the old city, making it a particularly remarkable and fruitful client meeting. On his return, Wright shared some doubts about the scheme with his associates – but, despite this, he proceeded to develop a personal fantasy that would be the culmination of his 60 years in practice.[94]

Wright's Plan for Greater Baghdad represented a singular vision for the identity of the city. He assumed the mantle of cultural arbiter as the original brief for an opera house became a full-blown Arabian myth. Yet, Wright was following a well trodden path, 'fantasy architecture,' involves 'reconstructed pasts, ruined presents and fantasy futures,'[95] and Wright acknowledged a rich heritage, citing the ancient region of Mesopotamia, and dedicating his drawings 'to Sumeria, Isin, Lars and Babylon.'[96] In addition, the court life of Harun Al-Rashid that was parodied in the *Arabian Nights* became a recurring theme for Wright[97] as myth, archaeology, architecture, and urbanism became entwined. As for the present, Wright stated that 'instead of flood or invasion, Baghdad is threatened by the increasing thousands of motor cars.'[98] This was a starting point for any urban analysis by Wright, in that the control of traffic was the means by which he developed urban plans. Yet Wright did not acknowledge the diversity of Iraq that was then composed of three old Ottoman provinces: Mosul to the north; Basra to the south; and Baghdad in the centre. Rather, he supported the imposed rule of the Hashemite. Thus, having invoked the historical past, and all but rubbished the present, Wright was ready to act out the fantasy. He was perhaps uniquely placed to deliver such a project considering his previous work in America, and his own mythical resurrection in the fields of Wisconsin and then the desert of Arizona.

Wright designed a number of fantastical schemes during his career, and he took on the persona of Aladdin to realise these magical projects. In *An Autobiography*, recalling the design of Midway Gardens in 1913, Wright could not contain his excitement as he imagined the brief and became a Midwestern Aladdin:

> Well, Aladdin and his wonderful lamp had fascinated me as a boy. But by now I knew the enchanting young Arabian was really just a symbol for creative desire, his lamp intended for another symbol – imagination. As I sat listening I was Aladdin. Young Ed? The genie. He knew apparently where all 'the slaves of the lamp' could be found. Well, this might all be necromancy but I believed in magic. Had I not rubbed my lamp with what seemed wonderful effect, before this? I didn't hesitate.[99]

The Barnsdall Cultural Centre (1916–21) (also known as the Hollyhock House) in Los Angeles, was another fantasy scheme, but one that was to be built in the land of make-believe: Hollywood. A block away from the Barnsdall site was the set for the film *Intolerance* (1916) by D. W. Griffith, a Babylonian fantasy.[100] In this way, Nebuchadnezzar and Babylon were literally next door.[101] This had a certain resonance for Wright's project, as the Barnsdall House and an extensive Cultural Centre (focused on the theatre) was developed into a 'monument.' Barnsdall encouraged Wright to 'put your freest dreams into it, won't you?'[102] Thus, Wright generated a new distinctive 'theatrical' identity in the 'desert of shallow effects,'[103] as he called Los Angeles. Despite the great prose and a remarkable abstract composition, these two 'entertainment' designs were given a classical symmetrical plan and spatial articulation, which proved a disappointing basis onto which Wright projected his freest fantasies.

During his professional estrangement that began in 1909, Wright had found work in Japan and California, but he also began to experience the distinctive quality of the American desert. He discovered this landscape while travelling across the continent from his home in Wisconsin to the west coast of America for voyages to Japan and to set up a new practice in the Sunshine State, following his Barnsdall commission. Charting his own Biblical narrative arc, Wright's career was resurrected by his encounter with the deserts of south-western United States. His desert schemes envigorated his architecture as he found a new freedom there. His architecture became more abstract and playful, as 'Usonia' became his new architectural language. One of his less well-known desert schemes was the rich geometric design for Six Beach Cottages / Tents on the Beach (1927), at Ras-el-Bar in Damietta, Egypt, a beach resort 48 kilometres (30 miles) west of Port Said and the Suez Canal. The single drawing sketch for the design shows six cottages arranged around a circular plan, with each cottage was rotated 60 degrees from its neighbours. Each cottage had a square plan laid out on a three-foot module concrete base, yet above was a playful origami-like structure made of prefabricated timber and canvas. The cottages emerged from this primal geometry into small shelters. They were bolted to a permanent concrete raft foundation and designed to be disassembled each year during the spring floods. The designs revealed a playful use of temporary lightweight structures set within a strict geometrical frame – perhaps even inspired by Islamic geometry and patterns? The cottages were a precursor to Wright's Ocatilla Desert Camp where Wright fully expressed his newly found freedom. The Octillla camp that Wright constructed in the Arizona desert, whilst he was designing his San Marcos in the Desert (1928–9) resort, was a startling statement of intent, with its free geometrical form and undulating façade.

Thus, Wright's entertainment projects and his 'desert rebirth' were points of departure for his ultimate Baghdad 'fantasy,' whereby he claimed inspiration from the original eighth-century circular 'City of Peace' within Baghdad, which he wrongly claimed was designed by Harun Al-Rashid[104] (it was in fact Al-Mansur). Nevertheless, the imposed idea of circular geometry dominated the project. Wright believed that traffic congestion could be alleviated by enhanced ziggurat traffic islands that surrounded the Opera Auditorium and the University Campus, which were to be used for both circulation and parking. Within the context of Iraq, with its ancient ziggurats forms, this had a peculiar logic. It was a solution that he had already developed in his Strong Automobile Objective project (1924–5), in which the ziggurat became an enhanced car journey with a planetarium at the top (see page 72). The scale of the intervention for Baghdad was overwhelming. Wright proposed an axial road, to be called King Faisal Esplanade, which would link the civic west bank of Baghdad directly to the opera house. He even orientated the road towards Mecca. For Wright, directing the car towards the Islamic shrine was reverential. The esplanade also contained a series of commercial kiosks, another form of the roadside market that Wright had advocated for Broadacre City, and the aerial rendering of the scheme was directed away from the old city towards a Broadacre-style paradise garden.

The outcast Pig Island that Wright had appropriated for his design was to become the Isle of Edena – a new Garden of Eden – and in this way Wright

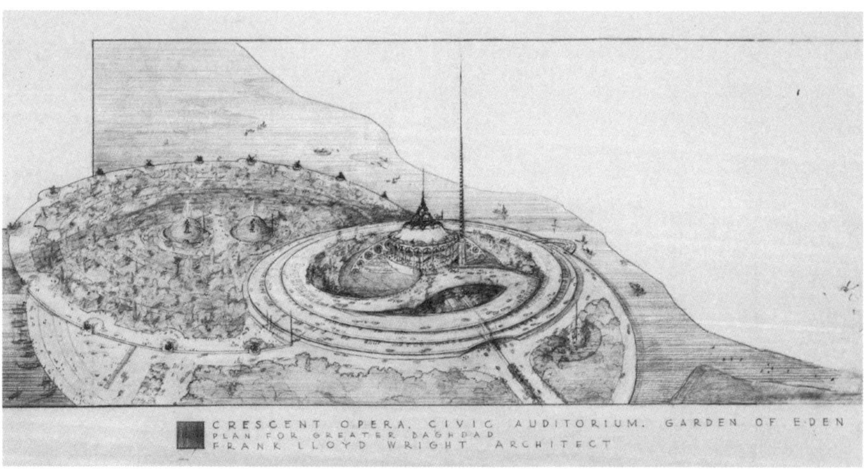

Perspective view of Crescent Opera, Civic Auditorium, Garden of Eden, Plan for Greater Baghdad, Iraq (1957) by Frank Lloyd Wright

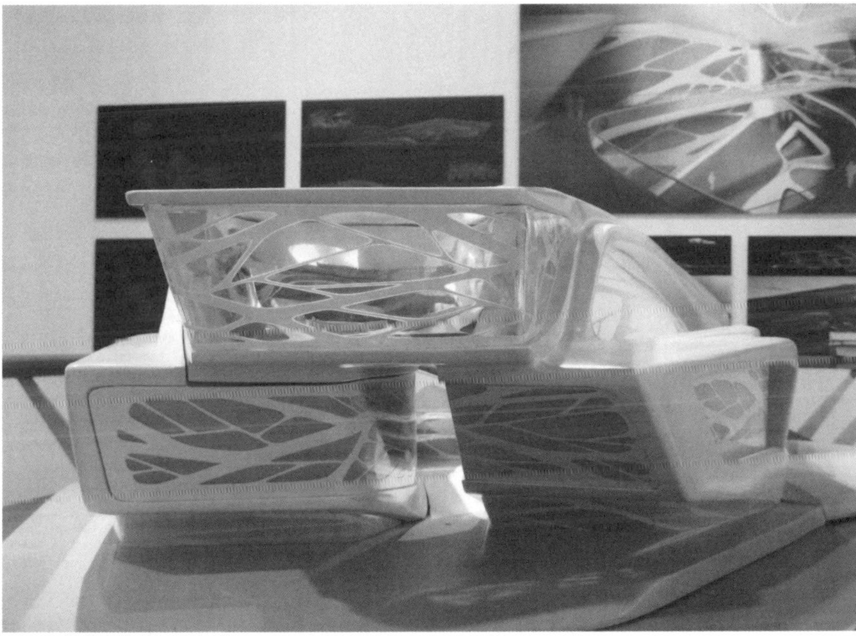

Model and images of Performing Arts Centre, Abu Dhabi, United Arab Emirates (2009) by Zaha Hadid

aimed to restructure and re-colonialise Baghdad into an Old Testament utopia. The centrepiece of the Cultural Quarter on the Isle of Edena was, of course, to be the Grand Opera and Civic Auditorium. This building was again orientated towards Mecca thus giving it a quasi-religious function that attempted to justify itself as a 'temple to culture.'[105] The auditorium had a defined circular geometry, and indeed most of Wright's theatre designs possess an overwhelming geometry (the Ginza and the Barnsdall Theatres were both octagonal). For Baghdad, Wright based his design on the intersection of two circles, one for a revolving stage and the other for an auditorium with 1600 seats for an opera performance, plus there were an additional 3700 seats for 'conventions or patriotic celebrations.'[106] The plan was an update of Sullivan's Auditorium Building, whereby two similar circles establish the relationship between the stage and the audience.[107] Another item reused from the Sullivan's Auditorium Building was the expressive proscenium, which Wright extended beyond the building to become an expressive 'great crescent arch,' springing from two pools of water and to be 'decorated with metal-sculptured scenes from the classic *Arabian* Nights.'[108] Whilst the

Crescent is a symbol of Islam, recalling the ancient 'fertile crescent,'[109] its use by Wright was decorative and not structural, and its articulation was yet another indulgence. And to crown the whole extravaganza 'above the auditorium, a crenelated dome shelter[ed] a golden figure of Aladdin [Wright] and his wonderful lamp, the symbol of human imagination.'[110]

In July 1957, however, there was a military coup led by General Abdul Karim Kassem, and King Faisal and his son were assassinated. Wright's fantastic scheme was unsurprisingly rejected by the new leaders, more than likely because of its references to the monarchy and its excessive decoration, which were not in keeping with the new republican ideals. The other modernist architects from the West (Gropius, Ponti and Le Corbusier), however, managed to continue their work under the new Iraqi military leadership. Wright's plan for Greater Baghdad was a fully blown 'Orientalist' project, with Wright as the 'white agent' of change who imposed his own set of Westernised cultural references and ideas onto the city and the nation. Furthermore, it was also a cathartic end for Wright's actual career, in that it was similar to the Wasmuth Folio and Broadacre City, whereby all his old designs (both real and imaginary) were integrated into a single idealised landscape – except that this time Baghdad was the recipient of Aladdin's last fantasies.

Similarly on Saadiyat Island, in 2009, Zaha Hadid was charged with producing a new Performing Arts Centre containing another expression of Western culture, the Opera House. Of Middle-Eastern origin herself, Hadid set out a less dramatic concept: '[the Performing Arts Centre] emerges from a linear intersection of pedestrian paths . . . gradually developing into a growing organism that sprouts a network of successive branches . . . the performance spaces, which spring from the structure like fruits on a vine and face westward, towards the water.'[111] Hadid claimed that her Performing Arts Centre's design 'will have five theatres, a music hall, opera house, drama theatre and a flexible theatre with a combined seating capacity of 6300'.[112] Wright and Hadid's 'organically' inspired designs for musical auditoria display a potent architectural image. Hadid's scheme may be considered more sensual and 'organically' inspired, but it also lacks any functional and material integrity. It is also a point of coincidence between two star-architects, fulfilling fantastical briefs for within the Middle East. For Wright, the Plan for Greater Baghdad was intended as a continuation of imagined cities from the past, whereas Hadid's scheme engages with the imaginary brand identity of a city belonging to the future and is rooted in computer-aided design.

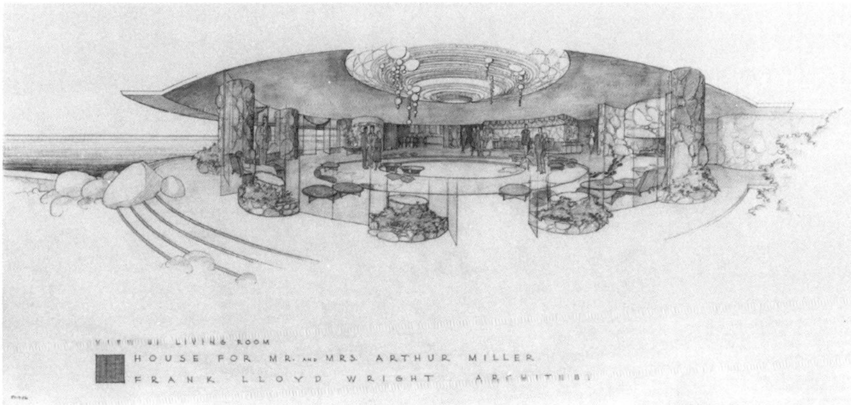

View of living room, Arthur Miller House (1957) by Frank Lloyd Wright

LEGACY IN IRAN

Wright's legacy practice, Taliesin Associated Architects (TAA), followed Wright's lead by engaging with the Shah of Iran. TAA designed two villas for Princess Shams Pahlavi, the sister of the Shah of Iran. The so called 'Pearl Palace' (1973) in Karaj, 17 kilometres (10½ miles) west of Tehran, is an extravagant home that was closely related to Wright's Baghdad scheme in all its bombast, and was 'borrowed' from an unwanted design by Wright for Arthur Miller and Marilyn Monroe – another Hollywood fantasy transplanted to Arabia.[113] The TAA's lead designer for this $6 millon scheme was Wes Peters, of whom Wright had quipped 'Wes is more!'[114] It is a truly excessive design, whereby a metaphorical 'pearls' appeared in countless circular motifs, that extends from the landscape into the formal plan of the palace, and culminates in a circular bed for the Princess. Two translucent domes and a ziggurat articulate an Arabian fantasy with the larger 36-metre (188-foot) diameter dome embracing a reception and exotic gardens, whilst the smaller dome covers a pool and lounge. Indeed, the Palace was the realisation of the 'pleasure dome' from Xanadu. A ramp within the larger dome ascends past a marble panelled banquet suite and a library, before reaching a spatial crescendo contained within a ziggurat in the princess's suite. Astonishingly, this was all built to plan! It was a fitting fulfilment to Frank Lloyd Wright, the Midwestern American Aladdin fantasist who became the first global architect.

7

MINORITY REPORTS

Frank Lloyd Wright was the prototypical architect of early globalisation and, it could be claimed, the first global architect. During his long and creative career, Wright realised many of his global ambitions, in that he designed and built examples of 'organic' architecture overseas, he lectured widely, and exhibited his ideas and presented his work to an international audience. Yet Wright's vision also became so overwhelming and singular that his overseas architecture ended up becoming a pastiche. When other architects, who were inspired by Wright, attempted to follow his 'organic' ideas in the different countries where he exerted an influence, they inevitably enriched the architecture by contributing a personal reflection to a specific site in a way that the 'master' never could do.

Thus we have seen the evident tension between Wright's globalising ambitions and the actual sites of his architecture outside America. All the sites of Wright's architecture that I found on my travels were places where his 'organic' mantra had been interpreted and translated, often with very different results to that which he had intended. The places that Wright had visited, designed for, and built in have also mutated and changed over the decades since his death, in response to much wider global trends and often complex local circumstances. In some respect my trips to these sites were a reversal of Wright's globalising tendencies, whereby the local places were the sources of new knowledge to analyse and deconstruct Wright's work. The different places that I visited possessed specific environments and conditions that were immediate and provided valuable insights into how 'organic' architecture came to be practised around the globe. Often, the most insightful knowledge was gained by engaging with local people who happened to have in-depth and relevant knowledge of these sites.

I was particularly fascinated by the way that architectural sites become places for multiple readings of human inhabitation and experience. I also enjoyed the tourist spectacle of sites where Wright's architecture is conserved as a museum of his creativity. During my journeys, they became pilgrimage destinations where one could view a modern relic and pay homage to Wright. But these museums were also lifeless, lacking the essential quality of a home. Meeting private owners in their homes was, for me, far more rewarding for the insights and reflection on 'organic' architecture. I felt that their stories enriched the discussion of what constitutes 'organic' architecture. In addition, this book responds to Wright's own method of articulating his architecture in a narrative form, and within *An Autobiography*, he challenges the reader to 'read between the lines.'[1] This is a wonderfully revealing admission, it implies that his life and architecture can be re-told and re-made as the occupant and the reader wishes. Likewise, this text is open for further interpretation and invention.

CONTESTED SITES

Having completed my journeys, and back home in London, I reflected on the diverse array of architectures I visited that were inspired by Frank Lloyd Wright's 'organic' architecture. They articulated many different ideas inspired by Wright, with some local architects seeking to make their buildings more democratic, while others were inspired by his dynamic forms and innovative internal spaces, and others still wished to exploit their local setting and landscape. Each site was its own 'minority report' – a call for independence from prevailing architectural and commercial forces of the day, just as Wright had proclaimed in London back in 1939. I was also heartened by the cultural diversity that I encountered during my visits, with each country requiring a negotiation of customs and language. Each site articulated an individual response to its own setting and had been given an inventive inflection by local architects who were inspired by Wright.

Wright was indebted to Japanese architecture in developing the first phase of his career, the suburban Prairie Houses, which laid the foundation for his remarkable career. Yet, the 'cross-cultural confusion'[2] that Isozaki identified in Wright's interpretation of Japanese architecture also highlights the difficulty that Wright faced in absorbing the cultural ideas from another country, especially at a time when there were great barriers to gaining such understanding (although maybe it was these very misunderstandings that led him into a creative dialogue). The act of translating architectural influences is always interpretative, critical and partial. At the Imperial Hotel in Tokyo, Wright created the original architectural icon, a hotel that had withstood an earthquake and put Tokyo on the international tourist map.

I found the Yamamura Villa (1918) in the city of Kobe to be a site that had experienced cultural translation, mutation, and adaptation (see page 40). The project can be seen as prophetic of a hybridised culture and processes that allow for an indigenous adaptation of globalisation. The Yamamura Villa was conceived by Wright in effect as a 'late' Prairie House, along with some hints of Secession influence, and it was then completed and adapted by his assistant on the Imperial Hotel, Arata Endo, to include a sequence of more ostensibly Japanese spaces. Hence it exposed two very different spatial conceptions within one house, a dialogue between Wright's Western material construction and Arata's immaterial sequence of spaces. The site can thus be seen as revealing an early global encounter in which cultural translation and interpretation – so fluid and nuanced in their operations – were made manifest through the medium of architecture.

At the turn of the 20th century, Wright's 'Prairie Style' houses with their innovative spatial layouts and dynamic elevational compositions encouraged two very different readings from architects in Holland. Today, it seems curious that Wright was simultaneously adopted as a rationalist and an expressionist, but that indeed was the case. Although Wright played a part in early modernist thought, modern architecture developed into a limited, self-referential projection of Western values and a globalising movement, the so-called 'International Style.' Wright's response to his exclusion from this kind of 'objective' modernism was simply to expand the remit of 'organic' architecture into a rival global manifesto. Both of these global visions sought to capture the zeitgeist of the assumed superiority of Western thought and practice. Yet, set against these rival global visions, far more interesting was the actual architecture built at a local level, such as the Meer en Bosch housing development in the suburbs of The Hague, designed by Duiker and Bijvoet (1920). They were inspired by what they saw as the progressive image of Wright's Robie House (1908–10), as an early expression of American modernity, and they wanted to adapt the design to their site. Furthermore, the suburb was planned with specific Dutch concerns in mind. The homes were built for multiple occupants and the houses used local materials; the use of thatch for the roof covering was particularly inventive, disturbing and fun. Duiker and Bijvoet openly grounded their modernist aspirations in the realities of their site.

Wright was a 'useful hostage'[3] to the Soviet regime or, more honestly, an unwitting apologist for Stalin. Wright's engagement with Stalin and Mussolini shows that many leading architects have scant regard for democratic rights or freedom of speech, just as long as their own designs are vocalised. Wright took his vision for the planned de-territorialised utopia of Broadacre City to Russia, as he knew that it needed a powerful state that was capable of restructuring capitalism to realise his ideal settlement. It was a fairly desperate attempt to fulfil his vision and part of his global persona, as an architect who was hawking around a de-territorialised city that claimed to be 'everywhere and nowhere.'[4] Magnitogorsk was the ultimate planned Soviet city, but the Soviet planned economy floundered due to a bureaucracy that was too remote and inflexible, and over the last 75 years the city has therefore experienced a dizzying sequence of modernist housing initiatives, idealised American suburbs, Stalinist neoclassical formal planning, and Khrushchev's massive super-blocks. As a result, it is best viewed as a contingent city that has managed to accommodate these different approaches to create its own varied urban environment and living spaces. However, Wright remained in favour of an architect-planned society along his own peculiar ideas, as exemplified in the cult of the Taliesin Fellowship, a society that was under his control. Wright had a singular and simplified view of a planned city, a settlement that could span across the world showed him to be the original global architect.

The plight of the urban poor in Chicago in the late 19th century was acute and Wright engaged with progressive and pragmatic movements based around settlement Hull House. Yet, it was Wright's Prairie School colleagues, William Purcell and George Elmslie, who developed a more affordable Arts and Crafts home, and realised William Morris's aspirations for an egalitarian suburb. In the economic turmoil of the 1930s, Wright did not engage directly with the New Deal programme, but he supported many of its radical aims, such as rural resettlement and some form of redistribution of wealth through spreading land ownership. So that when Wright came to visit the RIBA in 1939, ostensibly to promote his dispersed Broadacre City manifesto, it proved to be a kind of 'future shock' for the architectural profession in Britain. The technologically progressive Wright was confronted by an academic and anaemic British profession. His stream of 'organic' conscious thought was too much for his audience to comprehend, so they deemed him out of touch. Britain was not ready to accept or comprehend the arrival of the first global architect.

Yet, in postwar Britain, the nascent Welfare State was not the vision of social justice that Wright had been promoting in 1939, with its overbearing 'establishment' and its rigid official modernist language. Wright passed harsh judgement on his first homecoming to Wales through his rejection of the Brynmawr Rubber Factory. In the planned New Town of Milton Keynes, elements of Wright's decentralised utopia were adopted, and the results were characteristically bland. So Wright's influence in Britain was highly particular and specific. I found individual architectural admirers who designed modest homes for informed clients in the 1960s and 70s that were clearly inspired by Wright's 'organic' mantra, often in semi-rural or at least suburban settings. These 'organic' homes were a critique of the top-down Welfare State modernist doctrine and articulated a progressive alternative vision of modernism. There are only a small number of these 'organic' inspired properties in Britain, so Wright's influence was not widespread, but it was somehow more revealing that they were innovative, original homes and not generic production.

My contemporary Grand Tour from London to Rome was not a road of cultural discovery in the old classical style, but a modern-day road trip with Frank Lloyd Wright that questioned the old methods of producing architecture and recording history. In 1910, Wright embraced Italian vernacular architecture when he visited Fiesole, and he used Italian vernacular architecture to articulate a convincing anti-classical manifesto for 'organic' architecture. Yet on his return to Italy in 1951, Wright was a star-architect promoting his globalised Broadacre City in Florence. Then, in Venice, Wright's proposal for the Masieri Memorial on the Grand Canal was a scheme that compromised all his earlier ideas of 'organic' architecture.

The star-architect was desperate to realise his legacy on the Grand Canal, but he became mired in a debate with locals who were able to resist the might of his personality and fame.

The original 'organic' fabric of old Kuwait was displaced by a modernist city on the highway. It has since become a planned suburban city with a comprehensive road network and a seemingly equitable distribution of services, exactly as proposed in Wright's Broadacre City manifesto. And, having conquered the desert with road building and air-conditioned homes, Kuwait searched for an architectural identity with its innovative water towers and Parliament building. The search for a cultural identity within and other Middle-Eastern countries continues to this day with new daring architectural inventions. As a self-styled 'Aladdin' figure, Wright believed in his own magical powers and, for him, the Middle-Eastern region was waiting for him to appear on his magical Broadacre City carpet to provide architectural icons that might define a new cultural identity. When I visited the Saadiyat Island exhibition at the ostentatious Emirates Palace Hotel in Abu Dhabi, I found its scheme for a new Cultural Quarter there all too reminiscent of Wright's own Greater Plan for Baghdad (1957), with its own Cultural Quarter, full of Western cultural forms designed by the latest star-architects.

RECLAIMING 'ORGANIC' ARCHITECTURE

In May 2012, I gave a talk at the RIBA, in London on my research on Frank Lloyd Wright's architecture. The event brought together a good mixture of people of different ages, and in the follow up question-and-answer session, many in the audience rightly questioned the definition of 'organic' architecture. Some defined it as being related to the careful siting of a building, while others clearly believed that 'organic' buildings needed to display an environmental consciousness. Likewise, some regarded Broadacre City as an expression of 'organic' character from Frank Lloyd Wright, whereas the younger architects present seemed to view contemporary digital form-making as a valid exploration of 'organic' design. These are all valid interpretations, which show that 'organic' architecture is certainly able to embrace many different perspectives, supporting as it does what can perhaps be best defined as a complex overlaid palimpsest of architectural definitions and values. It was encouraging to think that

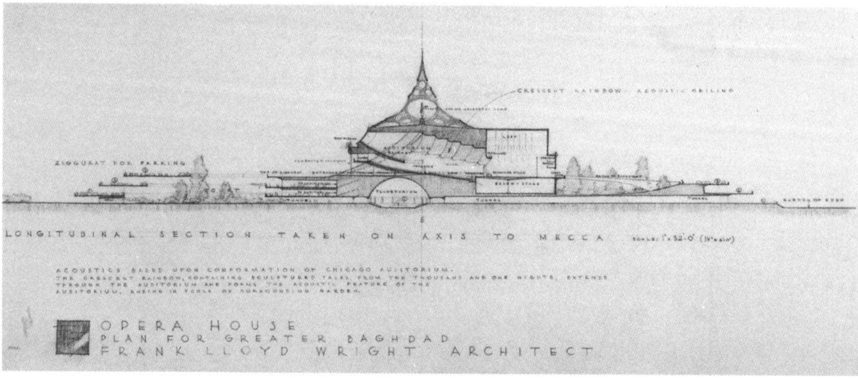

Cross-section of Crescent Opera, Civic Auditorium, Garden of Eden, Plan for Greater Baghdad, Iraq (1957) by Frank Lloyd Wright. Aladdin (Wright) and his wonderful lamp can be seen above the auditorium.

'organic' architecture can adopt the different histories as outlined in this book, and its definitions include different ideas that can be layered one upon the other.

Frank Lloyd Wright became the first global architect in the sense that he proposed and promoted a brand of globalised architecture that he claimed could be 'everywhere and nowhere.' This was despite an early career that responded to his local setting to produce architecture that was full of invention and progressive ideas about society. Yet, beyond Wright's rhetoric and bombast, there were specific and local instances of homes and buildings across the globe that sought to reclaim 'organic' architecture from a bland form of globalised architecture to become an alternative means of organising, practising and expressing architecture.

Even so star-architects continue to prosper and their fame is called upon to populate the globe with their signature forms. They should perhaps reflect on Wright's schemes for Venice and Baghdad, when his ego and eccentricity came to dominate his architectural work, and any semblance of 'organic' architecture was lost. These are warnings that global production, without local engagement and support, will not lead to universal approval or a lasting legacy.

NOTES

INTRODUCTION: ROUTE FINDER

1 F. L. Wright (1957) in B. Pfeiffer (ed.), *The Essential Frank Lloyd Wright: Critical Writings on Architecture* (Princeton: Princeton University Press, 2008), p.426.
2 C. Scarpa, cited in S. Los, *Carlo Scarpa: An Architectural Guide, Verona* (Verona: Arsenale Editrice, 2007) p.92.
3 Z. Hadid, cited in T. Kirk, *The Architecture of Modern Italy (Volume 2: Visions of Utopia 1900 – Present)*, (Princeton: Princeton University Press, 2005), p.243.
4 G. L. Jones, *12 Part Narrative*, Dissertation at Oxford Brookes University, supervised by Professor Murray Fraser (2000).
5 G. L. Jones, *Frank Lloyd Wright beyond America*, PhD thesis at University of Westminster, supervised by Professor Murray Fraser (2013).
6 J. Tomlinson, *Globalisation and Culture* (Cambridge: Polity, 1999), pp 27–8.
7 K. Nute, *Frank Lloyd Wright and Japan*, (London: Routledge, 2000).
8 K. Frampton, *Modern Architecture: A Critical History*, 3rd edn. (London: Thames and Hudson, 1992), pp 58–9.
9 Nute, op. cit., p.68.
10 A. Isozaki, *Japan-ness in Architecture* (Cambridge: MIT Press, 2006), p.5.
11 F. L. Wright, *An Autobiography* (London: Faber & Faber, 1945), p.150.
12 R. Twombly, *Frank Lloyd Wright: His Life and His Architecture* (New York: John Wiley & Sons, 1979), pp 186–7.
13 F. L. Wright (1908), in R. Twombly, *Frank Lloyd Wright: Essential Texts* (New York: W. W. Norton & Co., 2009), p.102.
14 Twombly (1979), op. cit., pp 304–11.
15 F. L. Wright, in Twombly (2009), op. cit., pp 135–57.
16 F. L. Wright, in Twombly (1979), op. cit., p.315.
17 Twombly (1979), op. cit., p.303.
18 F. L. Wright, *An Organic Architecture: The Architecture of Democracy* (London: Lund Humphries, 1970), p.36.
19 Wright (1957) in Pfeiffer (2008), op. cit., p.424

1: UNUSUAL VIEWS OF OUTSTANDING SITES

1 F. L. Wright, *An Autobiography* (London: Faber & Faber, 1945), p.173.
2 M. Tanigawa in M. Birk (ed.), *Frank Lloyd Wright's Fifty Views of Japan: the 1905 Photo Album* (San Francisco: Pomegranate Artbooks, 1996), pp 15–17, 19.
3 Wright (1945), op. cit., pp 173–4.
4 Wright (1945), op. cit., p.173.
5 ibid.
6 M. Secrest, *Frank Lloyd Wright: A Biography* (Chicago: University of Chicago Press, 1992), p.187.
7 B. Gill, *Many Masks – A Life of Frank Lloyd Wright* (London: Heinemann, 1988), p.185.
8 Wright (1945), op. cit., p.173.
9 A. Isozaki, *Japan-ness in Architecture* (Cambridge: MIT Press, 2006), p.3.
10 K. Okakura, *The Book of Tea* (Tokyo: Kodansha Int., 2005), p.59.
11 Isozaki (2006), op. cit., p.5.
12 K. Nute, *Frank Lloyd Wright and Japan* (London: Routledge, 2000), pp 22–5.
13 ibid., pp 22–5.
14 ibid., pp 36–46.
15 ibid., pp 38–44.

16 Okakura (2005), op. cit.
17 Wright (1945), op. cit., p.111.
18 Nute (2000), op. cit., pp 59–60.
19 Wright (1945), op. cit., p.183.
20 ibid., p.184.
21 B. Taut, *Houses and People of Japan* (London: Gifford, 1937), p.2.
22 R. Koolhaas & B. Mau, *S, M, L, XL* (New York: Monacelli Press, 1995), p.88.
23 E. Seidensticker, *Low City, High City: Tokyo from Edo to the Earthquake, 1867–1923* (London: Penguin, 1985), p.8.
24 *The Imperial Hotel – A Legend in Photos* (Tokyo: Imperial Hotel Ltd, 2003).
25 Wright (1945), op. cit., pp 190–200.
26 Seidensticker (1985), op. cit., p.37.
27 D. Stewart, *The Making of a Modern Japanese Architecture: 1868 to the Present* (Japan: Kodansha Int., 1989), p.22.
28 Seidensticker (1985), op. cit., p.97.
29 'The Hotels of Japan: Their Characteristics (The Welcome Society),' *The Times*, 19 July 1910, p.69.
30 Wright (1945), op. cit., p.172.
31 K. Smith in Nute 2000, op. cit., p.151.
32 Isozaki (2006), op. cit., p.8.
33 F. L. Wright, 'In the Cause of Architecture: The New Imperial Hotel, Tokyo', *The Western Architect*, 32, April 1923, in R. Twombly, *Frank Lloyd Wright: Essential Texts* (New York: W. W. Norton & Co, 2009), p.189.
34 ibid., p.192.
35 ibid., p.193.
36 Nute (2000), op. cit., p.153.
37 Isozaki (2006), op. cit., p.8.
38 Wright (1945), op. cit., p.194.
39 Wright (1923), op. cit., p.192.
40 Wright (1945), op. cit., pp 190–200.
41 ibid.
42 J. Quinan, 'Field Notes: Frank Lloyd Wright, Preservation, and the Question of Authenticity,' *Journal of the Society of Architectural Historians*, vol.67, no.1, March 2008, p.96.
43 Wright (1945), op. cit., p.198.
44 Gill (1988), op. cit., p.264.
45 A. Raymond, *An Autobiography*, (Rutland: Charles E. Turtle, 1973), p.71.
46 F. L. Wright (1922), *The New Imperial Hotel*, in B. Pfeiffer (ed.), *Frank Lloyd Wright: Collected Writings: Vol 1 1894–1930* (New York: Rizzoli, 1992), p.162.
47 Isozaki (2006), op. cit., p.8.
48 ibid., p.9.
49 G. Ponti, 'Tokyo Imperial Hotel, 1922–1967,' *Domus*, February 1968, p.511.
50 '"Myonichikcan" Honors its Name', *Frank Lloyd Wright Quarterly*, vol.13, no.3 2002, p.17.
51 ibid., p.16.
52 ibid., p.20.
53 ibid.
54 *New York Times*, 1992, cited in *Frank Lloyd Wright Quarterly* 2002, op.cit., p.21.
55 F. L. Wright (1908), in R. Twombly, *Frank Lloyd Wright: Essential Texts* (New York: W. W. Norton & Co., 2009), p.83.
56 J. Meech, *Frank Lloyd Wright and the Art of Japan: The Architect's Other Passion* (New York: Abrams, 2001), p.28.
57 Wright (1945), op. cit., p.173.
58 ibid., p.183.
59 Meech (2001), op. cit., pp 50–73.
60 J. L. Wright, *My Father Who Is On Earth* (New York: G. P. Putnam's Sons, 1946), p.98.
61 Meech (2001), op. cit., p.140
62 M. Ross, *Beyond Metabolism: The New Japanese Architecture* (London: McGraw Hill, 1978), p.8.
63 Wright (1945), op. cit., pp 175–9.
64 Taut (1937), op. cit., pp 181–6.
65 B. Shelton, *Learning from the Japanese City: Looking East in Urban Design* (London: Routledge, 2012), p.29.
66 Wright (1945), op. cit., p.175.
67 ibid.
68 ibid.
69 ibid.

70 Nute (2000), op. cit., p.44.
71 F. L. Wright (1931) in *Modern Architecture, Being the Kahn Lectures*, in B. Pfeiffer (ed.) (Princeton: Princeton University Press: 2008), p.175.
72 ibid.
73 M. Treib and R. Herman, *A Guide to the Gardens of Kyoto* (Tokyo: Shufunotomo Co. Ltd, 1980), p.185.
74 C. Jencks, *Late-Modern Architecture* (London: Academy Edition, 1980), p.101.
75 Wright (1945), op. cit., p.151.
76 K. Burns and L. Novick, *Frank Lloyd Wright: A Film*, 1998, PBS Home Video.
77 Stewart (1989), op. cit., p.124.
78 M. Tanigawa, *Measured Drawing: Frank Lloyd Wright in Japan* (Tokyo: Graphic Co., 1980), p.67.
79 M. Sasaki, *Morphologenesis of Flux Structure* (London: AA Publications, 2007), p.69.
80 ibid.
81 A. Wood and A. Davenport, *Tellytubbies* (Ragdoll Productions, 1997–2002).
82 www.mitsuihome.co.jp/product/heurtley/index.html (accessed 27 August 2008).
83 Wright (1908) in Twombly (2009), op. cit., p.85.
84 Taut, cited in Nute 2000, op. cit., p.149; Taut cited in Isozaki 2006, op. cit., p.13.
85 D. Treiber, *Frank Lloyd Wright* (Basel: Birkhauser, 2008), p.111.
86 Nute (2000), op. cit., pp 149–50.
87 Wright (1945), op. cit., p.188.
88 Wright (1922), op. cit., p.162.
89 Wright (1945), op. cit., p.198.
90 Taut (2006), cited in Isozaki (2006), op. cit., p.13.

2: VANITY FAIR

1 A. Rimbaud, cited in P. Childs, *Modernism* (London: Routledge, 2005), p.12.
2 J. Walsh (2006) 'Don't blame it on the concrete', www.theguardian.com/commentisfree/2006/apr/10/thismodernistlife (accessed on 12 April 2011).
3 F. L. Wright, *An Organic Architecture* (London: Lund Humphries, 1970), p.32.
4 F. L Wright, *An Autobiography* (London: Faber & Faber, 1945) p.323.
5 ibid.
6 ibid., p.145.
7 ibid., p.70.
8 ibid.,
9 J. L. Wright, *My Father Who Is On Earth* (New York: G. P. Putnam's Sons, 1946), p.136.
10 D. Hoffman, 'Frank Lloyd Wright and Viollet-le-Duc', *Journal of Society of Architectural Historians*, March 1969, vol.28 no.1, pp 174–5.
11 ibid., p.176.
12 Wright (1945), op. cit., p.71.
13 ibid., pp 71–3.
14 ibid., p.73.
15 V. Hugo, *Notre-Dame de Paris* (London: Penguin Classics, 2004), p.188.
16 ibid., p.189.
17 ibid.
18 ibid., p.197.
19 Wright (1945), op. cit., p.73.
20 R. Mallet-Stevens in F. L. Wright et al., *The Complete 1925 'Wendigen Series'* (New York: Dover Publications, 1992), p.163.
21 P. Joly in J-F. Pinchon (ed.), *Rob. Mallet-Stevens: Architecture, Furniture, Interior Design* (Cambridge: MIT Press 1990), p.41.
22 P. Joly in Pinchon (1990), op. cit., p.44.
23 Mallet-Stevens in Wright et al. (1992), op. cit., p.163.
24 ibid.
25 J-L. Cohen in A, Alofsin (ed.), *Frank Lloyd Wright: Europe and Beyond* (Berkeley: University of California Press, 1999), p.111.
26 D. Langmead and D. L. Johnson, *Architectural Excursions: Frank Lloyd*

Wright, Holland and Europe (London: Greenwood Press, 2000), p.22.
27 C. Ashbee (1911) in F. L. Wright *Frank Lloyd Wright: Early Visions, the Great Achievements of the Oak Park years: The complete Frank Lloyd Wright: Ausgefuhrte Bauten of 1911*, B. Goldstein, trans. (New York: Gramercy Books, 1985), p.4.
28 M. Casciato in M. Pollack (ed.), *The Education of the Architect: Historiography, Urbanism, and the Growth of Architectural Knowledge* (Cambridge: MIT Press, 1997), p.142.
29 R. Banham, *Theory and Design in the First Machine Age* (Oxford: Architectural Press, 2002), p.154.
30 P. Overy, *De Stijl* (London: Thames and Hudson, 1991), p.104.
31 ibid., p.20.
32 A. Colquhoun, *Modern Architecture* (Oxford: Oxford University Press, 2002), p.109.
33 K. Frampton, *Modern Architecture: A Critical History*, 3rd edn (London: Thames and Hudson, 1992), p.142.
34 J. J. P. Oud in H. Brooks, *Writings on Wright: Selected comments on Frank Lloyd Wright* (Cambridge: MIT Press, 1981), pp 135–7
35 Oud in Wright et al. (1992), op. cit., p.86.
36 ibid., p.87.
37 Langmead and Johnson (2000), op. cit., p.44.
38 ibid.
39 J. Wills in Brooks (1981), op. cit., pp 139–45.
40 '1928 Summer Olympics', Wikipedia, http://en.wikipedia.org/wiki/1928_summer_olympics (accessed on 28 April 2009).
41 N. Pevsner, 'Frank Lloyd Wright Peaceful Penetration of Europe', *Architects' Journal*, no.89, 4 May 1939, pp 731–4.
42 Banham (2002), op. cit., p.164.
43 Langmead and Johnson (2000), op. cit., p.72.
44 ibid., p.76.
45 Pevsner (1939), op. cit., p.734.
46 S. Polano, *Hendrick Petrus Berlage: Complete Works* (London: Butterworth Architecture, 1988), p.143.
47 Banham (2002), op. cit., p.145.
48 I. B. Whyte, 'Introduction' in H. P. Berlage, *Hendrik Petrus Berlage: Thoughts on Style 1886–1909*, I. B. Whyte and W. de Wit (trans.) (Los Angeles: Getty Center, 1996), p.50.
49 Langmead and Johnson (2000), op. cit., p.20.
50 ibid., p.87.
51 ibid., p.95.
52 Wright et al. (1992), op. cit.
53 Langmead and Johnson (2000), op. cit., p.97.
54 Berlage in Wright et al. (1992), op. cit., pp 80–82.
55 ibid.
56 Alofsin, A. *Frank Lloyd Wright: The Lost Years 1910–1922* (Chicago: University of Chicago Press (1993), p.30.
57 Wright (1945), op. cit., p.145.
58 ibid., p.146.
59 Alofsin (1993), op. cit., p.4.
60 ibid.
61 ibid.
62 ibid.
63 ibid.
64 A. Alofsin in K. Eggener (ed.), *American Architectural History: A Contemporary Reader* (London: Routledge, 2004), p.282.
65 N. Pevsner, *Pioneers of Modern Design: From William Morris to Walter Gropius* (London: Pelican, 1981).
66 B. Colomina, *Architecturalproduction* (New York: Princeton Architectural Press, 1988), p.6.
67 A. Alofsin, in F. L. Wright, *Studies and Executed Buildings by Frank Lloyd Wright* (New York: Rizzoli, 1998) p.6.
68 K. James, *Erich Mendelsohn and the*

Architecture of German Modernism, (Cambridge: Cambridge University Press, 1997), p.45.
69 A. Einstein in James (1997), op. cit., p.44.
70 James (1997), op. cit., p.46.
71 ibid., p.64.
72 ibid.
73 E. Mendelsohn in Wright (1992), op. cit., p.165.
74 ibid.
75 C. St John Wilson, *The Other Tradition of Modern Architecture : the Uncompleted Project* (London: Black Dog, 2007).
76 H. Haring in P. B. Jones, *Hugo Haring: The Organic versus the Geometric Stuttgart* (London: Edition Axel Menges, 1999), p.77.
77 Jones (1999), op. cit., p.84.
78 Colquhoun (2002), op. cit., p.163.
79 K. Kirsch, *The Weissenhofsiedlung experimental housing built for the Deutsche Werkbund, Stuttgart 1927* (Stuttgart: Deutsche Verlags-Anstalt, 1994), p.41.
80 ibid., p.17.
81 ibid., p.100.
82 D. Johnson, *Frank Lloyd Wright Versus America* (Cambridge: MIT Press, 1990), p.245.
83 Alofsin (1993), op. cit., p.56.
84 Jones, P. B. *Gunter Behnisch*, (Basel, Germany: Birkhauser, 2000), p.13.
85 ibid.
86 Wright (1945), op. cit., pp 145, 200–01, 360, 366–7.
87 ibid., p.366.
88 F. Dimster, *The New Austrian Architecture* (New York: Rizzoli, 1995), p.20.
89 O. Wagner in Alofsin (1993), op. cit., p.58.
90 Frampton (1992), op. cit., p.79.
91 H. Bisanz in R. Waissenberger (ed.), *Vienna 1890–1920* (New York: Rizzoli, 1984), p.122.
92 Alofsin (1993), op. cit., p.13.
93 V. Scully in Alofsin (1993), op. cit., p.58.
94 Alofsin (1993), op. cit., pp 58, 339.
95 H. Monroe cited in Alofsin (1993), op. cit., p.79.
96 A. & P. Smithson, *The Heroic Period of Modern Architecture* (London: Thames and Hudson, 1981), p.7.
97 Wright (1945), op. cit., p.217.
98 Frampton (1992), op. cit., p.92.
99 ibid., pp 90–91.
100 ibid., p.91.
101 Wright (1909) in R. Twombly, *Frank Lloyd Wright: Essential Texts* (New York: W. W. Norton & Co, 2009), p.106.
102 Frampton (1992), op. cit., p.91.
103 R. Schindler in L. March and J. Sheine, *R. M. Schindler: Composition and Construction* (London: Academy Editions, 1995), p.53.
104 E. McCoy, *Richard Neutra* (New York: George Braziller, Inc., 1960), p.11.
105 H-R. Hitchcock, and P. Johnson *The International Style*, (New York: W. W. Norton & Co., 1966), p.27.
106 Wright (1932a) in Twombly (2009), op. cit., p.244.
107 ibid., p.245.
108 ibid., pp 245–7.
109 Wright (1932b) in Twombly (2009), op. cit., p.253.

3: EGOR'EVSK CULTURAL CLUB

1 C. Cooke, *Russian Avant-Garde: Theories of Art, Architecture and the City* (London: St Martin's Press, 1995), p.18.
2 D. Udoviki-Selb, 'Between Modernism and Socialist Realism: Soviet Architectural Culture under Stalin's Revolution from Above, 1928–1938', *Society of Architectural Historians Journal*, vol.68, no.4, 2009, pp 267–495.
3 C. Williams-Ellis (1971), *Architect*

Errant: The Autobiography of Clough Williams-Ellis (Wales: Portmeirion Ltd, 1991), p.187.
4 F. L. Wright, *An Autobiography* (London: Faber & Faber, 1945), pp 468–9.
5 Williams-Ellis (1991), op. cit., pp 187–8.
6 ibid., p.188.
7 Wright (1945), op. cit., p.469.
8 S. Khan-Magomedov, *Pioneers of Soviet Architecture: The Search for New Solutions* (New York: Rizzoli, 1983), p.340.
9 A. Tarkhanov and S. Kavtaradze, *Stalinist Architecture* (London: Laurence King, 1992), p.94.
10 P. Hall, *Cities of Tomorrow: An Intellectual History of Urban Planning and Design in the Twentieth Century* (Oxford: Blackwell, 2002), p.215.
11 ibid., p.216.
12 Tarkhanov and Kavtaradze (1992), op. cit., p.90.
13 J. H. Bater, *The Soviet City: Ideal and Reality* (London: Edward Arnold, 1980), p.30.
14 F. L. Wright, 'Architecture and Life in the USSR,' *Architectural Record*, vol.82, October 1937a, p.60.
15 ibid., p.59.
16 Wright (1937a), op. cit., p.62.
17 ibid.
18 Wright (1945), op. cit., p.469.
19 J-L. Cohen in A. Alofsin (ed.), *Frank Lloyd Wright: Europe and Beyond* (Berkeley: University of California Press, 1999), p.102.
20 ibid. p.102 and S. F. Starr, *Melnikov: Solo Architect in a Mass Society,* (Princeton: Princeton University Press, 1978), p.23.
21 Starr (1978), op. cit., pp 26–7.
22 Cohen in Alfonsin (1999), op. cit., p.101.
23 ibid., p.102.
24 Wright (1937a), op. cit., p.59.
25 ibid., p.61.
26 Cooke (1995), op. cit., p.120.
27 Wright, F. L. (1932a) cited in D. Johnson, *Frank Lloyd Wright Versus America* (Cambridge: MIT Press, 1990), p.199.
28 ibid.
29 D. Arkin, cited in Johnson (1990), op. cit., p.201.
30 ibid.
31 Johnson (1990), op. cit., p.228.
32 Wright, F. L. (1937b) cited in Johnson (1990), op. cit., p.224.
33 ibid., p.226.
34 ibid.
35 ibid., pp 224–6.
36 ibid., p.226.
37 ibid.
38 Wright (1937a), op. cit., p.61.
39 B. Lubetkin, 'Recent Developments of Town Planning in USSR', *The Architectural Review*, May 1932, p.213.
40 Johnson (1990), op. cit., p.229.
41 Wright cited in Johnson (1990), op. cit., p.227.
42 ibid.
43 ibid.
44 Wright (1937a), op. cit., pp 58–63.
45 S. Breines, 'First Congress of Soviet Architecture', *Architectural Record*, vol.82, October 1937, pp 63–96.
46 ibid., p.65.
47 Tarkhanov and Kavtaradze (1992), op. cit., p.50.
48 Cooke (1995), op. cit., p.145.
49 Bater (1980), op. cit., p.56.
50 U. Altrock, 'The Lost Centre: Magnitogorsk Revisited', *Journal of Urban Design,* vol.3, no.2, 1998, p.203.
51 ibid.
52 Bater (1980), op. cit., p.56.
53 F. Engles cited in Khan-Magomedov (1983), op. cit., p.271.
54 V. Lenin cited in Khan-Magomedov (1983), op. cit., p.271.
55 Khan-Magomedov (1983), op. cit., p.284.
56 S. Kotkin, *Magnetic Mountain: Stalinism as a Civilisation* (Berkeley:

University of California Press, 1995), p.31.

57 M. Okhitovich cited in Cooke (1995), op. cit., p.199.

58 Khan-Magomedov (1983), op. cit., p.337.

59 C. Cooke, *Ivan Leonidov, Andrei Gozak and Andrei Leonidov – The Complete Works* (Rizzoli: New York, 1988), p.87.

60 Kotkin (1995), op. cit., p.42.

61 Wright (1945), op. cit., p.474.

62 H. Ford cited in J. R. Mullin, 'Henry Ford and Field and Factory: An Analysis of the Ford Sponsored Village Industries Experiment in Michigan, 1918–1941', *American Association Journal*, vol.48, no.4, Autumn 1982, p.426.

63 ibid. p.427.

64 Mullin (1982), op. cit. p.428.

65 Wright (1930) cited in Johnson (1990), op. cit., p.136.

66. G. Wright in R. McCarter, *On and By Frank Lloyd Wright: A Primer of Architectural Principles* (London: Phaidon, 2005), p.104.

67 ibid., p.106.

68 R. Twombly, *Frank Lloyd Wright: His Life and His Architecture* (New York: John Wiley & Sons, 1979), p.227.

69 F. L. Wright (1932b), *The Disappearing City* in B. Pfeiffer (ed.), *Frank Lloyd Wright: Collected Writings: Vol 3 1931–1939* (New York: Rizzoli, 1992), p.75.

70 ibid., p.84.

71 ibid., p.86.

72 ibid., p.91.

73 R. Banham, *Scenes in America Deserta* (London: Thames and Hudson, 1982), p.77.

74 Wright (1932b), op. cit., p.85.

75 ibid., p.79.

76 ibid., p.75.

77 Twombly (1979), op. cit., pp 227–9.

78 Wright (1932b), op. cit., p.90.

79 R. Friedland and H. Zellman, *The Fellowship: The Untold Story of Frank Lloyd Wright and the Taliesin Fellowship* (New York: Regan, 2006), p.564.

80 S. Peters cited in Friedland and Zellman (2006), op. cit., p.571.

81 J. Scott, *Behind the Urals: An American Worker in Russia's City of Steel* (Bloomington: Indiana University Press, 1989), p.3.

82 ibid., p.78.

83 ibid., p.70.

84 ibid., p.73.

85 ibid., pp 233–4.

86 ibid., p.232.

87 ibid., p.187.

88 Blacksmith Institute (2006) cited in 'Magnitogorsk', Wikipedia, http://en.wikipedia.org/wiki/Magnitogorsk (accessed on 30 June 2010).

89 Altrock (1998), op. cit., p.222.

90 Khan-Magomedov (1983), op. cit., p.434.

91 ibid., p.434.

92 I. Chepkunova, *Clubs built under the Trades Union Program 1927–1930*, Elek Urban (trans.) (Moscow: Shchusev Museum of Architecture, 2006), p.10.

93 ibid., p.12.

94 Cooke (1995), op. cit., p.27.

95 Cohen in Alofsin (1999), op. cit., p.110.

96 Johnson (1990), op. cit., pp 209–19.

4: WHATEVER HAPPENED TO FRANK LLOYD WRIGHT?

1 F. L. Wright, *An Autobiography* (London: Faber & Faber, 1945), p.15.

2 A. Saint, *The Image of the Architect* (New Haven: Yale University Press, 1993), p.37.

3 ibid., p.38.

4 ibid.

5 D. Hardy, *Utopian England: Community Experiments 1900–1945* (London: E. & F. N. Spon, 2000), p.3.

6 F. L. Wright (1901) in B. Pfeiffer (ed.) *The Essential Frank Lloyd Wright: Critical Writings on Architecture* (Princeton: Princeton University Press, 2008), p.23.

7 ibid., p.24.
8 ibid.
9 ibid., p.28.
10 ibid., p.30.
11 ibid., p.26.
12 A. Crawford, *C.R. Ashbee: Architect, Designer and Romantic Socialist* (New Haven and London: Yale University Press, 2005), p.97.
13 ibid.
14 ibid., p.98.
15 L. Blair, 'Choosing to Settle, Daring to Dream: the Settlement Difference through Henrietta Barnett's eyes', Selected Papers and Presentations from two seminars: *Toynbee Hall and Social Change,* 16 September 2000; *The Settlement Difference*, 22 September 2001, Toynbee Hall, London, July 2002, p.18.
16 Crawford (2005), op. cit., pp 100-101.
17 Hardy (2000), op. cit., p.118.
18 ibid. p.127.
19 'Lloyd Wright in Britain: Mr. R. Furneaux Jordan's Radio Talk,' *The Builder,* 24 November 1950, p.540.
20 ibid.
21 See introduction in S. Milkins and J. Mileur, *The New Deal and the Triumph of Liberalism* (Amherst: University of Massachusetts Press, 2002), p.3.
22 D. Ghirardo, 'New Deal, New City', *Modulus*, vol.16, 1983, p.17.
23 ibid.
24 ibid.
25 F. L. Wright (1935), 'Broadacre City: A New Community Plan,' *Architectural Record*, vol.77, April 1935, p.245.
26 G. Wright, *USA: Modern Architectures in History* (London: Reaktion Books 2008), p.132.
27 S. Davis, *The Architecture of Affordable Housing* (Berkeley: University of California Press, 1995), p.8.
28 F. L. Wright (1938a) in R. Twombly, *Frank Lloyd Wright: Essential Texts* (New York: W. W. Norton & Co, 2009), p.275.
29 ibid.
30 F. L. Wright, *Architectural Forum*, vol.68, January 1938b, p.78.
31 P. Morton Shand, 'Scenario for a Human Drama, VI: La machine-á-habiter to the House of Character', *Architectural Review*, vol.72, February 1935, p.62.
32 J. Gloag, 'Frank Lloyd Wright and the significance of the Taliesin Fellowship', *Architectural Review*, vol.72, January 1935, pp 1–2.
33 H. Seckel in D. Johnson, *Frank Lloyd Wright Versus America* (Cambridge: MIT Press, 1990), p.233.
34 F. L. Wright, (1938b), op. cit., pp 1–102.
35 'Frank Lloyd Wright: Architecture Club Dinner', *The Builder,* 5 May 1939, p.855.
36 F. L. Wright, *An Organic Architecture* (London: Lund Humphries, 1970), p1.
37 ibid.
38 ibid., p.1.
39 ibid., p.2.
40 ibid., p.4.
41 ibid., pp 4–5.
42 ibid., p.9.
43 ibid.
44 ibid.
45 ibid., p.10.
46 ibid., p.11.
47 ibid.
48 ibid., p.25.
49 ibid., p.31.
50 ibid., p.32.
51 ibid.
52 ibid., p.33.
53 J. Sergeant, *Frank Lloyd Wright's Usonian Houses: Designs for Moderate Cost One-Family Homes* (New York: Watson Guptil, 1984), p.129.
54 Wright (1970), op. cit., pp 33–4.
55 ibid., pp 35–6.
56 ibid., p.38.
57 ibid.
58 ibid., p.39.
59 ibid., pp 39–40.
60 ibid., p.40.

61 Wright (1945), op. cit., p.464.
62 Wright (1970), op. cit., pp 40–1.
63 ibid., p.41.
64 'Frank Lloyd Wright', *The Architects' Journal*, 11 May 1939, p.757.
65 'Frank Lloyd Wright', *RIBA Journal*, 22 May 1939, p.700.
66 P. Abercrombie, 'Correspondence: Frank Lloyd Wright', *RIBA Journal*, 11 December 1939, p.44.
67 ibid.
68 ibid.
69 Wright (1970), op. cit., p.40.
70 D. Johnson, *Frank Lloyd Wright Versus America* (Cambridge: MIT Press, 1990), op. cit., p.283.
71 Wright (1945), op. cit., p.464.
72 ibid.
73 F. L. Wright, 'London Rebuilt: How I Would Do it', *News Chronicle*, 17 February 1941, p.4.
74 ibid.
75 Edward Cullinan in conversation with Tony Chapman, 2008, pamphlet, p.8.
76 E. Cullinan, Royal Gold Medal address, RIBA, 13 February 2008.
77 Wright (1941), op. cit., p.4.
78 M. Fraser and J. Kerr, *Architecture and the 'Special Relationship': The American Influence on Post-war British Architects* (London: Routledge, 2007), p.145.
79 ibid., p.165.
80 M. Webber cited in Fraser and Kerr (2007), p.168.
81 Wright (1935), op. cit., p.244.
82 Fraser and Kerr (2007), op. cit., p.166.
83 'Annual Prize Giving: Presentations by Frank Lloyd Wright', *Architectural Association Journal*, vol.66, August–September 1950, p.32.
84 'Dinner to Mr. and Mrs. Frank Lloyd Wright', *Architectural Association Journal*, vol.66 August–September 1950, p.45
85 ibid. p.46.
86 ibid.
87 'Annual Prize Giving: Presentations by Frank Lloyd Wright', 1950, p.32.
88 ibid., p.34.
89 ibid.
90 ibid.
91 ibid.
92 'Lloyd Wright in Britain: Mr. R. Furneaux Jordan's Radio Talk', *The Builder*, 24 November 1950, p.540.
93 ibid.
94 F. L. Wright in A. Saint in A. Alofsin (ed.), *Frank Lloyd Wright: Europe and Beyond* (Berkeley: University of California Press, 1999), p.137.
95 ibid.
96 'Lloyd Wright in Britain: Mr. R. Furneaux Jordan's Radio Talk' 1950, op. cit., p.540.
97 V. Perry, *Built for a Better Future: The Brynmawr Rubber Factory* (Oxford: White Cockade Publishing, 1994), p.20.
98 ibid., p.88.
99 'Post-War Houses', *The Journal of the Twentieth Century Society*, Twentieth Century Architecture, Journal 4, 2000.
100 L. Campbell, 'Against the Grain: the Domestic Architecture of Robert Harvey', *The Journal of the Twentieth Century Society*, Twentieth Century Architecture, Journal 4, 2000, p.54.
101 Wright (1945), op. cit., p.151.
102 C. Williams-Ellis cited in B. Pfeiffer (ed.), *Frank Lloyd Wright: The Crowning Decade 1949–59* (Fresno: California State University Press, 1989), p.32.
103 ibid., p.29.
104 ibid.
105 J. Morris et al., *Portmeirion* (London: Antique Collectors' Club, 2006), p.22.
106 P. McGoohan, *The Prisoner*, ITV Production, 1967–8.
107 Wright (1945), op. cit., p.150.
108 ibid., p.151.
109 B. Gill, *Many Masks – A Life of Frank Lloyd Wright* (London: Heinemann, 1988), p.217.
110 Wright (1945), op. cit., p11.
111 ibid.
112 Twombly (2009), op.cit., p. 21.
113 ibid.

114 J. Alfrey, 'Themes and Sources for Public Housing in Wales, Housing the Twentieth Century Nation', *The Journal of the Twentieth Century Society*, Journal 9, 2008, p.79.
115 Wright (1945), op. cit., p.151.
116 Wright in Williams-Ellis in Pfeiffer (1989), op. cit., p.32.
117 K. Robinson, 'From Taliesin to Shepherds Bush', *Architects' Journal*, July 26 1956, p.65.
118 ibid.
119 M. Vidotto, *Alison + Peter Smithson: Works and Projects* (Barcelona: Editorial Gustavo Gili, 1997), p.16.
120 E. Harwood, *England: A Guide to Post-War Listed Buildings* (London: Batsford, 2003).
121 Interview with house owner, 2008.
122 Wright (1970), op. cit., p.11.
123 Harwood (2003), op. cit., pp 410–1.
124 A. Powers, *Aldington, Craig and Collinge: Twentieth Century Architects* (London: RIBA Publishing, 2009), p.35.
125 ibid.
126 ibid., p.56.
127 R. Rogers cited in K. Powell, *Richard Rogers: Complete Works Volume 1* (London: Phaidon, 1999), p.12.
128 ibid.
129 R. Stern, chapter in D. Jenkins (ed.) *Norman Foster Works 1* (Munich: Prestel, 2002), p.26.

5: WHEN FRANK MET FRANCESCO

1 M. Leapman, *Inigo: The Life of Inigo Jones: Architect of the English Renaissance* (London: Headline Book Publishing, 2004), p.20.
2 ibid., p.23.
3 G. Worsley, *Inigo Jones and the European Classical Tradition* (London and New Haven: Yale University Press, 2007), p.19.
4 Leapman (2004), op. cit., p.154.
5 C. De Seta in A. Wilton and I. Bignamini, *Grand Tour: The Lure of Italy in the Eighteenth Century* (London: Tate Gallery Publishing, 1996), p.18.
6 I. Jack and A. Jackson, 'Change here, and here, and here. . .', *Guardian, Travel*, 2 August 2008, pp 8–9.
7 F. L. Wright, *An Autobiography* (London: Faber & Faber, 1945), p.287.
8 Wright (1945), op. cit., p.289.
9 F. L. Wright (1932), in B. Pfeiffer (ed.), *Frank Lloyd Wright: Collected Writings: Vol 1 1894–1930* (New York: Rizzoli, 1992), p.85.
10 ibid.
11 M. Augé, *Non-Places: Introduction to an Anthropology of Supermodernity* (London: Verso, 1995), pp 77–8.
12 J. Tomlinson, *Globalization and Culture* (Cambridge: Polity, 1999), p.109.
13 Augé (1995), op. cit., p.94.
14 Wright (1945), op. cit., p.291.
15 Worsley (2007), op. cit., p.33.
16 Leapman (2004), op. cit., p.141.
17 K. Frampton, *Modern Architecture: A Critical History*, 3rd edn (London: Thames and Hudson, 1992), p.477.
18 R. Chicco, 'Tita Carloni: a Wrightian in the Canton of Ticino', *Architettura Cronache e Storia*, vol.50, no.579, 2004, p.45.
19 G. Brown-Manrique, *The Ticino Guide* (New York: Princeton Architectural Press, 1989), p.17.
20 Frampton (1992), op. cit., pp 315, 477.
21 A. Tzonis and L. Lefaivre in K. Nesbitt (ed.), *Theorizing a New Agenda for Architecture: an Anthology of Architectural Theory 1965–1995* (New York: Princeton Architectural Press, 1996), p.486.
22 J. Morris, *Venice* (London: Faber & Faber, 1993), pp 107–8.
23 B. Zevi in A. Alofsin, *Frank Lloyd Wright: Europe and Beyond* (California: University of California Press, 1999), p.72.

24 N. Levine, *The Architecture of Frank Lloyd Wright* (Princeton: Princeton University Press, 1996), p.374.
25 ibid., p.375.
26 R. Moneo, *Frank Lloyd Wright: Memorial Masieri, Venice 1953* (Madrid: Editorial Rueda, 2008), pp 133–4.
27 F. L. Wright, 'The Masieri Memorial,' *Metron*, no.49–50, 1954, pp 14–26.
28 ibid.
29 Moneo (2008), op. cit., pp 82–4.
30 C. D. Medina in Moneo (2008), op. cit., pp 36–7.
31 ibid., pp 19–44.
32 ibid., pp 45–63.
33 F. L. Wright cited in C. D. Medina in Moneo (2008), op. cit., p.35.
34 E. Hemingway cited in Levine (1996), op. cit., p.382.
35 F. L. Wright cited in Levine (1996), op. cit., footnote 54, p.493.
36 J. Ruskin, *The Seven Lamps of Architecture* (New York: Dover Publications, 1989), p.178.
37 J. Ruskin cited in D. Howard, *The Architectural History of Venice* (London: B. T. Batsford Ltd, 1980), p.94.
38 Howard (1980), op. cit., p.95.
39 J. Ackerman, *Palladio* (London: Penguin, 1991), p.50.
40 ibid., p.172.
41 V. Scully, *Frank Lloyd Wright* (New York: George Brailler, 1996), p.18.
42 J. Ackerman, *The Villas: Form and Ideology of Country Houses* (London: Penguin, 1990), p.253.
43 Ira Levin, *Stepford Wives* (London: Random House, 1972).
44 M. Par, 'Recenti Constrzioni de Marcello D'Olivo', *L'Architettura*, 1958, p.296.
45 A. Rossari and F. Lehman, *Wright e l'Italia 1910–1960 Wright and Italy 1910–1960* (Milan: Edizioni Unicopli, 2002), p.89.
46 T. Furlan, 'A Free Community for boys in Trieste', *Metron*, no.47, December 1952, p.60.
47 F. L. Wright, *An Organic Architecture* (London: Lund Humphries, 1970), p.39.
48 E. M. Forster, *A Room with a View* (London: Edward Arnold, 1908).
49 L. Sullivan, *The Autobiography of an Idea* (New York: Smith, 1949), p.236.
50 A. Alofsin, *Frank Lloyd Wright: The Lost Years 1910–1922* (Chicago: University of Chicago Press, 1993), p.49.
51 R. Bencini and P. Bulletti, *Frank Lloyd Wright a Fiesole cento anni dopo 1910–2010: dalle colline di Firenze al 'colle splendente'* (Florence: Giunti, 2010).
52 Wright (1945), op. cit., p.147.
53 ibid., p.148.
54 ibid., p.149.
55 F. L. Wright (1910) in B. Pfeiffer (ed.), *The Essential Frank Lloyd Wright: Critical Writings on Architecture* (Princeton: Princeton University Press, 2008), p.52.
56 ibid., p.52.
57 ibid.
58 ibid.
59 ibid.
60 M. Casciato in Alofsin (1999), op. cit., pp 76–99.
61 ibid., p.84.
62 ibid., p.85.
63 ibid., p.86.
64 N. Fasola, footnote to M. Casciato in Alofsin (1999), op. cit., p.239.
65 ibid., p.239.
66 Rossari and Lehman (2002), op. cit., p.66.
67 ibid., p.67.
68 M. Casciato in Alofsin (1999), op. cit., p.78.
69 F. L. Wright, 'Message from Frank Lloyd Wright', in Atti ufficiali: XIII *Congresso internazionale architectti, Roma, 22–28 Settembre 1935 – XII* (Rome: Accademia Nazionale de San Luca, 1935), p.736.

70 B. Zevi, *Towards an Organic Architecture* (London: Faber & Faber Ltd, 1950), pp 66–76.
71 L. Sullivan cited in Zevi (1950), op. cit., pp 68, 66.
72 S. Giedion cited in Zevi (1950), op. cit., p.67.
73 Goethe cited in Zevi (1950), op. cit., p.69.
74 Vasari cited in Zevi (1950), op. cit., p.68.
75 Zevi (1950), op. cit., pp 72–3.
76 B. Zevi, *The Modern Language of Architecture* (Seattle: University of Washington Press, 1978), p.5.
77 ibid., p.65.
78 ibid., p.112.
78 ibid., p.96.
80 ibid., pp 209–10.
81 B. Zevi in Alofsin (1999), op. cit., p.78.
82 A. Blunt (ed.), *Baroque & Rococo: Architecture and Decoration* (London: Granada Publishing, 1982), p.45.
83 ibid, p.38.
84 ibid.
85 S. Kostof, *A History of Architecture: Settings and Rituals* (Oxford: Oxford University Press, 1985), p.515.
86 '*Papal Rebuke*', *Building Design* website, www.bdonline.co.uk/story.asp?sectioncode=437&storycode, (accessed 13 December 2009).

6: A SHORT TAXI RIDE AROUND THE PERSIAN GULF

1 F. L. Wright (1937) in B. Pfeiffer (ed.), *The Essential Frank Lloyd Wright: Critical Writings on Architecture* (Princeton: Princeton University Press, 2008), p.283.
2 F. L. Wright, *An Autobiography* (London: Faber & Faber, 1945), p.38.
3 ibid.
4 ibid.
5 Wright (1945), op. cit., pp 70–1.
6 K. Frampton in R. McCarter (ed.), *On and By Frank Lloyd Wright: A Primer of Architectural Principles* (London: Phaidon, 2005), p.174.
7 F. L. Wright (1937) in B. Pfeiffer (ed.) (2008), op. cit., pp 276–91.
8 ibid., p.282.
9 ibid.
10 ibid.
11 Wright (1928) cited in Pfeiffer (2008), op. cit., p.135.
12 W. Lethaby, *The Church of Sancta Sophia* (London: Macmillan, 1894)
13 Wright (1937), op. cit., p.282.
14 ibid.
15 ibid.
16 C. W. Thomsen, *Visionary Architecture: From Babylon to Virtual Reality* (Munich: Prestel, 1994), pp 69–70.
17 Wright (1937), op. cit., p.283.
18 'Aladdin', Wikipedia, http://en.wikipedia.org/wiki/Aladdin (accessed July 2011).
19 Wright (1937), op. cit., p.283.
20 ibid.
21 ibid., p.288.
22 ibid.
23 ibid., pp 277–8.
24 R. Lewcock and Z. Freeth, *Traditional Architecture in Kuwait and the Northern Gulf* (London: Art and Archaeology Research Papers, 1978), p.12.
25 ibid.
26 ibid.
27 ibid.
28 ibid.
29 ibid.
30 ibid.
31 Raunkiaer cited in Lewcock and Freeth (1978), op. cit., p.25.
32 S. Kostof, *The City Shaped: Urban Patterns and Meanings Through History* (London: Thames and Hudson, 1991), p.64.
33 Lewcock and Freeth (1978), op. cit., p.15.
34 Kostof (1991), op. cit., p.95.
35 B. Rudofsky, *Architecture without*

Architects: a Short Introduction to Non-Pedigreed Architecture (New York: Museum of Modern Art, 1965), preface, p.1.

36 R. Chadirji, 'The Identification of Architectural Needs in the Middle East', *RIBA Transactions*, vol.4, no.2, 1983, p.89.

37 Minoprio in S. Gardiner, *Kuwait: the Making of a City* (London: Longman, 1983), p.35.

38 ibid., p.37.

39 K. Jamal, 'Kuwait: A Salutary Tale', *The Architects' Journal*, 12 December 1973, p.1456.

40 Y. Mahgoub, 'Globalization and the built environment in Kuwait', *Habitat International*, vol. 28, 2004, p.514.

41 Gardiner (1983), op. cit., p.88.

42 Y. Mahgoub, interview with the author in Tareq Rajab Museum, 18 September 2009.

43 ibid., see also Gardiner (1983), op. cit., pp 22–6.

44 P. Hall, *Cities of Tomorrow: An Intellectual History of Urban Planning and Design in the Twentieth Century*, (Oxford: Blackwell Publishing, 2002), p.316.

45 F. L. Wright (1932), *The Disappearing City* in B. Pfeiffer (ed.), *Frank Lloyd Wright: Collected Writings: Vol 1 1894–1930* (New York: Rizzoli, 1992), p.94.

46 F. L. Wright, *An Organic Architecture* (London: Lund Humphries, 1970), p.36.

47 K. Frampton in McCarter (2005), op. cit.

48 Gardiner (1983), op. cit., p.67.

49 F. L. Wright cited in J. M. Siry, 'Wright's Baghdad Opera House and Gammage Auditorium: in search of regional modernity', *Art Bulletin*, vol.87, no.2, June 2005, p.281.

50 ibid.

51 L. Vale, *Architecture, Power, and National Identity* (New Haven: Yale University Press, 1992), p.221.

52 ibid., p.224.

53 ibid.

54 Wright (1937), op. cit., p.283.

55 Vale (1992), op. cit., p.233.

56 ibid., p.231.

57 'Arab League states: a recent history of protests', *Guardian*, www.guardian.co.uk/world/2011/mar/22/arab-league-states (accessed 27 October 2011).

58 K. Boucher et al., 'The Great Metro Race', *The National: Arts and Life Sunday*, 13 September 2009, pp 1–5.

59 E. Grube in G. Mitchell (ed.), *Architecture of the Islamic World: its History and Social Meaning* (London: Thames and Hudson, 1978), pp 10–13.

60 ibid., p.13.

61 J. Lipman in McCarter (2005), op. cit., pp 264–85, and K. Nute, *Frank Lloyd Wright and Japan* (London: Chapman Hall, 1993), pp 40–41.

62 E. Grube in Mitchell (1978), op. cit., p.13.

63 ibid., p.14.

64 K. Frampton in McCarter (2005), op. cit., p.181.

65 ibid., p.184.

66 ibid., p.189.

67 M. Marefat in A. Alofsin (ed.), *Frank Lloyd Wright: Europe and Beyond* (Berkeley: University of California Press, 1999), p.209.

68 K. Frampton in McCarter (2005), op.cit., pp 176–7.

69 G. Abdul-Ahad, 'We need slaves to build monuments', *Guardian*, www.guardian.co.uk/world/2008/oct/08/middleeast.construction (accessed 12 November 2009).

70 Mahgoub (2009), op. cit.

71 'Frank Lloyd Wright: Selected Projects, Mile High Tower', Guggenheim Bilbao website, www.guggenheimbilbao.es/microsites/frank_lloyd_wright/secciones/frank_lloyd_wright/proyectos_seleccionados/torre_oficinas_mile_high.php?idioma=en (accessed 10 November 2009).

72 F. L. Wright cited in B. Gill, *Many Masks: A Life of Frank Lloyd Wright* (London: Heinemann, 1988), p.477.
73 Thomsen (1994), op. cit., p.28.
74 ibid., p.299.
75 ibid.
76 H. Hartman, 'Masdar', *Architects' Journal,* 11 February 2010, pp 26, 29.
77 F. Poli, 'The Museums of the Island of Happiness,' *Lotus*, no.134, May 2008, pp 6–10.
78 'Saadiyat Island', TDIC website www.tdic.ae/Projects/Saadiyat_Island/Overview.aspx (accessed November 2009).
79 F. Poli (2008), op. cit., pp 2–4.
80 ibid., p.6.
81 R. Booth, 'From Desert to Cultural Oasis, Complete with Louvre, Guggenheim and Ferrari', *Guardian*, 3 September 2008, www.guardian.co.uk/world/2008/sep/03/middleeast.art (accessed July 2009).
82 M. Marefat in Alofsin (1999), op. cit., p.186.
83 N. Levine, *The Architecture of Frank Lloyd Wright* (Princeton: Princeton University Press, 1996), p.384.
84 M. Marefat in Alofsin (1999), op. cit., p.188.
85 ibid., p.189.
86 J. M. Siry (2005), op. cit., p.271.
87 M. Marefat in Alofsin (1999), op. cit, pp 189–90.
88 F. L. Wright (1999) cited in M. Marefat in Alofsin (1999), op. cit., p.190.
89 ibid.
90 F. L. Wright, 'Wright to Design Baghdad Opera', *Architectural Forum*, May 1957, p.91.
91 D. Haskell, 'Wright to Design Baghdad Opera', *Architectural Forum*, May 1957, p.89.
92 M. Marefat in Alofsin (1999), op. cit., p.194.
93 ibid., p.194.
94 ibid., pp 194–5.
95 C. Carolin in N. Bingham et al., *Fantasy Architecture 1500–2036* (London: Hayward Gallery Publishing, 2004), p.8.
96 Wright (1957), op. cit., pp 90–91.
97 Wright (1957), op. cit., p.91.
98 ibid.
99 Wright (1945), op. cit., pp 158–9.
100 Levine (1996), op. cit. p.126.
101 ibid., p.127.
102 ibid., p.124.
103 Wright (1945), op. cit., p.209.
104 Wright (1957), op. cit., p.91.
105 Siry (2005), op. cit., p.277.
106 Wright (1957), op. cit., p.93.
107 Siry (2005), op. cit., p.276.
108 Wright (1957), op. cit., p.93.
109 Siry (2005), op. cit., p.276.
110 Wright (1957), op. cit., p.93.
111 Z. Hadid cited in Poli (2008), op. cit., p.6.
112 ibid.
113 Gill (1988), op. cit., p.275.
114 Wright cited in Freidland, R. (2006), op. cit., p.559.

MINORITY REPORT

1 F. L. Wright, *An Autobiography* (London: Faber & Faber, 1945), p.322.
2 A. Isozaki, *Japan-ness in Architecture* (Cambridge: MIT Press, 2006), p.5.
3 J-L. Cohen in A. Alofsin (ed.), *Frank Lloyd Wright: Europe and Beyond* (Berkeley: University of California Press, 1999), p.100.
4 F. L. Wright, *An Organic Architecture* (London: Lund Humphries, 1970), p.36.

BIBLIOGRAPHY

Ackerman, J., *Palladio* (London: Penguin, 1991)

Ackerman, J., *The Villas: Form and Ideology of Country Houses* (London: Penguin, 1990)

Alofsin, A. (ed.), *Frank Lloyd Wright: Europe and Beyond* (Berkeley: University of California Press, 1999)

Alofsin, A., *Frank Lloyd Wright: The Lost Years 1910–1922* (Chicago: University of Chicago Press, 1993)

Augé, M., *Non-Places: Introduction to an Anthropology of Supermodernity* (London: Verso, 1995)

Banham, R., *Scenes in America Deserta* (London: Thames and Hudson, 1982)

Banham, R., *Theory and Design in the First Machine Age* (Oxford: Architectural Press, 2002)

Bater, J. H., *The Soviet City: Ideal and Reality* (London: Edward Arnold, 1980)

N. Bingham, et al., *Fantasy Architecture 1500–2036* (London: Hayward Gallery Publishing, 2004)

Blunt, A. (ed.), *Baroque & Rococo: Architecture and Decoration* (London: Granada Publishing, 1982)

Brooks, H., *Writings on Wright: Selected comments on Frank Lloyd Wright* (Cambridge: MIT Press, 1981)

Colquhoun, A., *Modern Architecture* (Oxford: Oxford University Press, 2002)

Colomina, B., *Architecturalproduction* (New York: Princeton Architectural Press, 1988)

Cooke, C., *Russian Avant-Garde: Theories of Art, Architecture and the City* (London: St Martin's Press, 1995)

Crawford, A., *C.R. Ashbee: Architect, Designer and Romantic Socialist* (New Haven and London: Yale University Press, 2005)

S. Davis, *The Architecture of Affordable Housing* (Berkeley: University of California Press, 1995)

Eggener, K. (ed.), *American Architectural History: A Contemporary Reader* (London: Routledge, 2004)

Frampton, K., *Modern Architecture: A Critical History*, 3rd edn (London: Thames and Hudson, 1992)

Fraser M. and J. Kerr, *Architecture and the 'Special Relationship': The American Influence on Post-war British Architects* (London: Routledge, 2007)

Gardiner, S., *Kuwait: the Making of a City* (London: Longman, 1983)

Gill, B., *Many Masks – A Life of Frank Lloyd Wright* (London: Heinemann, 1988)

Hall, P., *Cities of Tomorrow: An Intellectual History of Urban Planning and Design in the Twentieth Century* (Oxford: Blackwell Publishing, 2002)

Hardy, D., *Utopian England: Community Experiments 1900–1945* (London: E. & F. N. Spon, 2000)

Hitchcock, H-R., and P. Johnson *The International Style*, (New York: W. W. Norton & Co., 1966)

Isozaki, A., *Japan-ness in Architecture* (Cambridge: MIT Press, 2006)

James, K., *Erich Mendelsohn and the Architecture of German Modernism* (Cambridge: Cambridge University Press, 1997)

Jenkins, D. (ed.), *Norman Foster Works 1* (Munich: Prestel 2002)

Johnson, D., *Frank Lloyd Wright Versus America* (Cambridge: MIT Press, 1990)

Jones, P. B., *Gunter Behnisch* (Basel, Germany: Birkhauser 2000)

Jones, P. B., *Hugo Haring: The Organic versus the Geometric Stuttgart* (London: Edition Axel Menges, 1999)

Khan-Magomedov, S., *Pioneers of Soviet Architecture: The Search for New Solutions* (New York: Rizzoli, 1983)

Kirk, T., *The Architecture of Modern Italy (Volume 2: Visions of Utopia 1900 – Present)* (Princeton: Princeton University Press, 2005)

Koolhaas R. & B. Mau, *S, M, L, XL* (New York: Monacelli Press, 1995)

Langmead, D. and D. L. Johnson, *Architectural Excursions: Frank Lloyd Wright, Holland and Europe* (London: Greenwood Press, 2000)

Leapman, M., *Inigo: The Life of Inigo Jones Architect of the English Renaissance* (London: Headline, 2004)

Levine, N., *The Architecture of Frank Lloyd Wright* (Princeton: Princeton University Press, 1996)

Lewcock, R. and Z. Freeth, *Traditional Architecture in Kuwait and the Northern Gulf* (London: Art and Archaeology Research Papers, 1978)

Los, S., *Carlo Scarpa: An Architectural Guide, Verona* (Italy: Arsenale Editrice, 2007)

McCarter, R., *On and By Frank Lloyd Wright: A Primer of Architectural Principles* (London: Phaidon, 2005)

Meech, J., *Frank Lloyd Wright and the Art of Japan: The Architect's Other Passion* (New York: Abrams, 2001)

Mitchell. G. (ed.), *Architecture of the Islamic World: its History and Social Meaning* (London: Thames and Hudson, 1978)

Moneo, R., *Frank Lloyd Wright: Memorial Masieri, Venice 1953* (Madrid: Editorial Rueda, 2008),

Nute, K., *Frank Lloyd Wright and Japan*, (London: Routledge, 2000)

Okakura, K., *The Book of Tea* (Tokyo: Kodansha Int., 2005)

Overy, P., *De Stijl* (London: Thames and Hudson, 1991)

Perry, V., *Built for a Better Future: The Brynmawr Rubber Factory* (Oxford: White Cockade Publishing, 1994)

Pevsner, N., 'Frank Lloyd Wright Peaceful Penetration of Europe', *Architects' Journal*, no.89, 4 May 1939

Pevsner, N., *Pioneers of Modern Design: From William Morris to Walter Gropius* (London: Pelican, 1981)

Pfeiffer, B. (ed.), *Frank Lloyd Wright: Collected Writings: Vol 1 1894–1930* (New York: Rizzoli, 1992)

Pfeiffer, B. (ed.), *The Essential Frank Lloyd Wright: Critical Writings on Architecture* (Princeton: Princeton University Press, 2008)

Pinchon, J-F. (ed.), *Rob. Mallet-Stevens: Architecture, Furniture, Interior Design* (Cambridge: MIT Press 1990)

Polano, S., *Hendrick Petrus Berlage: Complete Works* (London: Butterworth Architecture, 1988)

Powell, K., *Richard Rogers: Complete Works Volume 1* (London: Phaidon, 1999)

Powers, A., *Aldington, Craig and Collinge: Twentieth Century Architects* (London: RIBA Publishing, 2009

Raymond, A., *An Autobiography* (Rutland: Charles E. Turtle, 1973)

Ross, M., *Beyond Metabolism: The New Japanese Architecture* (London: McGraw Hill, 1978)

Rossari A. and F. Lehman, *Wright e l'Italia 1910-1960 Wright and Italy 1910–1960* (Milan: Edizioni Unicopli, 2002)

Rudofsky B., *Architecture without Architects: a Short Introduction to Non-Pedigreed Architecture* (New York: Museum of Modern Art, 1965)

Ruskin, J., *The Seven Lamps of Architecture* (New York: Dover Publications, 1989)

Saint, A., *The Image of the Architect* (New Haven: Yale University Press, 1993)

Scott, J., *Behind the Urals: An American Worker in Russia's City of Steel* (Bloomington: Indiana University Press, 1989)

Scully, V., *Frank Lloyd Wright* (New York: George Brailler, 1996)

Secrest, M., *Frank Lloyd Wright: A Biography* (Chicago: University of Chicago Press, 1992)

Seidensticker, E., *Low City, High City: Tokyo from Edo to the Earthquake, 1867–1923* (London: Penguin, 1985)

Sergeant, J., *Frank Lloyd Wright's Usonian Houses: Designs for Moderate Cost One-Family Homes* (New York: Watson Guptil, 1984)

Shelton, B., *Learning from the Japanese City. Looking East in Urban Design* (London: Routledge, 2012)

Smithson, A. & P., *The Heroic Period of Modern Architecture* (London: Thames and Hudson, 1981)

St John Wilson, C., *The Other Tradition of Modern Architecture: the Uncompleted Project* (London: Black Dog, 2007)

Stewart, D., *The Making of a Modern Japanese Architecture: 1868 to the Present* (Japan: Kodansha Int., 1989)

Sullivan, L., *The Autobiography of an Idea* (New York: Smith, 1949)

Tanigawa M. in M. Birk (ed.), *Frank Lloyd Wright's Fifty Views of Japan: the 1905 Photo Album* (San Francisco: Pomegranate Artbooks, 1996)

Tarkhanov A. and S. Kavtaradze, *Stalinist Architecture* (London: Laurence King, 1992)

Taut, B., *Houses and People of Japan* (London: Gifford, 1937)

Tomlinson, J., *Globalisation and Culture*, (Cambridge: Polity, 1999)

Treiber, D., *Frank Lloyd Wright* (Basel: Birkhauser, 2008)

Twombly, R., *Frank Lloyd Wright: Essential Texts* (New York: W. W. Norton & Co, 2009)

Twombly, R., *Frank Lloyd Wright: His Life and His Architecture* (New York: John Wiley & Sons, 1979)

Tzonis A. and L. Lefaivre in K. Nesbitt (ed.), *Theorizing a New Agenda for Architecture: an Anthology of Architectural Theory 1965–1995* (New York: Princeton Architectural Press, 1996)

Vale, L., *Architecture, Power, and National Identity* (New Haven: Yale University Press, 1992)

Williams-Ellis, C., *Architect Errant: The Autobiography of Clough Williams-Ellis* (Wales: Portmeirion Ltd, 1991)

Worsley, G., *Inigo Jones and the European Classical Tradition* (London and New Haven: Yale University Press, 2007)

Wright, F. L., *An Autobiography* (London: Faber & Faber, 1945)

Wright, F. L., *An Organic Architecture: The Architecture of Democracy* (London: Lund Humphries, 1970)

Wright, F. L., 'London Rebuilt: How I Would Do it', *News Chronicle*, 17 February 1941

Wright, F. L., 'Architecture and Life in the USSR', *Architectural Record*, vol.82, October 1937

Wright, F. L., 'Message from Frank Lloyd Wright', in *Atti ufficiali: XIII Congresso internazionale architectti, Roma, 22–28 Settembre 1935 – XII* (Rome: Accademia Nazionale de San Luca, 1935)

Wright (1935), F. L., 'Broadacre City: A New Community Plan,' *Architectural Record*, vol.77, April 1935

Wright, F. L., et al., *The Complete 1925 'Wendigen Series'* (New York: Dover Publications, 1992)

Wright, G., *USA: Modern Architectures in History* (London: Reaktion Books 2008)

Wright, J. L., *My Father Who Is On Earth* (New York: G. P. Putnam's Sons, 1946)

Zevi, B., *Towards an Organic Architecture* (London: Faber & Faber Ltd, 1950)

Zevi, B., *The Modern Language of Architecture* (Seattle: University of Washington Press, 1978)

INDEX

Page numbers in *italics* refer to illustrations.